GO AND SERVE

YOU WILL NEVER REGRET IT

JAMES "JIMBO" WILLIAMSON

EDITOR: KEITH GILBERTSON

"We are designed to serve and it makes us happy when we do this. The only way we can know for sure is to go and serve."
James "Jimbo" Williamson

authorHOUSE®

AuthorHouse™
1663 Liberty Drive
Bloomington, IN 47403
www.authorhouse.com
Phone: 833-262-8899

Published by AuthorHouse 07/14/2020

ISBN: 978-1-7283-6665-4 (sc)
ISBN: 978-1-7283-6693-7 (e)

Print information available on the last page.

CONTENTS

CHAPTER FIVE

CHAPTER SIX

CHAPTER SEVEN

FROM THE EDITOR

James "Jimbo" Williamson gets a "kick out of uplifting people and seeing the good side of them." About twenty years ago, he realized he was at a crossroads in his life and "wanted to help others."

At a flea market in South Carolina, he found a book about a Catholic priest's work in Eastern Kentucky with the Christian Appalachian Project (CAP). Father Beiting was asking for help, so Jimbo decided to go to Kentucky and see what he could do. He wasn't sure CAP would allow him to help because he was not a Christian. Jimbo started to go to prayer meetings during this time and was telling one of his new friends about wanting to volunteer with the Christian group. His friend replied, "You can do that if you want to, but it won't amount to nothing. You need to get saved."

Well, Jimbo had a "spiritual experience and accepted Christ as his Savior." I've met many people who have accepted Jesus Christ but few who seem to embrace their new life as much as Jimbo has. He lives his beliefs. He shares his love of the Lord with people and serves. He talks about the Lord. He writes devotions to share with others, and now he has a book of many of his thoughts, reflections, and prayers for the greatness and goodness of God's creation. I feel like Jimbo is on a "Mission from God."

Jimbo began working as a volunteer with CAP in 2003 as a member of the home repair crew. I had been working with CAP for many years. When Hurricane Katrina ravaged the Gulf Coast in September 2005, the leaders at CAP decided to send some of our workers to help in the cleanup and relief efforts. This gave me an opportunity to travel and to work to help get people back on their feet. This is when I first crossed paths with Jimbo: on a bus with a group of CAP workers on our way to Christus Victor Lutheran Church in Ocean Springs, Mississippi. The members of this church had organized several ways to serve those who had lost nearly everything in the storm.

Those who have had the pleasure to meet Jimbo know he often tells funny, uplifting stories and generally likes to talk. This ride on the bus was my introduction to a true "character with character." What you see and what you hear is what you get with Jimbo. He demonstrates a genuine, caring heart that matches his understanding of the words the Lord tells us about how to serve. Matthew 25:35-40: "The King will reply, 'Truly I tell you, whatever you did for one of the least of these brothers and sisters of mine, you did for me.'"

My favorite title in this book is: "That ain't no White Guy, that's Jimbo." When you read this and the rest of his stories, you will see how country-boy Jimbo fits in most anywhere as he spreads his love, cheer, laughter, and words of the Lord to uplift all of God's creation. Also beware: Jimbo uses a lot of four-letter words in this book........ Love, Hope, Good, Glad, Calm, Rest, Easy, Well, Kind, Lord, Have, Holy, Book, Heal, Care, Tend, Pray, Free, Gain, Heat, Cool.

These encouraging stories Jimbo tells and his spiritual words of wisdom will inspire you to follow his lead. Jimbo is an example of a person who sees the good in all God's creation and does his best to live out his personal goal to lift everyone he meets. The title "Go and Serve" is the call for others to enjoy opportunities to serve others' needs in times of disaster, floods, hurricanes, and everyday life's ups and downs.

Listen to Jimbo. "Go and serve. You will never regret it."

ABOUT THE COVER DESIGN

By Amanda Morris, Graphic Designer & Illustrator

The cover design incorporates the following symbolism:

- While the background house, wood- and junk-pile including the duct-taped refrigerator (per request) allude to the act of service of rebuilding homes after a natural disaster, the central focus is on the prayer circle.
- God's power is represented by the brightest value of the sun and three rays of light (the Holy Trinity), which reach into all boundaries – the house, the earth, and the people… The people reflect His light because they are "children of the light".
- The shadows cast by the people are all the same color despite a diverse group as suggested by the silhouettes of different genders and ethnicities – as in Christ, we are not judged by the surface because our identity is in Him.
- The shadow shape also alludes to "in the shadow of the cross" because those in the prayer circle are doing good works in the path that God has prepared beforehand and carrying the cross so to speak.

- The held hands occur in the center of the illustration, which symbolize how community and God's church are at the center of one of his two greatest commandments – to love others as we have been loved by Him.
- The color palette is minimal yet warm like the messages of service and love, and the red sky reflects the sailor's adage: "Red sky at night, sailor's delight; red sky in morn', sailors take warn" to reveal God's sovereignty over nature.
- The style is a woodblock print with flat planes of color to suggest minimalism and resourcefulness, referencing the materials in the wood pile as well as the timelessness of prayer and service – they are fundamental and doable even without modern luxuries.
- The font and layout are also inspired by the Hatch Show Print, one of America's longest running letterpresses, now housed in the Country Music Hall of Fame, so as to connect to the woodblock style and to announce the message loud and clear: "Go and Serve!"

INTRODUCTION

GO AND SERVE: YOU WILL NEVER REGRET IT

What the Lord Wants for Me and You Today

He wants me to be healthy and happy. He wants me to meet one of his children (my brothers and sisters) and encourage them and to be encouraged by them. He wants me to enjoy his handiwork of nature. He wants me to get to know one of His other children better. He wants me to get to know myself better. He wants me to get to know Him better.

He wants me to enjoy the gift of life he gave me.

Living for the Lord is the best thing I have ever done. He fills my heart with joy. Sometimes I get distracted but I don't have to because I know my job doesn't change depending on the political party in office, my circumstances or anything else. My job description it to feed the hungry, clothe the naked, visit the sick and imprisoned and to tell people the Good News: We have a risen Savior who will comfort us, guide us, and provide for us.

When I got to the Owsley Volunteer House, the welcoming lady had put a banner on my door. It said, *"Welcome Jimbo."* I was 58 years old and I had never been called Jimbo before. Because I'm in housing I had to work with young college students who came down on spring break. They seemed to enjoy yelling, JIMBO, when they needed something and were more likely to talk to me, probably a lot more than if I had been called "Brother James."

Words for reflection from Jimbo's Stories

1. Life is an adventure. Some good adventures and some bad ones. We learn from them all.
2. The reason I want to write about mission trips is so others will see the need, and the joy in serving.
3. The more I share, the more I meditate, and the more I write, it seems more thoughts come that are inspiring to me
4. God is in control and he has a job for all of us.
5. Let's all be servants and meet new people and learn new things.
6. Come down, have a life changing experience, go back, and tell others, help people where you are, come back and bring others
7. Whatever the storm, our job stays the same; to feed the hungry, clothe the naked, visit the sick and imprisoned, and to tell everyone the "good news."
8. We may need the Bible, talks, examples, walks, and time alone among other things to fix a problem in our life or to help others.
9. We are all in this together; so, let's try to calm someone's storm today.
10. The Bible has given us all the instructions we need. And even if we didn't have the Bible, if we would just love one another, we wouldn't go wrong.
11. Say and do things to encourage people to be the person God created them to be and we will be following the instructions of Jesus.
12. Man, it is an emotional roller coaster just coming here and volunteering.
13. As usual in my life, a semi miracle happened and I was going again. I testified once that not only did I believe in miracles; I depend on them.
14. I keep hearing about how hard it is to be a Christian.
15. When we look for these things in ourselves and do them, and we look for them in others and encourage them we will see the J E S U S in ourselves and others.
16. Who knows when what we learned years ago will come in handy?

17. Some lady behind me said "I could listen to you for hours; with that accent."
18. We have limited resources when it comes to finances, but we are not limited on love, compassion, peace, joy, and we won't be limited on our finances if we use them for the Kingdom.
19. Out of every disaster there is rebirth of some kind or other.
20. The old life sounded exciting; and was but it doesn't compare to my life now as a Christian.
21. There are angels watching over us. It reminds me I'm to be generous and to help whoever I can whenever I can.
22. I guess getting rid of bitterness, worry, pride, envy (among a few) and reacquiring love, compassion, empathy, and contentment might do it.
23. I get a bigger kick out of uplifting people and seeing the good side of them.
24. Being grateful is good because the more grateful we are, the happier we are.
25. The next time you have a chance to do good; do it.
26. There is no greater feeling than helping others.
27. We have been created to serve, so if we don't serve, we are not living life to the fullest.
28. . The joy we have when we help one person is worth the pain we have for all the times things didn't work out.
29. I used to could barely pass a bar without stopping and going in. Now I can barely pass a church without stopping and going in.
30. The cogs in my head are turning.
31. God probably made the earth pretty much like He wanted it to stay.
32. The good thing about volunteering. You don't expect to get rewarded and it is a bonus when we do.
33. The more we share, the more we are given

CHAPTER ONE

HOW I GOT TO WHERE I AM; JIMBO'S AUTOBIOGRAPHY

On December 11, 1945 around 9:00 PM I was born out on a ridge next to Owingsville, Kentucky. The doctor had to drive through Harrisburg (called that because George Harris was the de facto representative of the blacks in town) which was the black section of town and then walk out a muddy lane to deliver me. We didn't have electric power so the doctor had to deliver me in the light of "coal oil" lamps. We moved into town when I was three. I don't remember the birth or the moving, but my mother said I would crawl out the lane when she took a nap and they had to go look for me.

The good thing about being born out on that ridge was my dad had to walk through the colored section of town. He got to know everyone so I had no prejudice against black people (of course they were called colored then). As the oldest child I was responsible for my younger two brothers and a sister. I figured if anything happened to my parents we would just go out and live with the colored people because they treated me so well. I called the older black people Aunt and Uncle. I had to call the older white people, Mister and Miss, so I guess I figured the black people were more like family. They were poor also and seemed to be more like us than our white neighbors. My daddy drank and worked with them so I knew the good people and the ones that were "trifling." I didn't have to call the drunks uncle or aunt. I just called them by their names. My dad taught me that your word was the most important thing and you did what you said you would do.

When I was three, we moved to Owingsville, Kentucky. Population 1,000. I was fortunate to be able to remember stuff so when I went to school it was easy and I got bored. I went to school during the first two grades in a building next to the jail. It was like the western movies where the prisoners are looking out the door. You could walk up to them and talk and touch them. They finally had to put some kind of mesh over the door because there was so may wine bottles in the cells. There was only a driveway between the school yard and the jail door so we could talk to the prisoners. We would ask, "What are you in jail for?" They sneered back their lips and yelled, "MURDER", "RAPE." We didn't know what rape was, but we would laugh because we knew they were in there for being drunk.

My dad worked for a guy who bought and sold everything (metal, walnuts, roots, cowhides, rags, if it could be sold he would buy it. On Saturday I went with my dad when we made rounds buying eggs in various neighboring communities. During the summer I would get to go with him to Ashland and Lexington to sell scrap metal.

Once we went somewhere to get some cow hides. Fresh cow hides don't smell good and the blood is running out of them. We were parked in front of a department store and someone came out and asked us to move. My dad usually had a beard and the other guys who worked with him looked rough and all of them drank every day. They drank cheap wine in pint bottles that they hid. I watched where they hid it and then could sneak a drink every now and then. Sometimes I would move the bottle and when they couldn't find it, I would and they might give me a nickel of dime to get a bottle of pop.

So, to me this was how life was. Men worked and drank. My dad always chewed twist tobacco. I stole some and tried it. It tasted horrible and hurt my mouth, so I never tried that again and never got addicted to tobacco. I sure am glad he didn't smoke.

My dad seemed to know the Bible pretty well, but he didn't like preachers and he gave them a rough time when they came around. I joined the Boy Scouts so between the Boy Scouts, church, and my dad I was pretty moral. Of course, he drank so almost everyone I was around were poor people who drank. I thought that was a part of life so I would take a sip of wine every now and then when my dad wasn't watching.

When I was in high school, we moved into the country to a place called Pea Sticks where there were actually poor white people. Tar paper shacks were not uncommon. The area was noted for moonshining and gambling. My dad said, "In the old days, the moonshiners wore badges so they wouldn't try to sell to each other." I had already learned to shoot pool for money, so now it was cards and dice too. When I was a senior in high school, I skipped so much that the bus driver wouldn't let me ride the bus. I would have quit school except my dad was going to make me work if I did. I had failing grades but when I took my finals I did good, but I think they may have allowed me to graduate so they wouldn't have to put up with me another year.

Not all the teachers thought I was a loser. One of them even tried to get me to go to school to be a teacher. I definitely didn't want to be a teacher. I wanted to be a drunk. I know there are some teachers who are drunks; our principal was, but most of the high school students weren't very respectable to the teachers so I didn't want to put up with that

I got seasonal jobs to have money to drink and gamble. I got a job with the Kentucky Highways in the engineering department. The people who hired me meant for it to be political, but I didn't take it that way. I learned how to survey and test soils and concrete. When the administration changed, I lost my job but I got a job at the Cave Run Reservoir working for a contractor with the Corps of Engineers. I learned a lot more stuff about surveying and testing materials, but at the same time I was drinking so much and getting into jail, fights, and wrecks, my bosses were threatening to make me stay on the job site. They said they would bring me booze so I could drink there. I was doing my job fine because I had integrity and worked hard.

When the dam got finished they offered me a job in Mississippi and I took it to get out of Kentucky. I went with them and took my pregnant girlfriend. We went to Vicksburg, Mississippi and worked in the delta building a flood control project. I was unhappy with the job and a bartender at the Holiday Inn told me her husband worked at the Grand Gulf Nuclear station. She said they were going to kill an inspector, so his job would be open. Now I don't think they were really going to kill him (but after I got to know him I could see why they wanted to), but I figured they needed inspectors. Besides, it was dangerous living in Mississippi having long hair and a beard and so liberal he thinks blacks are as good (maybe better) than whites. I got a job and ended up working with people who were somewhat like me (long hair and into partying). I drank a lot there and learned I liked marijuana. I had smoked in Kentucky but it didn't affect me then.

Nothing changed about my drinking, but I did get a job testing materials on a construction of a nuclear plant. I went from nuclear plant to nuclear plant in various states and marriage to marriage getting caught for drunken driving in various states.

As nuclear plants get built and I meet more people, I move around from place to place, until I am in South Florida in 1981 and the drug culture is almost normal. I stop at the Holiday Inn for happy hour and then come home and smoke some grass. Drugs are cheap so cocaine is readily available so I learn how to do that too. It looked like we would be there forever but fortunately our company lost the contract and I came back to Kentucky. I meet another woman and we get married and go to North Carolina. That job gets finished and I come to South Carolina to work for Duke power. They are building a dam and it is great. The area is more red neck than Kentucky so a lot of my in-laws move down. Plenty of redneck bars around, but then I get transferred to an operating nuclear plant where getting arrested for driving and drinking is frowned upon, and drug tests are given randomly.

In 1994 I left Duke Power as a Reactor Operator Technician at the Catawba Nuclear Station. Before I worked in Operations I had spent my life inspecting and testing construction materials at nuclear plants, roads, and dams. During that time, I thought success was making money to buy alcohol and other drugs and doing what I wanted. But working at an operating plant had stressed me to the max. It was dangerous (but that part didn't bother me) and I had to go to classes two weeks out of every ten. I also had to do shift work which was four weeks on night shift and four weeks on days. A mistake while working could cause the plant to shut down costing the company a million dollars a day until it got back online. We also had to take random drug tests which interfered with me doing all the drugs I wanted. Did I say I was stressed? Duke wanted to cut down on employees and offered a buyout plan. I said, "Show Me the Money.".

Now I didn't have to worry about random drug tests but I didn't have money to buy any. I was trying to help my stepdaughter go to school. This resulted in me in going to school also. I was taking electronic classes and got a part time position with Michelin as a Technical Scholar until I graduated. I really didn't have an aptitude for electronics, so I didn't pass the employment exam. Now I can party all the time but of course I don't have much money. I do get turned on to crack cocaine, but fortunately for me it didn't do anything for me and I didn't like it. I helped cut cane to make sorghum syrup.

My stepdaughter had to go to school to get her GED. I would go cut some cane and then come back and pick her up, but after she gets her GED, she has to go to a college or technical school and it is too far away for me to drive back and forth twice. I talk to the people at the college and find out I can take classes for free because I don›t have a job. I decide to do that and get a job with Michelin as a technical scholar. Man, that sounds impressive, but I didn't have an electronic aptitude so I failed the test to get a full-time job. Probably one more fortunate thing in my life.

I realized I was at a crossroads in my life where I wanted to help others. Obviously up until now I have seen plenty of people who need help. Maybe I can be a counselor. I take psychology classes and meet my last wife in an abnormal psychology class. She wants to be a counselor too, so it looks like this will work out fine. WRONG. We broke up almost immediately and that ended the counseling career for both of us. Well for me, she continued on with her courses for a while. It seemed she had problems with me. Imagine that.

So now I was back to square one, but while I was at the Pickens's South Carolina Flea Market, I saw a book by Father Beiting telling about his work in Eastern Kentucky with an organization called the Christian Appalachian Project (CAP). It seems he was asking for help so I decided to go to Kentucky and see about helping him. I was concerned whether he would allow me to help or not because I was not a Christian.

I went to Kentucky to find him. I went to Whitesburg, Kentucky to look for CAP. I don't know why I went there except for the fact it was poor. CAP wasn't there. I went on to Ashland to a library to see if I could look up Father Beiting's number. There were three listings in a couple of towns. I figured one of these phone numbers was for his son. That shows what I knew about a Father in the Catholic Church. Now, CAP is not a Catholic organization, but it is a Christian organization with a lot of Catholics involved. Not only was I not a Catholic I was not a Christian. Because of that I wasn't for sure they would let me volunteer with them.

There were two other guys I wanted to see in Kentucky. One was a guy who I wanted to ask forgiveness from for slapping him over a drink of whiskey in the 60's. I didn't want him to go to hell because he hadn't forgiven me. There was another guy I wanted to thank because he had protected me when I got my face smashed in during a bar room fight.

I am also in Kentucky looking for a guy, Billy, who helped me when I got my cheek broke in a bar room fight in 1974. He was in jail for a few minor things; threatening a judge and something else.

While I am wandering around looking for these two guys, I run upon some school mates who tell me about a beautiful woman who I had always figured kind of wanted me. They told me she was working at JC Penny's as a beautician. The last time I talked to her she owned a couple of beauty shops. I figured this meant there had been a divorce so I drove over to JC Penny's. She wasn't working that day so I left, but as I was leaving, I noticed a lady shopping and it happened to be her. I asked her, "Joyce?" At first, she didn't recognize me. I guess we had changed a little in the years we hadn't seen each other. She told me she was going to church and invited me to go. There were no churches there because it was in an area where the bars are. She mentioned she was working in the church.

I knew no one works in a church so I figured she was in a cult. I also thought; maybe I can get her out of that. I drove by on a Saturday night. The lights were dim and I saw people scurrying around inside. Yep, cult, no one has church on a Saturday night. I went on to the bars and had some drinks. The next day I went to the church and when I walked in, greeters welcomed me like they were waiting on me. I asked, "Where's Joyce?" and they told me. I walked over to her and she introduced me to Keen Johnson who is a judge. I looked at him and said, "I should have been here long ago."

This was the first judge I had ever looked in the eye on the same level. Always before I had to look up at them. Now I was confused. I didn't think a judge would be in a cult, but these people were different from what I knew church people to be. They acted like they were glad to see me. They were milling around and talking to each other before the service. Everyone seemed to be happy. A friend of mine, Mitch, came up and said to me, "I thought I recognized that voice." I asked him, "What are you doing here?" I knew he had started going to church. I just didn't know where. He told me, "I didn't want to go to hell." It didn't make any sense to me, but whatever.

Then the preacher preached and it was very entertaining. He could have been a comedian. Even though he was funny, the sermon was inspirational. I kept going to that church even though I knew I should get back to South Carolina and get a job. I really couldn't understand this. Finally, I went to the jail during visiting hours to see Billy and I found out he was in another jail.

Later, I called Mitch because I thought maybe we could talk about this religion thing. He invited me to come out to his home and eat. We did and then he told his wife they had to leave in 20 minutes. I was upset because I was wanting to talk. He told me, "The church is having 54 nights of prayer because of someone having a revelation from the Lord." It was Saturday night and now I realized what was going on when I drove by on a previous Saturday night. Mitch invited me to the prayer meeting. I didn't think there would be any way I would be interested in going to where people are praying. Singing, preaching, maybe, but prayer? What would I be doing? For some reason, "Sure" came out of my mouth.

So, I drove over and we went in. There was some singing and then someone brought out a prayer shawl. Keen Johnson, the judge, was explaining about the shawl. It came from Jerusalem and it was what Jesus is wearing in his pictures. It can be stretched over your head to separate you from the rest of the world while you are praying. Each tassel is used to keep up with what you are praying about. Then he said, "You will get a blessing if you pray under the shawl. I said to myself, "Sure." I couldn't imagine anything happening if I prayed under a piece of cloth.

They passed the prayer shawl around. The lights were down. It was quiet because people were praying silently. The church was across the street from a drive-in liquor store so as the cars drove through, their lights would shine into the church. The bar where I got my cheek broke was just past the liquor store and I was thinking about how I almost got killed there and also in the parking lot once. And how ironic it is I survived those two instances and I am now sitting in a church a few feet away while people are praying.

We had been there for a good while, but I was enjoying myself just sitting in the darkness. The preacher asked, "Who has not prayed under the prayer shawl?" Three people said they had not. Mitch and his wife hadn't and some person behind me hadn't. Mitch and his wife were at the end of the pew where I was sitting. They took the shawl together and prayed for a short time. Mitch took the shawl to the next person and as he walked past me, he looked at me questioning.

I just kind of shrugged my shoulders, "Why not, I've been sitting here for hours. I might as well let him put that piece of cloth on my head. Well when he did, weird things started happening. The cloth was as thin as a sheet, but when he put it on my head, it felt hot. I started sweating and crying. Mitch laid his hand on my shoulder and started praying. His hand was so hot I could barely stand it. After a minute of this (or maybe just a few seconds). I stuck up my hand to show I have had enough. Now I was confused. I had no idea what happened. I pondered this in my heart. Later I talked to my cousin about it. She shared the experience with her brother who told her, "It was the Holy Spirit moving on Jim."

Well, I didn't know so much about that, but a week later I was looking for Mitch's sister and brother in law, Teresa, and Stanley Ray. I knew they lived in a housing development, but I didn't know the apartment. I was driving through and saw Teresa running across a yard. I stopped and yelled at her. She didn't recognize me so I introduced myself. Stanley Ray got out of the car and I didn't recognize him. He had a gaunt look of a prophet. He said, "Let's go inside and talk." Well of course that was right up my alley.

We went inside and I started telling him about all kinds of stuff and about wanting to volunteer with the Christian Appalachian Project (CAP). He looked at me and said, "You can do that if you want to, but it won't amount to nothing. You need to get saved." I was confused. I didn't remember Stanley Ray being religious. He was with me the night I slapped a guy over the drink of whiskey (and he probably was the cause of it). Now I looked around the apartment and noticed Bibles everywhere. Stanley Ray said to me, "You may not believe. Do you mind if I pray for you?"

I was too confused to answer so I just nodded my head. He grabbed my head and started praying for the Holy Spirit to reveal the truth to me.

Before it was over he had me say the sinner's prayer. And now I am saved. Or at least Stanley Ray said I was. I was shaking as Stanley prayed, but it was nothing like how I felt when that prayer shawl was on my head. Teresa asked me, "How do you feel?" I told her, "Pretty good, I guess." She fixed us some food and Stanley told me, "We were leaving when you drove up and the only reason we were still here was I had forgotten my billfold and sent Teresa back in to get it." I got kind of scared then thinking I would have missed getting saved. He looked at me, "You didn't have anything to worry about. You were searching. The Lord would have revealed Himself to you"

As it came out, I never found either one of these people. While I was in Kentucky, I had a spiritual experience and accepted Christ as my Savior. When I did this, it seemed as if I forgot everything about wanting to work with CAP. I went back to South Carolina, got a job, went to church almost every night, read my Bible, prayed, and witnessed to everyone I could. There was going to be a lay off so I decided to take it to go back to Kentucky and witness to my old drinking buddies. Some people at work didn't want me to leave when almost everyone there was closer to the Lord because of seeing Him work through me. Just after I took the layoff, I found out I had cancer of the thyroid so I had my thyroid removed instead of going to Kentucky. There had been all kinds of weird coincidences happening to me to know I had cancer. When I was told, I knew the Lord was in all of this so I was ecstatic. That sounds weird, but I just knew it was going to be something I could witness about.

Things were going well. My sister told me about her two grandchildren who almost drowned when they went down to a flooded creek. They survived because some man helped them across. No man was there when they were found. She told me because she knew I talked to a lot of people and she wanted me to share with them how quickly one's life can change.

After she told me about her grandchildren being rescued, I bought small angels at the Dollar Store. When I saw a family, I asked if I could give the kids an angel and then I told the parents to appreciate their children. One day as I was driving, it seemed as if the grass was greener and everything was so beautiful and I was so appreciative of how my life was. I thought, "if nothing ever happens good to be again, it will be worth it just thinking my great niece and nephew were not drowned.

After I had been a Christian for three years, going to church almost every day, and two or three times on Saturday and Sunday, I was randomly talking to a lady and she asked if I knew about an organization she donated to. It happened to be the Christian Appalachian Project (CAP) and all at once something just flooded over me. I told her I did know about the organization. Her daughter downloaded an application form for CAP. I filled it out to volunteer for a year. I wanted to go into the elderly program, but due to my driving record and the fact I had been arrested for criminal domestic violence I couldn't work in that program. They accepted me into the housing program because it is the only program where people who have beat other people up can go. I can't hurt anyone in the housing program and I can hammer nails. I was not allowed to drive but there were other housing people in the volunteer houses who I could ride with.

When I got to the Owsley Volunteer House, the welcoming lady had put a banner on my door that said, "Welcome Jimbo." I was 58 years old and I had never been called Jimbo before. Because I'm in housing I had to work with young college students who came down on spring break. They seemed to enjoy yelling "JIMBO" when they wanted something and it seem they were more likely to talk to me (probably a lot more likely than if I had been called Brother James). So now I am learning some construction skills and being somewhat of an influence to these young people. They all have email, so I get the email addresses of the people who worked on my crew and keep them informed about what is going on after they left.

There was a flood in Eastern Kentucky and CAP responded to it, so I got a taste of disaster relief. Later, they went to Mississippi after Katrina and I knew I was supposed to go. After I got there, I knew I was supposed to go back after my obligation to CAP was up. I also knew more people needed to be there so I emailed a lot of people informing them of what was going on and trying to explain the experience of serving; of how fulfilling it was. We are designed to serve and it makes us happy when we do this. The only way we can know for sure is to go and serve.

I was trying to write stories and words so people would be encouraged to serve. As I was doing that, Keith Gilbertson was there with CAP taking pictures of some of the things going on and writing about them. I am somewhat of a character and I was around when he was taking pictures. I told him I wanted to be a "character with character" so he took little snippets of things I had written and put photos with it and made an eBook called, "Jimbo, A Character with Character." He encouraged me to write even more.

We were in Mississippi for four months and I was there during that time as much as they allowed me to stay. CAP left Ocean Springs, Mississippi in January and I had committed to staying with CAP until the end of April so I went back to Kentucky in the housing program but I knew I was supposed to be on the Gulf Coast. At the end of April, I went back to Ocean Springs and other communities on the coast. Christus Victor Lutheran Church where CAP had been working from and staying, offered me a job. I took it and stayed there until the end of March 2010.

There is no way to really share the experience of serving. If I can share the feelings and emotions, along with the actual facts of the experiences, maybe more people can understand. The more I share, the more I meditate, and the more I write. It seems thoughts come to me that are inspiring. They don't seem to be there before I start telling someone about an experience or as I start to write. When I try to share what little bit of wisdom I may have, the Lord gives me more to say. I think it is like that with everything. The more we share, the more we are given. That seems to work in the emotional and physical and spiritual.

When we share our possessions, it seems we still have plenty. When we listen and try to help people who are grieving or discouraged, it seems we grow stronger emotionally. When we talk about the Bible and how the Lord has blessed us, it seems our faith grows. The more we share, the more we get. It seems to happen the other way too. When we hoard up stuff it seems we are more worried we won't have enough. When we won't talk to others about problems they have, it seems as we have more problems ourselves. It may work on the fact, when we hear about other's problems, we realize ours aren't as bad as we thought.

When I get a thought about something and don't write about it immediately, I can't seem to get the same feeling later to explain it as well as I would like. It seems as if when I write something down as soon as the thought comes to me, more thoughts come as I write. If I wait, I'm struggling to relay it. This kind of proves delayed obedience is disobedience and isn't rewarded.

CHAPTER TWO

MISSION TRIPS

Why go on Mission Trips?

Why go on mission trips? I guess people go for various reasons. Some go from duty. Some go to serve the Lord. Some go because others go. Some of us tease; we go for the food. I say, I go for the stories. Why? And what are the stories I'm looking for? I don't know. Sometimes it is a story to show how interesting the mission is. Sometimes it is a story to show others how bad some people have it.

Sometimes it is a story to motivate others to do something. What would I have people do? Well I would like for them to get more involved in what is going on in the world. I would like them to get involved in helping their fellow man. I mostly would like to show how joyful it is to go on mission trips. How one gets a feeling like no other. It doesn't happen to every person who goes somewhere, but it happens to a bunch of people.

To some of us it is addicting. I just worked with a guy who said he had to work to feed his addiction. He showed me some pictures of his Alaska trip and I could see how it could be addicting; and how it could be expensive. One has to fly to Alaska or take a long time driving and buy a lot of gas. So far, I have only gone where I could drive. One thing I didn't mention was, sometimes it is very spiritual.

The most spiritual day of my life was on the Gulf Coast cleaning up after Katrina. And I believe it is always emotional. There is no way I can explain it. I can't explain anything in any story I write, so I guess it is like Jack Webb in Dragnet, "Just the facts." Well, there are too many facts, too many feelings, too many emotions. I could just write the facts; and day to day, they would appear differently as my emotions or memories change.

I can't figure out why I go on mission trips. How in the world would I be able to figure where to go and how long to stay? Well, that one is a little easier. I go where someone asks me to go and stay until the end or until some prior obligation comes up. Last week I got a text from Samaritan's Purse wanting volunteers in Texas or Mississippi. I had to go to Mississippi anyway because my driver's license is from there and it expires at the end of December. It seemed to be a hassle trying to change it to another state. So, I can go to Mississippi, renew my driver's license, work a few days, and then go to a doctor's appointment on Jan 6th.

I try to follow the leaning of the Lord, so I don't change appointments because the Lord was with me when I made the appointments. I figure I'm not supposed to change them. It may sound weird but it works for me. It also keeps me from staying anywhere too long. If I make an appointment, I need to see the doctor. If I have to see him, I should see him at the scheduled time so he can tell me what I should do to be as healthy as possible so I can continue to go on mission trips.

Before I could schedule my trip, my buddy calls and says he is having a revival and he asks me to come. I have to stay a minimum of three days with Samaritan's Purse so I can go there on Wednesday night and work Thursday, Friday, and Saturday and drive back to South Carolina on Sunday so I can go to the service on Sunday night.

Going to church is my other addiction and while there may be more than one mission trip going on at the same time; there is more than one church service going on so I do have to make decisions where I'm going? If I stay for the Sunday morning service at the Ashland Baptist Church I won't be able to get to Walhalla, South Carolina for the six o'clock service.

We Need More Volunteers

November 30, 2016

We only had one team yesterday, but we did manage to remove HVAC ducts from four houses. I didn't have to go under any of them and felt a little guilty, but not guilty enough to volunteer. There are certain hazards and inconveniences about going under houses. The crew found a dead opossum, a dead cat, and a dead rat. Well finding dead animals is better than encountering live ones. In one of the HVAC units we found a bunch of 'possum poop.' How did we know that was what it was? I'm not sure but it was big and a bunch. The people who live there should be glad their

HVAC unit got flooded because otherwise they would still be breathing foul air.

Two of the units were electric and two were gas. One of the gas had the meter removed so we had no danger from the gas. It had such a small opening to go in we had to remove the HVAC unit to go in. When Jerimiah crawled in, he said the was still in the duct work. That was the first I had heard of that. The other gas line was turned off at the unit. We had to disconnect it beyond the cut off which was okay, but as we were taking the hood off, we hit the cut off and turned it back on. We heard the gas and turned it off. We were teasing; otherwise we would have been seeing each other fall out and then be talking about how lazy they were taking naps in the middle of work. We informed the owner he needed to put a plug into the line in case someone turned the gas on again.

We had one lady, Donnie, who came down for two days. She had been here before and she didn't want a 'girls job' then. I notice this time, she didn't volunteer to go under the houses. I guess she is realizing there are no girl jobs or guy jobs. Everything has to be done, and it is just as hard to clean up as anything else when one is removing wet insulation or sheetrock.

I wish we had more volunteers. I hope after people read this and see how enjoyable it is, we won't be able to handle everyone who comes. I know it sounds weird, but it actually is very enjoyable. One gets joy beyond imagination.

Go and Serve, You Will Never Regret It

Nov 18, 2016

So many times, we feel we should do something to help others. We hear someone is going on a mission trip and we feel like we should go. We see someone standing beside the road with a sign that says, "homeless" and we feel like we should stop and give them some money and tell them God loves them. We see someone broke down and we think we should stop and help.

Then what happens? Well we realize we don't have the skills, or the money and time to go on a mission trip. We realize the person on the side of the road will probably drink up the money. We will be late for an appointment if we stop and help and besides, they most likely have a cell phone to call for help, and people have been mugged when they stopped to help people.

So then when we don't do these things we seem to think the Lord didn't want us to do them. We are thankful the Lord gave us a discerning spirit to not waste our money or time that would have been better spent doing the things we did. We would have been late for church or we would have given money to a drunk when we could have used it for something Godly.

Well then, 'why in the world did we get the first thought anyway'? Who was it from? It probably was from the Lord. The reason we didn't obey was because our flesh didn't want to go through the inconvenience or we didn't want to spend our money. We tell ourselves, the Lord didn't want us to do something when things come up to keep us from doing things. Well, we will always have things that come up against any plan.

There will always be a reason not to do good. That is why we should stay focused. We seem to not get discouraged from going hunting or whatever we really want to do. There is always inconvenience is doing good. If it was simple, there would be no reason to do it. And the good thing is, when we do what we were supposed to do, we will feel so much better.

One of the bad things is when we don't do what we were guided to do by the Holy Spirit, he will not continue encouraging us to do things. The Holy Spirit will see our hearts, that we don't really want to do anything and he will quit bothering us. This is called 'quenching the Holy Spirit' The sad part about this is, later we will be saying things, like "I would like to go do something for the Lord; and for people, but I'm just not able, or can't afford it" and we will believe this. We will never know what we are missing. There is no greater feeling than helping others. Words can't describe it; and no one can understand when you are telling a person who hasn't served.

So, the next time you have a chance to do good; do it. Hey, what have you got to lose? A little money; a little time. What were you going to do with that money anyway? Buy some skinny Lattes? What were you going to do with the time? watch TV? Go and serve. You will never regret it.

That Ain't No White Guy…That's Jimbo

I'm in Moss Point, Mississippi and possibly the only white person for a mile around. I'm thinking of the time I needed topsoil and a black guy who was a wheeler and dealer told me I could have some. I drove behind his place where he sold African American clothing and started shoveling the topsoil into the truck. Some little girls who were having a garage sale ran and told him, "There is a white guy back there stealing your dirt."

He came around the corner and told them, "THAT AIN'T NO WHITE GUY; THAT'S JIMBO." Then he told me, "Don't get that bad dirt, I've got better dirt at home", so we went and got the better dirt. I was fortunate when driving up at a time he was getting the dirt a few weeks earlier; especially being I had damaged a guy's yard and he had come out yelling at me, so I really needed to fix his yard. That guy didn't know I was "Jimbo." He thought I was just some uppity white guy who thought he could just back into some person's yard with a dump trailer. That was another experience; Too bad I can't write about them all

Greetings in Christ, I am a Follower of Christ

January 20, 2006

Ocean Springs, Mississippi

I have been writing about what has been going on or my thoughts or both. This is the same but more important. I take some Bible classes. In this class, three things were brought up that I found interesting and wanted to share. I won't quote scripture because I may not get it just right, and you guys know it better than me, and you can "read the Book".

First, Paul says he is a bond servant to Jesus Christ. Second, he is indebted to the Jews and the Gentiles; the wise and the foolish. In other words, indebted to everyone. Indebted to what? Indebted to teach the Gospel. Third, he is not ashamed of the Gospel of Christ. What does this mean to us?

Well, if we are followers of Christ we should be the same as Paul. I think most of us would say we believe the same except maybe the part about being in debt to everyone. If we believe this why don't we do it? Maybe we don't do it because we are lazy. The teacher gave us an example of how we should do it.

First thing in the morning, go to your neighbor; ask him if there is anything he needs praying for, then go to the next house, ask them if there is anything they need prayer for. By noon somebody will offer you lunch. After lunch, go to the next house and so on. By dark somebody will ask you to stay overnight. After a few days there will still be people following you and you will have a church. Sounds pretty simple. Maybe I will do it tomorrow.

Jesus didn't tell me to follow him tomorrow. He said to follow Him today. To not wait until I retire or I have more money in my 401k. I will concede I am lazy but maybe just today I will at least ask one person if they have something that they want me to pray about. Where we work, we pray before we start work so I will knock on their door and ask if I can pray for them. After all I am indebted to them. If I would look at it like this maybe I would be more likely to see people.

If we looked on the fact we are indebted to the people on the Gulf Coast, maybe we would go with more a servant attitude. Rather than, "we are going to help," we should go with the attitude we owe them and this will help pay the debt. Everyone we meet we are indebted to share the gospel, so let's pay the debt and share the gospel with everyone.

Third, are we ashamed? I would have to say, we must be. Sometimes I meet people and after talking to them a half an hour or so, I mention I am a follower of Christ. Usually they tell me they are too. That bothers me because I am so undiscerning. How could I have talked to them so long and not known they were a Christian? If we both were, they might have been ashamed of it and I might have been ashamed too. They told me they were Packers fans and had trouble with their son-in-law and a lot of other personal things. I told them I was against the war in Iraq and I had a step-daughter on drugs. Obviously, I wasn't ashamed of these things, why didn't I share Christ?

It seems easy enough. A conversation starts. Almost immediately we can say we have Christ for a Savior, we can tell them how they can have him for a Savior also. If they already do, we can witness to each other about how blessed we are and other people will hear our conversation and realize we are Christians by our love for one another. Others may get people to ask us to pray for them. Anyway, if we cannot be ashamed, not be so lazy and realize we are indebted we can further the Kingdom. I have to go.

Love in Christ, Jim

Typical Day Ocean Springs, Mississippi

November 11, 2007

I open the tool room at 6:45 am. The group leader of a crew from North Carolina who has been here before asks me if I can deliver some material to one of his job sites. He has 37 people in his group and is working at three sites. He says he knows it is not one of my jobs but it is only a few blocks away and the material is already on a pallet ready to be delivered. I have never been to the job before but I had read a description of it. An extended family of eight is living in the three rooms that are livable and this is the kind of job I think we should concentrate on so I readily agree.

I ask Jon Biggs, the site director, if he will use the forklift to load the material. The sheet rock, insulation and trim are all on one pallet. Jon says he will and this is the way we should try to do all our projects. I have never been to the job before so I drive down School Street until I see the volunteer's vehicles. I drive around to the back of the house and ask where they want the materials unloaded. They tell me when they tore off the old sheet rock, they discovered there was damage to the ceiling joists that couldn't be discerned before.

After a discussion, we decided to take the pallet of materials back to warehouse. Another estimate of materials would be done and somebody else would deliver it. I had told another guy with the same group on another project, I would drop off three pieces of sheet rock to his job and I should have it there within the hour. This also was not one of my projects but it was kind of on the way. After I got the pallet unloaded and loaded the three pieces of sheet rock, another crew who have been here various times before needing a wheelbarrow. They are gutting out a house we have not worked on previously.

They are driving a car and could not carry a wheelbarrow. This job is on the same street as the one I had previously gone to but there are no numbers on the houses so I drive the length of the street and come back to the first house on the street, which is where it was. There is no Dumpster there to throw debris in, so I call Mary to order one and ask her if maybe the city will pick up the debris if we just put it out by the street. There is no room on the house side of the street to put a Dumpster

She says the city has been cooperating but this is a lot of debris so she will tell them to put the Dumpster across the street. The volunteers tell me they found a loaded shotgun (which they unloaded) in a closet. They asked me if this typical and what furniture should they throw away. I tell them the loaded gun wasn't typical and they should call the supervisor who had the project about what to throw away.

I realized the project I was taking the three pieces of sheet rock to, needed some debris picked up. It had to be picked up soon because the volunteers had piled it up on someone else's property. I stopped at another site to pick up the dump trailer. I didn't think the trailer would be full so I would be able to go and pick the material that was in the wrong place and take it to the land fill. Well, it was pretty full, plus it had a lot of food products that had been cleaned out of the kitchen but were not allowed in the landfill. We had to unload these.

The volunteers wanted to keep the trailer another day so they could get everything loaded up so they wouldn't have to waste garbage bags. I told them, while they had the most important job, they didn't have the only job, so it was better to take the trailer and bag up the rest of the stuff. It was a dead-end street and pretty tight quarters so it was a little hassle getting it turned around.

Okay, so now I am going to have to dump the trailer before I go pick up anything else. The landfill is on the way, but they only take cash and I don't have any. I drive a few miles out of the way to get to a bank. I pull the trailer in to the bank lot and then the ATM won't give me any money. I walk across the street to a filling station. They have an ATM and I get some money. I go back to landfill. It seems the dump trailer is raising slow because the battery is low. I figure it will charge up before I dump again.

I also notice one of the truck tires is a little low. I stop at a filling station and get something to eat and decide to get some air. Naturally, somebody else has the air pump blocked but they move after a while. Well something is the matter with the air hose and more air is coming out of the tire than is going in. I go in and tell them and they give me my 75 cents back and tell me they will report it so someone can fix it.

I have never been to the job before. It is in subdivision where there are some canals and the streets run kind of weird. The street is Dead River Road. It crosses Roy Street, which I am on. I know the house is elevated so I turn down the street, which I think is the closest to the water. Well it was the wrong way and a dead end. I had to turn around and a mail truck was in my way. I get turned around and go the other way. It winds around and the house is at the complete end where it looks like there is not a house.

Another feat is to get this trailer turned around. The volunteers are teasing me about being there in an hour like I first said. They have run into some problems and need more materials. They had called the supervisor and were hoping I had the materials. We unloaded the sheet rock and picked up the debris that was on the wrong property. They questioned me about a pile of debris they had piled on the owner's property in a 'burn pile'.

Man, if that pile had burned, the fire department would have been called. We loaded it on the trailer and it was full. Actually, it was over the top and we put a piece of carpet on it and tied it down to cover it. I called the supervisor and asked him about the materials the group needed. He was tied up getting stuff for another project in another town. I told him I would go back to Camp Victor and get the material. I had the dump trailer full and I hated to drive all the way back with it so I called the warehouse manager and asked him if he could bring the materials out. He said he could so I went back to the landfill.

Guess what, it wouldn't dump. The battery was too low. It raised some and then quit. I would wait awhile and rev up the motor and try again and it would raise it a few more inches. Well it never got it high enough for it to slide out, so I got in the truck and tried to run out from under it. That worked.

I think maybe I should take it back to camp and put it on charge, except if I did that, I would never get to any of my projects. I figure I can get it loaded again and come back to Camp Victor and charge the battery and dump it tomorrow. I go to one of my jobs I had heard the volunteer ask about some debris being picked up. It is on a dead end. Actually, it is not a street. It is an alley.

We like to never found this house the first time we went there. I park on the street and walk down to the house. There is a long-term volunteer working there who has a trailer with his tools. There are actually two long-term volunteers there. One from Tennessee with the tools, and a young lady from Minnesota who is unskilled. The guy says he has already put the debris in his truck. I like that because I won't have to back the trailer into the alley. While I am there, I get a call from the warehouse manager with the materials for the other job, asking me where it is because the numbers on Dead River Road don't seem to be right.

I tell him to drive to the end of the street where it looks like there is not a house and he will find the volunteers; unless they have all decided to leave because we have had so much trouble getting to them. I was thinking another young lady was at that site with the guy and girl; a young lady who was here a year ago with AmeriCorps. I was aiming to get her to help load some more stuff but she was on another job.

Now I go to the job I actually got the dump trailer for. It is also on a dead-end street. It seems like every job we have is on a dead-end street, but they are not. The house had very little debris, but the house next door is getting a new roof and when the group tore the old roof off they threw the debris on this lady's property. The group is from NC and working with the Methodists. I thought it would be nice to cooperate between two different faith-based groups.

Naturally, they don't know what is going on when I pull into the yard and turn the trailer around. They also didn't seem to have as many people there today and they didn't just jump on the idea of throwing the trash into the trailer. It seemed they were more interested into nailing shingles. Imagine that. One lady offered to help me. One woman! I was imagining they would just load it and I wouldn't have to do anything and they would tell me what a nice guy I was for bringing the trailer. Oh man, expectations are a killer.

Now because my expectations are not met, I am kind of mad. I go into the house we are working on and take them some cabinet material. The group was putting some doors in. None of the door openings were plumb and the guy was having to plane part of the stud to get the doors to fit. Hardly ever is anything plumb or square. Hey, a hurricane hit these houses and it shook them up pretty good. Plus, a lot of the houses were built by poor people who were not professionals.

I go back out and start loading the trailer with the lady. Then another lady comes over and helps and then a guy comes over. We load it fairly full. We could have gotten more on it but it appeared I could get it all in the next load and I have to go check on another job. One of the ladies puts a 20-dollar bill in my shirt pocket to pay the dump fee and she thanks me for coming by to get the shingles. Then I feel kind of guilty about getting mad at them. I need to check on a job I thought was finished because the lady called and said the roof was leaking.

The lady's name is Mary Green. She is usually in a hospital bed and reaches out her hand to me when I go there so I can pray for her. I had not been there forever and I kept aiming to check on her but it seems as if I am always busy. I was really glad when Mary, the job coordinator had sent me there. I wasn't glad she had a leak, but I was glad to see her. Mary was not in bed, she was in a wheelchair and she looked pretty good and of course she was glad to see me.

She showed me where the roof was leaking in two different places. She also showed me the door on her refrigerator wouldn't stay closed. She had to keep something against it to keep it closed. She also said she had no water pressure on her hot water. Her house is settling and I could see where the trim is separating from the ceiling. Plus, she showed me how the wheelchair just rolls to the back of the house when she allows it to.

I go up on the roof and see where one of the vent covers has a hole rusted in it. I also see the shingles are not overlapping the drip edge so water might be running under them. I want to go up into the attic to see if I can see water stains but I don't have a stepladder. Tony, the construction superintendent, had bought me an extension ladder that morning but I told him not to get me a stepladder. I was aggravated at myself because I had not let him get me a stepladder. I walked around behind the house and could see where the blocks were starting to settle and lean.

All at once I felt kind of blah. I don't know if I was tired from loading and unloading so much stuff or depressed about Mary's house. We can fix her roof, but the settling is not a result of Katrina, so I am not sure we can do anything about that. I am not a plumber so I don't know what's the matter with her hot water, but I know her house is very low and it will be hard to get under the house to get to the water lines. I also don't know how to fix her refrigerator door. I tell her I will be back the next day to put another vent cap on. She says she will leave about 1:00 PM, but the door will be unlocked. I leave without praying with her and that also bums me out.

I get back to Camp Victor and it is dark. There are about 100 people who have come from Texas to work at Waveland and the parking lot is pretty full and it is a tight squeeze getting the dump trailer to where I can hook the battery charger to it. Some of the new guys help me back it in. I have to get under it to hook the battery charger up. I get it hooked up and the dinner bell rings. Just right. I go into the dining room and Jessica Doyle tells me to get in line.

They are having Shepherd's Pie and it is "yummy." Jessica is such a blessing. She was with the first AmeriCorps group that was in this building. At that time, we were all in one dorm. She works at a hospice in New Jersey and she is just down for a week. She definitely brightens a person's day and I know she is a blessing to the people she works with.

Just as I start to get in line somebody wants me to take a group picture. It is the group from Tennessee. There are 37 people in it and of course it takes a while to get them in one spot. Then the camera doesn't work correctly. It was on a wrong setting or something. I get the picture taken and go back and sit with Jess. The food is good. After the meal, the young people from a group out of Pennsylvania are going to have a fashion show. The group's name is HAM. It stands for Hellertown Area Mission. It is comprised of various churches and denominations from the Hellertown, Pennsylvania area.

The group was here a year ago. Some of the young people had gutted out a house behind the camp. An old black gentleman lived it in by the name of John Mills. Mr. Mills is also a blessing. The house was a rental and we were aiming to fix it so he and long-term volunteers would have a place to stay. As it came out we could not get money to fix it because it was a rental and the owners were not interested enough in fixing it to buy the materials. We had a camper trailer Mr. Mills was staying in until the house got fixed. Finally, the house got razed so the people who owned it could make it into a storage area.

We have tried to find a place for Mr. Mills and finally we found a rental he could afford, but we had to do some work on it. The work is finished and the young people were doing the fashion show to get donations to buy curtains and whatever else Mr. Mills needed to get into his house. His birthday is Saturday and he will be 79, so this was a birthday present.

The group was sent to do some other job early in the week and it fell through and they were sent to move somebody. They were surprised and elated when they knocked on the door and saw Mr. Mills again. And of course, Mr. Mills was glad to see them. They said, "Last year when we were leaving, he was crying and we stopped the van and hugged him again before we left."

The fashion show consisted of three girls and two boys. They had gone to the thrift show and got some wild clothes to model. The girls had some really wild hairdos. The boys had put two bottles in the girl's hairdos to make them stick out. The other girl had paper plates and plastic forks and spoons to make it a cuisine coiffure. Seth, the asst. house manager, and Jess were in charge of the runway music. The timing of the music didn't match the runway walk, but of course that made it even funnier. Each person modeled three or four different sets of clothes. It was pretty hilarious.

The thrift store did well because I doubt they would have ever sold what the kids were modeling. I don't know how much money they got in donations, but one of the ladies said they bought quite a bit of stuff for Mr. Mills. I told them to come back. They all agreed, "Well, next year Mr. Mills will be 80 so we have to come back for that."

Maybe this was not a typical day because it was the first time we have had a fashion show, but the typical part of it is; there is not a typical day except every day is different and every day is an adventure.

Volunteers

Come down, have a life changing experience, go back and tell others, help people where you are, come back and bring others.

Biloxi, Mississippi
June 16, 2007 at 3:26 AM

This morning I went into the dining room. It was_4:14 am. I saw a

Bible and a book of devotions laying open. Nobody was there but I heard someone in the dorms as I walked by. As I came back from the bathroom, I saw a bald-headed guy with a walrus mustache at the place where the Bible and devotional were. He had an open tin box there with various bottles of pills. I guess he went back to get his daily meds. I went on back to my bunk and thought about all the different people who come to volunteer here.

I am going to attempt to tell about some of the volunteers who are either here now of have been in the last few days. The guy with the walrus mustache is from Austin, Texas. He had been here before. He definitely isn't young and he got sick that day. He couldn't work the next day which was a Wednesday but by the time supper was served he felt well enough to go around ringing the bell for supper.

He felt bad about not being able to work and couldn't figure out what it was. I told him I figured he got dehydrated. Last week a lady working with me got headaches and had to sit in the AC for a while as we were loading trash. I got kind of dehydrated myself because when I got in, I couldn't seem to get enough water.

We have some long-term volunteers. I guess that is what we call anyone who stays here a month or more. Maybe it is anyone who stays two weeks. Last week I went to the airport to pick up a girl who flew in from Washington state. She is going to be here all summer. Her name is Noel. She is 23 but looks 17 and has too much energy. She had been to the coast before and worked in Pascagoula. I think she may have stayed in a Baptist church but wherever she stayed, she felt like coming back and staying longer.

Noel had construction experience working with her dad and on mission trips but I think they are going to have her work in the distribution center because the guy who was running it left today. His name was Doug. He is in his 60's He had been here for about two months. I met him in April of 2006 when I guess he first came down. We bunked together in the media room of Christus Victor Church. He is from Connecticut and comes down for a couple of months at a time.

Doug brings his kayak and takes it out almost every weekend into the ocean and bayous. He rides his bicycle or runs early in the am. He is a vegetarian and does yoga every week. He lives a pretty Spartan life while he is here. I think he lives a healthier lifestyle while he is here than he does in Connecticut. This may be another reason he comes. Today as he was leaving, he told us he may come back with the Red Cross if a hurricane or even a tropical storm comes to the Gulf.

This week another return visitor came back. His name is Guillame. I can't pronounce it. He is from Belgium. We call him Will. He is young; in his low twenties I guess. He talks very little. He was here last year for a month about this time. He may be quiet because he is not real fluent in the English language. We were talking tonight and he said about how last year he was talking to a lady abut a black person and he said they were A-fric-a A-mer-i-can. I guess it threw her off for a while because she asked him to repeat it. He didn't realize at the time it was pronounced Af-ri-ca.

Will drew a picture of Jesus on the wall pointing up, it says, "I am the light and the way." When he drew it last year, it was one of the first pictures on the wall. Now the wall is covered with drawings, names and sayings. Will usually goes out on work crews. I haven't asked him why he comes. I assume he would tell me, "God sent me."

Today a lady came on the bus from Fort Wayne, Indiana. She has been down here twice before with a group. It was the first group to be here in this building. The group was supposed to be here the first week of this month but they had to cancel because of school being extended.

When they were here last year, her husband painted a bunch of murals in the building. He got sick and was afraid to come back because he might get sick again and he doesn't have insurance. The group came down between Christmas and New Year's and he sent a painting of the Biloxi lighthouse with his wife. This time he sent a painting of the gulf with her. I don't know how hard it was carrying that painting on the bus.

This Friday morning, three groups left. This is kind of unusual. The groups that left were Moravians (two groups from Winston-Salem North Carolina and one from North Dakota). One of the groups from Winston - Salem had been here before and the other one had not. I didn't realize there were so many Moravian churches in Winston - Salem. There have been a half dozen Moravian church groups from the Winston-Salem area.

The guy for North Dakota said there were only four Moravian churches in his state. He said there is one in California and one in Arizona. The group from North Dakota was mostly young people. I guess they worked hard but they didn't have a lot of construction skills. They went out to a lady's house we have been working on for a while. When the adult supervision left, the youths put on some of the drywall mud with their hands instead of a trowel. The lady liked the look so they put it all on that way. She was showing me and bragging on it so I figured if it looked good to her, it was fine with me.

Last night the Moravians had a cookout. They bought a house down here and are fixing it up. They still need the flooring put in, but it looked like that was about it. They are going to use the house to stay in while they are working down here. They have a big trailer all loaded up with construction equipment at their house. It would be neat if more churches bought houses down here. They could use them to house volunteers or for spiritual retreats or mission outreach; and then they could sell them and make money if they wanted.

This is what it is going to take to fix the coast; churches committed to sending volunteers over and over again. The cookout was pretty neat. Some of the people in the neighborhood came over and got acquainted. There was a couple in their 80's and the lady told me how she prayed for all the volunteers who had come and helped fix her house. She was telling me, "some of whoever you meet rubs off on you."

It was kind of ironic because the neighborhood was the first place I worked in when I came down here in September 2005. I should have gone and invited those people over except I couldn't remember their names. I heard more stories about what was going on during the storm. One guy said he and his family were up in the attic and he kept hearing the car float around in the garage and bump against the garage door.

Finally, it knocked he garage door open and then the wind blew through it into the attic. He said, "It was kind of neat when it did because it cooled the attic off. "He just kept watching the water rise on the ladder rungs. He had an axe to cut through the roof if he had to but didn't need it. I guess there were a lot of people in the neighborhood who stayed during the storm.

Well back to the Moravians. I had never met a Moravian before I came here. I knew they were around Winston-Salem but I didn't know anything about them. I thought they were like the Amish but that was completely wrong. I guess they are a lot like the Lutherans. Someone from Pennsylvania told me they were Protestants before that was the word. They were before Martin Luther. I guess they started when John Huss left the Catholic Church. They started in 1557 so they are celebrating their 450-year anniversary.

One of the ladies (Adrianne) with them was excited to get to "muck out" a house. She definitely did not appear to be a "mucker outer" She looked like she was just coming back from a beauty salon or something. She had to wear a 'Tyvek' suit which is a paper suit to keep stuff from getting all over you. She said it should be called a "asbestos keeper offer." Well I don't know how much work she did but I when I went over to the job one of the guys said she was in the dumpster rearranging it. I believe she got a lot out of being down here and that is what it is about. Come down, have a life changing experience, go back and tell others, help people where you are, come back and bring others.

There is another group from North Carolina but they were from an Episcopalian church. I didn't know that until they invited me to worship with them tonight. The guy they had with the most carpentry experience happened to be a schoolteacher. He had been down here a couple of times before and he is sad that he can't come back in October when the church is coming again but he has to teach then.

Their leader was a lady who also seemed to have too much energy. She was very gung ho except, she didn't think they could repair some laminate flooring and wanted to leave it for another crew. After we discussed it for a while, they tried it and were very proud of the fact they got it done. I wasn't going to insist they do it because when somebody tells me they can't do something, I figure they may try to prove themselves right and mess it up.

There was another group of three women and two guys. They were here a year ago this week. I thought surely it hadn't been that long. They worked with me last year but didn't this year. They were doing mudding where they were working. They were teasing me, "We did a good job because we had such a good teacher." I didn't know what they were talking about but they said I taught them last year.

I probably just told them what to do and they caught on because I know I am one of the worst in the world. Maybe this is where the maxim comes in: "When you can't do; teach." One of the ladies said she went back and they sheet rocked one of the rooms and she did the taping and mudding. One more good thing about coming down here; you learn how to do something that is useful later.

A woman and two daughters came down from Pennsylvania. They caulked and painted and then caulked and painted some more. I talked to the mother tonight and she said, "It was a life changing experience." She said it was so humbling. She couldn't explain it. I told her I knew exactly what she meant. She said she was going to tell everyone about it when she got back home.

Two of the women in the Episcopalian group worked in the kitchen. One of them was a little old lady with white hair who was here before. I heard the other say she was worried bout coming here because she couldn't bend her knees much and she was afraid she might not be able to do what was needed. I told her if the Lord sent her down here, He would use her. I told her I overheard another lady talking about going to work somewhere and a neighbor lady wanted her to come over and drink tea and listen to her story. I said the most important thing she did was to drink tea with that lady and listen. That may have been the main reason the Lord sent her.

Last week one of the ladies who came down had cancer. She got her purse stolen in Granada while the group was on the way back to Illinois. I was really moved by the fact she came down here to serve even though she was sick. I felt bad I couldn't picture her when somebody told me about her. It just proves, even though I talk a lot a lot of the time to a lot of people, I still don't pay enough attention to what is going on.

I am so thankful to be a part of the operation and I have to ask the Lord to forgive me for how much I have not done. So many more people I could have talked to, kept in touch with, visited more, prayed for, etc, etc.

Next week over 200 youth are coming from Nebraska. They are 14 to 18 years old, so of course they don't have much construction experience. Well, I have to believe the Lord has sent them so it will work out fine. I just let the Lord work. It will be a life changing experience for us and them.

We have had a person in a wheelchair down here before and she contributed very well. We've had healthy people who complained and couldn't find things to do to make use of their abilities, but that is the exception and I truthfully don't believe someone was listening to the Lord when this happened.

It may sound like from the above that there haven't been many skilled people here lately. They were quite a few last week, it just wasn't a high percentage. A roof was put on a house so that's pretty good. Well it all works out. The skilled ones were here when we needed them.

A few weeks back we practically built a house in three weeks replacing most everything in the house. I would really have liked to have had a time delay camera taking pictures of the house getting worked on. It was unbelievable. The crew that started it will be back in October and there will be another house their expertise will be used on.

If you feel you should come to the coast, come on. Obey the Lord and He will use you.

Love in Christ, Jim

Every Day is an Adventure

Houston, Texas

May 31, 2016

Each day is usually a series of adventures. Today I'm near Houston, Texas. I put in an application to help clean up after the flood this weekend. SP said on Facebook they were taking volunteers starting Wednesday. I knew I wasn't going to get a call about it until tomorrow, Tuesday, because today is a holiday and there won't be anyone in the office to call me today. I had driven down yesterday and gotten a room. I was hoping I wouldn't have to get one but one more night and I would get to stay at the church on Tuesday night.

It seemed as if I was having difficulty finding the church. It was Woodlands Church at The Woodlands near Conroe, Texas. Well I couldn't get that to come up in my GPS. It would come up on my Google Map so I had a general idea of where it was. Well exactly as a matter of fact, but as I drove around all over the place in Conroe, looking for a cheap motel and a laundromat, I wasn't for sure where I was, much less how to get somewhere else.

I stop at McDonald's and check Google Maps one more time. I see where the church is and start to drive there so I can talk to someone with

SP to see if I can come Tuesday night. The problem was, I didn't know where I was and as I started to drive, I saw I wasn't on the road I thought. The good news was, I was on the road I was supposed to be looking for, so I could drive straight to the church. I missed the drive, but I remembered someone saying this wasn't the best way to get in anyway so I drove to the next intersection and came around behind the church. I knew it was on a pretty big complex because they have 20,000 members.

I get into the parking lot and see Don Hall. He tells me someone is in the office trailer. I told him I hadn't gotten confirmation about staying yet. The director comes out and welcomes me. I told him the same thing and he said, "Don't worry about that. I'll show you where you are supposed to sleep". Wow, I won't have to get a motel room. The bad thing is… I will have to work tomorrow.

He takes me into the building and tells me to go upstairs and pick a place. I have to walk past a foosball table and a pool table to get there. the pool table isn't regulation size, but I guess we are supposed to be roughing it, so I can manage. As I come in, I see some young people playing volleyball in an area labeled "The Beach." In the activity center I see they also have some kind of arcade game. The big problem is I can't get the internet to come on.

I also hadn't washed my clothes from being up in West Monroe so I still needed to go to a laundromat. We are supposed to have supper at 6:00 and then I can go. I didn't realize SP had worked today. They didn't get here until last night, but the pastor had mentioned at the Sunday service that they wanted help so about 30 people showed up to work. I guess they worked on four houses and they already have 70 work orders and 20 people to call back to check on their requests. Man, this thing is starting out fast.

We didn't start supper until 6:30. The cooks had worked in the morning mucking out houses so I guess they could be excused. They cooked more than was needed because they thought there would be 25 people here to eat and there was only about a dozen of us. We had also moved chairs and tables around to accommodate this larger number and we had to move them back.

During our share time, it was brought up that we hadn't washed our clothes since West Monroe, so we could use the washing machines in the shower trailer. I didn't figure I would get to it, because there were people from the site leadership team and the chaplains so I decided to look for a laundromat. It is 8:15 and I know I have to be back by 10:00 because the gates to the compound may be shut and/or the building may be locked up. I drive back the way I came and stop at a filling station to ask directions to a laundromat. There is a guy in the parking lot and he tells me he doesn't know one for miles around. I go on inside and ask the guy there. He tells me there may be one in the Kroger lot which isn't so far away.

When I come out, the other guy is still there and when I tell him, he says, I go to that shopping center and I don't remember any." Well I drive up there; and pass it because it is hidden back in the woods. I guess The Woodlands is a high-class area with a lot of gated communities. I drive a few blocks past and come back. Sure enough, there is no laundromat, but there is a laundry. Oh well, I'll drive back and do whatever. Well someway I get disoriented and go in the wrong direction. Of course, I don't know that until I can't find the church. I drive past three other mega churches set back in some compounds.

I finally see the name of the street I'm on and realize it was the crossroad street where the shopping center was. I have to drive back. The street goes from a divided four lanes to single two lanes and I almost have an accident. Well, more like aggravate some people and have them convinced I don't know how to drive. For a while I was kind of in a panic; well I thought I might have to sleep in the van. I get back and check the washing machines in the trailer. Wow both are empty. The two married chaplains are just putting their clothes in the dryers. I met this couple in West Monroe. They are from Virginia; and are oceanographers when they are not being chaplains.

They also told me I could stay at their house when/and if I ever come by the east coast of Virginia. (maybe a hurricane will hit in the area, or maybe I should schedule a trip in the area). I don't want to aggravate them but I'm happy I can get my laundry in. I do; and it is finished now, but they are waiting on their clothes to get dry; which of course takes longer than it does to wash.

I come into the activity center to write about all of this and see some books for sale. The book is *Beauty Begins* and it is by Chris Shook and her daughter Megan Shook Alpha. Chris is the co-pastor of this church along with her husband Kerry and they have written two New York Times best sellers, *One Month to Live*, and *Be the Message.* Both sound interesting and I would like to read them but is seems I have met so many authors who I haven't read their books yet. I will have to live a long time to read them all. I guess I need to write a book (or two or three). I would have to get more concise and say they are fiction, because no one would believe I do all the goofy things I do.

What a Day: I Took a Breath Every Now and Then

Texas

What a day. Well they are all unique, but this may have been more so. We were tearing down a house and burning the wood. The fire department came out because someone said we were burning sofas and all kinds of stuff. The fire chief checked it out and said everything was fine. He gave me a brochure saying what could be burned and thanked me for us being here.

Christ in Action had an excavator and a skid loader doing the work and two laborers (me and a pastor from Galveston) dragging stuff and piling wood to be burned. I knew the guy was from a church but I don't guess I realized he was a pastor so I "preached to him all day." His words not mine; but hey he could have jumped in there and preached any time. I took a breath every now and then. Then he got hit by a 2x4 from the excavator. I don't think I have seen so much blood from a head wound before. I had to run up and get the first aid kit.

The excavator operator, Denny, was cleaning the wound as I kept opening antiseptic packs. They were very small. We didn't have any bandages that would stick to his head, so we took some gauze, put it on his head and told him to put his cap on to hold he gauze in place. Later he took his cap off and asked me if it had bled through the gauze. Yep, it had and bled through the cap also. I couldn't figure how why I hadn't noticed it before.

The skid loader broke a hydraulic hose and Mike, the operator, had to take it to Kyle, Texas to get it fixed but they didn't charge us anything. Then the person who called the fire department called the police on us because we were burning stuff on his property. Two deputy sheriffs came out and talked to us. The lady next door said it wasn't exactly the guy's property. The neighborhood association owns it and they voted to allow us to burn stuff. While the sheriffs were there, the skid loader put a big log on the pile and the guy who was upset got really upset. He was yelling, "Don't put that on there," but the operator couldn't hear him, and he came up and started talking to the sheriffs and they told him they couldn't get into any neighborhood arguments.

Just as we were getting ready to leave, the next-door neighbor came over and brought us some homemade blackberry ice cream. We really thanked her, but she said it was left over ice cream. Who cares? It was ice cream; and we had been working in the heat. Well, it was actually cloudy most of the day and we were wearing raincoats for a while. Somewhere in there I realized I had lost my phone. We just had moved some big pieces of the roof tin, so I figured I had lost it then. The skid loader had just run over the area. I looked and found it smashed down into the mud. I cleaned off the mud and it was still working. Then I did what I should have done earlier and took it off and put it in a safe place.

We went back to camp. A couple we worked for last week came over and cooked supper for us, brisket, potato salad and baked beans. It was very good. Three of their grand kids came over with them to help them serve. Then for dessert, they brought ice cream and peach cobbler.

We had some of the cobbler left over and as we took it to the cook trailer, we saw a rainbow. Second one in a week. This one was before the rain. There is a big rain supposed to be coming, so I guess the rainbow is a sign there won't be flooding. Then it started raining and we saw another piece of a rainbow, but it didn't materialize into much of one.

After we got back to the camp, the sheriff came out and apologized to Denny about them having to come out and talk to us because of some guy acting like a jerk. The sad thing is, if he would have called other people in the neighborhood association first, he would have understood what was going on.

Oh well, just another example of how it takes all kinds to make a world. The guy who was complaining had no damage from the flood and I would have thought he would have been glad to have helped his neighbors. I wrote earlier about so many people having survivor's guilt. I don't guess he was having that problem; but he had some worse ones, like not having empathy or sympathy, or compassion. I guess we should feel sorry for him rather than get mad at him. He is bound to be miserable tonight.

Washing in "All Hands" Washers
I'm a problem solver

Denham Springs, Louisiana

August 29, 2017

I've put up with this phone not working long enough. It is 3.2 miles to the Verizon office and it is raining, but I am going to walk over there and get this straight. The directions are simple enough. Just walk east on 190, then turn south on some other road with three numbers in it, and the Verizon store will be in a shopping center. Sounds simple enough so I don't write the directions. Should be kind of major traffic in the area and if nothing else I can follow it.

Before this I plan to wash clothes. It is our day off so I can use "All Hands" washers. I get there early to do that but someone has left their clothes in from last night. It is an AmeriCorps lady's stuff so I start folding it. She has a bunch of little underwear stuff which I don't know how to fold. While I am trying to do this a guy comes in with his stuff. He is supposed to leave for Houston in an hour or so and he is agitated the washer and dryer is full.

I'm a problem solver so I say, "Well ok, let's fix the situation. We have to take the stuff out of the washer so you can use it. Where can we put this stuff in the dryer?" There isn't much room for anything, so he wants to throw it out in the rain. Then he says he is teasing, but I know he is agitated and would kind of love to do that to make a point if it wasn't so mean. I take what is left and put it on the clothes I have folded. Which was good for me because this meant I could quit trying to figure out how it was supposed to fold stuff. We took the stuff out of the washer and put it in the dryer and then he put his stuff in the washer.

So now we are going into the dining room of the building and it has a lock box. I didn't know the combo. He couldn't remember but it was on his phone. He looks it up, but it doesn't work. We can tell it is supposed to be the right combo, but the stupid thing won't pull open. So now he is getting really agitated. I'm glad I'm there to keep him from blowing up. We try another door, which also doesn't open. There are some people sleeping in the rec room, but they are young and can sleep through anything. Someone does come over and open the door. We go in and he starts fixing some breakfast because he is working today driving to Texas. It is my day off so I'm not supposed to eat the food, but I do make some coffee.

While I'm doing this, Mike from California who has come here to monitor the job and see where things can be improved, comes in. We talk a little. I tell him I'm going to eat breakfast at James' Grill and Cafe which is on the corner of the building. It is local place so people are hanging out and teasing each other. I see they have tomato gravy on the menu so I know I'm going to get that, along with some grits, eggs, and some kind of meat. They put the tomato gravy on the meat. After we eat, Mike offers to pay for mine and of course I accept.

Well time is moving on. It is over three miles to Verizon place and it is raining a little harder than it was. Hey, there is a tropical storm and it is flooding Texas. I should get going before it gets worse and I know it will get worse before I walk six miles plus.

Decisions, decisions.

Stay tuned to see what happens.

Boas, Tattoos and Syrian Refugees

Jan 10, 2017

Gatlinburg, Tennessee

In Gatlinburg, Tennessee helping clean up after the fires and wondering what I'm going to be doing. I look at the jobs board and it says, Knoxville. I find out a young lady, Morgan, and I are going there to work in a warehouse because it is where everything goes before it gets distributed to other distribution centers.

First, we have to stop at the VRC (volunteer registration center) in Pigeon Forge to pick up some stuff and get instructions on what we are to do. We also have to drop off a young lady, Sarah, at the Knoxville bus station. She has been here for a few weeks and she is going back home to Ohio. They show us the stuff and there are three big boxes, a lamp, a tall table, and a dresser. We are in the minivan so this looks like it will be a tight fit. We start to move the dresser and the top comes off. It is amazing what junk people donate. Well that should take care of that. Nope, we are still told to take it. The back seat of the minivan goes down and one of the middle seats is already down so we manage to get it in. Then we are told to pick up another person in Knoxville who is going to work with us. Sarah says she can sit on the floor so we can fit the other person in.

The lady with us has worked at the warehouse before, but we still have trouble getting to it. We can see it, but there is a gate that is closed. We finally drive down a road that looks like it dead ends at the river but actually winds around to the warehouse. We tell the people there we have some stuff to deliver and they tell us we have to drive in and around. I am amazed. There are boxes, and boxes, and boxes of clothes and whatever else.

Our job is to sort out this stuff, backpacks, and purses in one spot, belts in another, shoes, baby clothes, new toys, used toys, new clothes and some other categories in various locations. But the clothes in general are going in some big boxes that will get chopped up and made into insulation. Then I was told the clothes will be sold by the pound and the proceeds will go to Gatlinburg. Man, we are throwing all kind of designer clothes into these boxes. It was about to make me sick. We were told if we see anything we wanted, we could take it. I was thinking how sad and wasteful this was. There were hundreds of tons of clothes. Of course, not all of them were nice. Some of the stuff was donated instead of taking it to the dump.

People are told not to donate clothes. It takes too much effort to separate them. If people have lost their homes there is no place to put a bunch of clothes anyway. A better thing would be to have a garage sale in the town they were donated and send the money to the disaster area. Not all the clothes were disposed of. If they were new, we kept them. The only way we knew this was if they had price tags on them.

I salvaged a few things, a couple of boas; those skinny, furry scarves. One is light green and one is pink. I put them around my neck. They kind of interfere with me throwing stuff in the boxes, but "hey, if you are going to look weird, it requires some effort". I know it isn't so easy for those guys to wear their pants so low either.

All is not lost on these clothes. The two ladies say they heard about some Syrian refugees needing some winter clothes, so we confiscate a box of coats for them. I get a blue jean jacket for myself. Morgan picks it out. I think she was determined I get a jacket or coat. She kept having me try on stuff. I asked where she came from and how come she was here. It was kind of confusing; just like it is when people ask me where I'm from. She is from Minnesota, but she lives in Chicago.

She was teaching kids but lately she has been a nanny. She usually tries to go to Columbia in the winter. I asked her if that was dangerous. She said, "not anymore." The FARQ had been subdued and tourists are usually protected. She had some tattoos and told me she is 30 years old. She used to know a tattoo artist (before he was an artist) and he practiced on her. She showed me the first one he had done her neck. It looked like a cassette. I asked her what it was. She said, "It is a cassette." I didn't ask why she had a tattoo of a cassette. She showed the last one on her arm. It was in color and looked much better. She said the tattooing was over a ten-year period, so that was only three tattoos a year.

I meet interesting people even when I have to do boring and sad jobs. All the jobs are necessary so I'm not complaining. One can't work in the mud and crawl under houses all the time. It is all interesting. I got to wear some boas, get some coats for Syrian refugees, and work with a tattooed lady. Not bad for a day so early in the year.

I could listen to you for hours; with that accent".

May 29, 2017

I'm getting ready to go to the laundromat and do some other things. Bill asks if I need some detergent. I say "Sure." He says, "Ok, I'll get it.... Oh, maybe I'll just go with you.... if that is okay." I had other plans, but hey, he doesn't have a vehicle. He flew down from Massachusetts and has been here over two weeks so I should accommodate him. Besides if I'm going to act like a Christian, I have to give people what they ask for.

When we get down to the laundromat a couple of other volunteers are there. One of them, Travis, asks me where I was this morning, because they were looking for me to go to breakfast. He said, 'I could hear you talking, but I couldn't find you." I asked, "What time was that?" "It was after 10:00, he said. I told him, "I was in Sunday School and had to apologize a couple of times for talking so much. The Sunday school teacher said it was okay because it was good we were adding comments. I was amazed someone didn't mind me talking".

Some lady behind me said "I could listen to you for hours; with that accent," I said, "Accent?" Then Travis says, "Wow that's good, I thought maybe I was just hearing you in my head" I guess he may have been influenced by our ghost stories from last night.

The lady who had made the comment was with another lady who happened to be her sister. As we talked, we learned that one of the sister's houses had been destroyed by the flood. She said she had a handicapped son is in his 40's and because he is in a wheelchair she always takes him to their church when bad weather happens. She knows she won't be able to handle him by herself in a storm. While they were there in church, her house was washed away.

She seemed to be very upbeat about the situation. She said she had decided to move closer to where her son's doctors are. She said, "I have been praying wrong. I was praying for the rain to stop and I should have been praying for wisdom." She seemed pretty wise to me, but I guess she knows what she should have been praying about. Her and her sister were joking about all kinds of stuff. The sister gets change to do laundry and when the quarters start coming out, she yells, "JACKPOT." She acts like she has won a bunch of money. She tells us about her neighbors getting some of her clothes out of the house and washing them before they got too moldy. She said, "Maybe some of the towels got moldy and I might have to throw them away, but it seemed as if the rest of the clothes are good."

I was inspired by these two ladies so I asked if I could pray with them. They said, "Sure we accept prayers from everyone." I was mostly thanking the Lord for getting to meet these ladies and seeing their tenacity and their positive attitude. Of course, I asked the Lord to bless them and to give them wisdom in making decisions.

While I was at the laundromat I asked Travis about his job and how he could take off and volunteer like he did. He was in Gatlinburg in January.

He said, "I retired from deep sea diving." I was amazed because he is so young. I guess in his 40's. He told me, "I saved my money and lived a frugal lifestyle." He rode a bicycle until he bought a motorcycle. He said he also works a few months in the winter in New Orleans when it is cold elsewhere.

If I had not taken Bill with me, I wouldn't have met the two sisters or heard Travis's story.

He Can't Handle Snakes, Well on Second Thought, I Guess He Can

Eastern Kentucky

What happened today that was different? We had to go back to the trailer where we were removing the insulation. It has dried out some. Well that is relative. A local volunteer, Amber, got her foot stuck in the mud and she had trouble getting it unstuck. Even though it was drier than yesterday it wasn't where we were trying to get in and out. No big deal. We just went in somewhere else. When you have a nasty job, you just have to see how you can enjoy it. Hey ain't mud bogging, or mud wrestling fun? "Just a slippin and a slidin"

Earlier someone had mentioned watching out for snakes. I figured snakes wouldn't want to hang around in old nasty mud. I told the volunteers, "You don't have to worry about the snakes because the alligators ate them." Well that was wrong, or there are no gators here because we found a snake under the trailer. It was small and Carmen from New York caught it, but we had to crawl out so we could look at it and determine what it was. It appeared to be a garter snake. That's good because it isn't poisonous, so therefore if he had a momma or papa around we won't get bit and die. A young snake gets scared and uses all the venom when they bite.

Okay, now that we know we are not going to die of snake bite, we go back underneath the trailer again. We had originally planned on going from end to end taking out insulation, but decided going cross ways, backwards and forwards, would be more effective. Carmen and I cut the plastic and insulation and the ladies pulled it out and disposed of it. We also had a tarp we thought we could put the insulation on and drag it out. The problem was how to get the tarp back under again in the mud.

Finally, we decided to lay on the tarp and used a rake to push the wet insulation to where the ladies could use another rake to pull it out. The second time they try to pull the wet insulation out, the rake breaks. Then when we move the tarp to go back across and are in the next bay. We realize there is a hot wire. Carmen is telling me about it. He felt a tingle when he was in the mud on the last bay but thought it was his hand getting weak or something.

Now we realized it was electricity. I could hear the wire sparking and see it out of the corner of my eye. So now we have to get out again, trying to be as careful not to touch the frame of the trailer. Before I was watching to not knock my brains out, and now it's not to get electrocuted. I know neither one is a big deal. Just aggravating. When we get out and tell the owner he says a breaker tripped. That means there is no electricity going into the wire now. Well that may depend on which way the electricity was coming.

Carmen crawls back under to check to see if wire is hot; it isn't and we go back under. This is Carmen's last full day at work so he wants to get as much done as possible and he decides to work through lunch. He stays under the trailer cutting out insulation while we are eating. When we get through, we pull out the tarp with the insulation on it. He says it will take us all to pull it out. The insulation is so heavy when it is wet, plus when we crawl on the tarp in the mud the mud wants to suck it in and it is hard to just pull it out of the mud.

Earlier in the day we had cut a piece of flex duct out. It was full of nasty water so we were trying not to spill any. I'm pulling one end and then Carmen is holding the other end up so it won't pour out under the trailer and make it worse than it is. I get to the edge and some spills out but at least it isn't under trailer.

With more contact of the duct on the mud and causing more friction, it is harder to pull and we can't pull it with the four people who are tugging. It appears we are going to have to dump it all beside the trailer and have a mud hole.

I yell for Gladys who is the smallest person there to grab hold somewhere and pull. It isn't budging and it seems a futile effort, but when she gets hold and pulls, it seems as if a tractor or something is pulling. It almost flies across the grass as we are going to the creek to get it dumped. We are all laughing and staggering over each other as we pull that flex duct full of water. Just goes to show; if it weren't for the weakest person in a team, the team couldn't do as much. The weakest appeared to be the strongest because until she put out her effort, nothing was happening. Seems like there could be a lot of lessons and sermons out of that. I'm tearing up as I type this. It actually was very emotional at the time.

When you are straining your guts out and another person comes along side to help in whatever way they can, it makes you appreciate them and it adds to the feeling when you realize something is getting accomplished. You are not just a strain with no results. I think that is what is hard sometimes. We work and we see no results. When we work together, we can encourage each other; and we can rejoice together when we see results. Man, I'm going to miss the team, because Gladys and Amber are only here for today. They were here yesterday also. Carmen is leaving also.

On the other side, if we were having to pull out wet insulation all the time, I'm not too sure I would want to be on that team. Just not a job one wants to do for ever. Right now, that is what it looks like. I was carrying a bag of wet insulation to the road and a guy stops and asks how many of us are there. I think maybe he is going to bring us a lunch or something. I tell him "Six." I forgot our lead had left. He says, "Well I'm going to have my stuff moved out in a few days and the insulation taken out from under my trailer." I tell him there is going to be a big crew coming in on Saturday so he has to get his request in before then. I can't believe I was so civil when I had anticipated good stuff from him and he tells me he wants me to crawl in the mud instead.

That may be the reason we get upset with people. We expect them to do something for us and they want something instead. This is the good thing about volunteering. You don't expect to get rewarded and it is a bonus when we do so we enjoy it more. I wasn't disappointed when he asked for help instead of feeding us. We had lunches anyway. I just kind of hope there are more people to do it and I'm doing something else that day. I guess I don't have the servant heart I could have.

After lunch, the ladies decide they don't have enough to do so they suit up to go under the trailer. "Carmen," I say, "they can do the edges around it and that way they won't have to move the insulation as far; especially now that they just have one person carrying it to the road." Before it was finished they got farther back under the trailer. I was amazed they seemed to enjoy it so much. Gladys kind of amazed me anyway. On her first day, she said, "I know I am going to enjoy myself because I enjoy helping people." Too bad she could only work two days.

Even with them helping we didn't get finished. We had to leave a little early because we were going to a benefit concert. I didn't know it at the time, but Carmen was preaching. It was his first time. Earlier when Gladys asked him what his goals in life were, he said. "I'm going to spread the gospel" I agreed this was the goal for all of us.

"Sunday Best" was playing as a fund raiser for Johnson County Flood Relief. I got a T-shirt out of the deal and the music was good, but I missed hearing Carmen preach after I had been with him in the mud with snakes and hot wires. Maybe that was the more exciting part anyway. I am impressed with him and a church also that allows a 20-year-old preacher from New York. Wow. I guess I could say, "What are these eastern Kentucky churches coming to anyway? Allowing a young Yankee to preach. You know he can't handle snakes, well on second thought, I guess he can.

Well, I have to go to work. The dryer quit working so my clothes are wet. I guess that shouldn't make much difference. If I put them on and get wet it will save the time of having to work up a sweat.

House on Fire / July 4th
Fear as Motivation

Wimberly, Texas

Well, I didn't believe it could get any more exciting than being in the 4th of July parade in Wimberly, Texas. Not only exciting; but more emotional to see so many people thankful *Christ In Action* is there to allow the Lord to work through them helping people to recover from the Blanco River flood. I wasn't thinking of it at the time but the flag on the float was the one Christ in Action had when they were at the Pentagon after the plane crash.

Or course there are all kinds of emotions. Pride is one and can be bad when used in the wrong way to think one is better than someone else. I'm proud to be able to contribute what little bit I can to allow the Lord to work through me. I'm proud of Him. He is so awesome and sends me places I would never get to go otherwise and takes care of me when I go there.

Another emotion is fear. That can also be bad, but it can be good when it motivates one to do something to protect someone's person or property. The thing is, when one gets a good dose of both of those on the same day, it makes one very tired and one needs sleep to recuperate. That is one reason I haven't written about the rest of the day on July 3rd.

After the parade we eat some hamburgers and hot dogs. Definitely Independence Day stuff. Don't know why; it just is. Then we muck out a house that had nine feet of water. That means it was in the rafters so the sheet rock was removed from the ceiling; which as it comes out was a good thing. There was a big pile of brush in the back yard about 60 feet from the house. People on the outside set it on fire and moved some brush from another pipe to burn also. I was trying to get some stuff out of a tree.

At the time I thought I was being kind of goofy trying to get something out that wasn't a big deal and the skid loader could have done it easier. As I'm doing this, I'm amazed how high the water got and I notice a water spigot with two places a hose could be fastened and there is a hose fastened to one of them. I got the stuff out of the tree and went inside to help take out tile and pull nails. Suddenly a lady who can't hear very well starts yelling, "There are sparks in the air!!!" I'm thinking it was just smoke or something coming from the brush fire. Then she says, "There is fire in the rafters!"

No one is quite sure what happened but it seems as if an ember blew up on the roof, which was tin, and blew up under the ridge cap and caught some debris on fire. Whatever happened caused some adrenaline to start flowing. We could see smoke coming out of the top of the house so one of the young guys, Brad, started to try to get up there. There was no ladder so another young guy, Peter, used his hands as a step but it wasn't enough and then he pulled his hands up as far as he could and basically threw Brad up on the house.

I'm remembering the waterspout so I run over there and turn the water on, but there is no pressure so I figure it is off at the road and I start looking for the cut off. I'm used to looking for these but it is usually when we have to cut it off because of a broken water line. First time I have had to look because we needed water.

In the meantime, Peter is throwing bottles of water to Brad who is trying to throw the water under the ridge cap. Inside Bobby, our leader, is up in the rafters and someone is throwing him bottled water which he is using to douse the rafters that are on fire. I find the cut off, but I can't turn in on by hand so I yell for Sharon, who noticed the fire in the first place to get me some pliers. She does and I get the water turned on. I run to the hose and grab it and yell for Brad to come to the edge of the roof to get it. For a second or so I'm thinking it may not reach but it does.

The problem is, it doesn't have a cut off at the end so the water is going up on the tin roof and I'm afraid Brad won't be able to stand on the roof and get the hose. He does and runs up to douse the fire. Now the water is flooding the house because some of the cut-offs in the bathrooms are broken, so this is causing more excitement. They get some of them cut off and one of them is broken so they can't get it cut off, Denise manages to get a water bottle and cut a hole in the side and tape it on the spout so the water is diverted down through the floor.

Well it doesn't take long to get the fire out now and I can cut the water off. In the meantime, the fire department has been called. Before they get there, it flares up again and I have to turn the water back on. I have to turn it on and off a few times. Seems weird when it flares back up. There could be more debris in the ridge cap. Brad tore up part to the ridge cap to get to the fire, but figures he needs to take up some more so he yells for a crowbar. I grab one and am going to throw it, but Peter is afraid I will bust out a window.

I'm sure I won't but this delays me enough so we decide not to take off any ridge cap. The fire department comes and get a heat sensor to check to see if it is out. It is and the fire chief tells us, "You all did a good job." We weren't really expecting that. We were concerned he would be upset we allowed the fire to get to the house. He joked, "Do you want us to leave the fire truck with you?"

I was amazed everyone worked together so well to put the fire out. No one panicked and everyone played a part. Adrenaline set off by fear is a good thing. Relief the fire department was happy with us was good.

One fear is replaced by another. We worried about what the homeowners might think about their house catching on fire and their ridge cap being damaged. Well the next day, the 4th of July, they came out and worked with us. They said they had gotten an email from their neighbor about their house being on fire and they couldn't figure what it meant.

They were very happy it had happened when we were there to put it out; and they were glad to know there was debris in the ridge cap that needed to be cleaned out. I don't think they were glad it was there; but they were glad they knew about the problem. Well it is good people appreciate things. We were amazed at their attitude of gratitude. It makes our job so much easier and satisfying. So, hey, so far this has been an exciting holiday. Tomorrow three people get baptized before we go to work. That will be exciting also. Stay tuned.

Everything is Important

Columbia, South Carolina

Dec 20, 2015

I'm in Columbia, South Carolina cleaning up after a flood. It is Saturday, so that means there are plenty of local volunteers. I have been here a week and we have a new supervisor today. The third one this week. Somebody teased me this week about me being the cause of three different supervisors in a week. This is my last day. I'm driving to Pascagoula, Mississippi tomorrow to meet with the *Heavenly Helpers*, which is a group from a couple of different churches in Pennsylvania that started doing Katrina repair and still keep going back to the Gulf Coast. It is a long10-hour trip from here. Driving is hard on me and maybe I should not work today so I can drive today and have a day's rest before starting Monday. Hey, maybe I can even go to church at Christus Victor in Ocean Springs, Mississippi. That way I could see some people I haven't seen for a while. I actually stayed in that church for months during Katrina clean up and repair.

The only problem is I would have to change my schedule. I know people don't believe I have a schedule and I don't normally. But I believe when I sign up as a volunteer, the Lord is in it and if I wasn't supposed to work my schedule, why would I have made it. I meet with my supervisor, Vic, and tell him, "I'll get the ice for the coolers while you're talking to the local volunteers." I guess I'm the only volunteer in his group who has been working on previous days. I get the ice and he comes out with the group and tells me we have to go up to the tool trailer to get tools to put in his truck. I amazed he doesn't know we have rental trucks with tools and tell him we don't need to get any tools. We will look to see what is in the rental truck to make sure of course.

We have enough so we are on our way. I ride with him and when we pull up to the job where we had been at the previous day there are so many people in the yard it looks as if there is some kind of convention or something going on. There was no water in the lady's house of residence but water had gotten around it and ruined her hot water heater which was in a shed against the house. She had a rental behind her house that had been flooded. It had been a garage and they had converted it to a 4-room apartment. We had gotten most of the stuff out and we had more people than could get in the house and move around.

I'm really not seeing why I should be here. As I am walking into the yard, I see a truck and tool trailer with a logo saying they are from the First Baptist Church of Simpsonville, South Carolina. I know they are not happy that there are so many people here to do a job so small and maybe even shouldn't even be done.

Besides being a rental, the owners may not even restore it to an apartment again. Well, Vic sends them to another job and as I see them walking back to their truck, I realize I have met these guys before in Park Isle, NY doing repairs after Sandy. I tell them this and they say they thought I looked familiar. Well I talk to them for a few minutes and I'm envious I can't go with them because they are going on a more important job. They are going to clean out a house where someone actually lives and needs it to be gutted out so they can repair it and move back into it. Well, I know I'm to do everything as to the Lord, so I have to do the best job I can at this rental, regardless of what is going to happen. We get finished in a couple of hours and we go on over to the next block to see if there is anyone there who needs help. Well there are plenty of people who need help, but because their houses have been flooded and now they are moldy, no one is at these houses.

There is a group from Kentucky getting ready to go under a house to remove insulation. They have removed everything else. We could help them, but we wouldn't be able to go under the house and working with another disaster relief group is kind of tricky. What is one's responsibility? What about the legal ramifications?

I get to talk to one local resident who said he had been trapped for three days in his house. The water had not gotten in his house, but it was under it and all around where he couldn't go anywhere or no one could get to him. Every time I'm involved with disaster relief I learn something or at least get a different perspective about what the people go through who are living in the area. Of course, each person has a different experience. Some are scared. Some are thankful. Some grow closer to the Lord.

We eat lunch and go to an area we had worked in before. The house we go to just needs a tree cut up and hauled to the curb. We have more people than we need again and I start cleaning up debris in the yard. It isn't a big deal, but the yard look better than it did before. I talk to a guy from another disaster relief group and I find out some stuff about his organization. I actually get emails from them, but I have never volunteered with them.

The tree gets cut up and carried to the street and we leave to go to the next job. It is after 3:00 pm and we are going to Lexington, SC which is at least 30 minutes away. Hard to believe we will start so late on a new job. It is the only house in the neighborhood that got flooded and it didn't get in every room. That always seem weird when the rooms are all on the same level. I guess the water starts going down before it spreads to each room. The lady who lived there was using a walker. She seemed to be a little overwhelmed. Well why not? Your house has been flooded. It is moldy. And now here is a big group of people here from all over the place. One of the groups was from a Pentecostal church.

Getting Emotional Thinking About It

Ocean Springs, Mississippi

December 31, 2005

Fear not and have faith is the mainstay of the Bible it seems to me. A lot of the writers seem to fear and by fearing it show we don't have much faith.

Starting with emotions again. We worked at Escatawpa, Mississippi, a small town north of Pascagoula and north of I-10. As we were getting ready to go home, the lady next-door came out of her FEMA trailer and asked where we were from. We said Iowa, Pennsylvania, and Kentucky. She said, "That's so nice."

She had been worried the guy next door wouldn't get any help and she was so glad we had come so far to help and we were so nice. I am getting emotional thinking about it. It's one of these things that can't be described. She was an older white lady who was walking with a cane. Her neighbor who we were helping was a middle aged black guy who works in Gulfport which is pretty far away. She said, "I should be ashamed because I don't have my teeth in while I'm talking to you all."

She told us, "Some contractor was supposed to put door facings in for me but he skipped out." She got somebody else and he hadn't been around for a few days either but would be back after the holidays because in her words, "He had a good heart." After that she went back to her house I walked onto the street and looked around. I realized, as far as I could see the water had covered everything.

I thought about how many times and how many places I had stood in the street (Moss Point, Biloxi, St Martins, Pascagoula, D'Iberville) and had seen that same thing and how little of the area that got flooded I had seen. I was very emotional as I kept looking around. I think some of the guys thought I was "weirding out" standing in the middle of the street and turning and looking in one direction and then another.

While I was doing that, a guy came riding up on a bicycle. He told us he had lost everything he had and I thought he was going to start crying. I asked him if he needed us to clean out his house. He said, "Oh, no. A group came and they were from everywhere." He got animated then. He said, "they had been everywhere, to Costa Rico and who know where to do things but they came here to help me." And they sent him a Christmas card and invited him to visit them at Christmas and offered to pay for him to come. He said, "if it hadn't been for us (volunteers) and the Red Cross I wouldn't have made it." He was crying then and I was too because I am now while thinking about it. We gave him the number of the church so he could call them and put in a request for a rebuild.

The crew was taking off a little early because they wanted to take some pictures. I told them how to get to where the highway 90 bridge to Biloxi was down. It is so impressive a storm could tear a concrete bridge up so bad. And it tore up at least two more just like it. Because it wasn't so late I went by Gautier and drove by the Presbyterian Disaster Assistance (PDA) compound. I talked to some of the people who had come from Illinois.

When the ladies realized I was with CAP they started telling me how much they enjoyed and appreciated our shower trailer. I hated to tell them but I was afraid CAP might be taking the trailer back shortly because we were leaving. They jokingly said, "We may have to throw our bodies in front of the truck taking it. That is a big deal."

We don't have enough here at the church. We have four showers for almost 200 people right now. That will change with fewer people next week. I hope and pray CAP and PDA can work out something beneficial for everyone. Going to Pascagoula earlier I had seen kids along the road cleaning it up. Some of them were from a Wesleyan church from Alabama. As I was leaving Pascagoula I noticed kids at the southern Baptist church getting into a van to go to work. Seeing all these different people from different places and different churches doing different things to help people: giving up their time during Christmas break filled me with joy. I think all that emotional stuff tired me out and I couldn't write about it then plus at night there are a lot of kid at the computers and it is hard to get on.

The next morning when I am trying to write about it, I am interrupted by someone who tells me the breaker the coffee pot is on has been tripped. The breaker is in a room that is locked. The guy who has the key comes in early sometimes but he wasn't here then. I think I can break in but I can't.

Finally, Arturo gets an extension cord to get juice from another receptacle. It has knots in it of course and the guy plugging it in thinks he has to get everyone out before he can use it. This is aggravating me so instead of leaving, I torture myself by standing there and watching him get each one out. Then he plugs it directly to the coffee pot instead of to the plug-in strip. This confuses the ladies because they don't have anything to plug the warmers into. I am getting more aggravated.

During this time, I went back to the computer. Instead of sending what I had written to myself I had just minimized it and went to check on the breaker. Naturally, some kid is at the computer and I lost what I had wrote. I go back to the kitchen and I was telling somebody how many emotions I had gone through. Joy, compassion, love, but now I was back to hate and discontent and that was a lot easier to deal with. I was more used to that. I don't know how to handle those other emotions. It felt like I had to do something.

With the negative emotions I don't have to do anything. I just can feel sorry for myself because life is so unfair. When I feel compassion, I may have to do something to help the people I feel compassion for. When I feel anger, it is all about me. When I feel compassion, I have to realize it is not all about me. This means I am not as important. I am much more important if everything is about me. And doesn't everyone want to feel important.

Man, what a dilemma: to do good makes us lesser. People don't notice us as much. They don't give in to us as much when we are nice and you can't tell people how important you are when you are being nice. You ain't got time to be nice. Get to the front of the line, through the stoplight, because you are important and need to be places where people can see you. Sometimes through all this, we feel joy, compassion and it almost overwhelms us. We say we are having a spiritual experience. Humans having a spiritual experience. This is so awesome. But why?

Are we not actually spirits having a human experience? After our body dies, don't we go on to something else forever and ever and ever and ever? Is this not living in the Kingdom when we are filled with the Spirit; experiencing joy and peace? Why don't we just stay there all the time? All we have to do is release all the fleshly junk.

Oh, but if we release everything WE would not be in control. We would have to release the control to a higher power. Of course, the Higher Power should be able to make better decisions and we would feel safe knowing we were protected. Safety, peace love, vs, fear, anger, anxiety. Why do we pick the latter? And why do we pick it so often; especially after we have experienced this spiritual peace?

I guess it is because we are only humans for a short time. It is like being on vacation. being at Disney World of something. We have to stand in line, miss sleep, get in traffic, spend money, rush, rush, rush. We are on vacation. We have to pack all this stuff in before we go back to the real world. Maybe we are to pack all these negative emotions in before we go back to the spiritual world. If this is what we are supposed to do, most of us are doing a good job.

Well, I don't know if any of this makes any sense but maybe it will make you think. Maybe I am just getting too emotional. I really enjoy being able to cry and laugh. Here you get the chance to do both pretty much at the same time. Now the lusts of the flesh are overpowering me and I am going to eat. I'll write more factual things later.

Love in Christ, Jim

Flat Gap Flood: Your Life Has Changed

July 22, 2015

Paintsville, Kentucky

It is amazing the stuff that can happen in a couple of days. So much stuff happens to me. I can't remember it or record it. I have been in Paintsville working with Christian Appalachian Project for two days, but I didn't write what happened yesterday so I don't remember and I doubt if I know everything that happened today.

If I think two days is a long time, I wonder what the people were thinking as they got flooded here in Flat Gap. One minute you are watching TV, visiting someone, having a conversation, worrying about how you are going to finish remodeling your house, or yelling at the kid for leaving his bike near the road. All at once none of this is important. Your stuff just got washed away, the bikes got washed away. Cars got washed away.

The remodeling is about to become a rebuild. The conversation becomes trivial. Who cares about flags, politics? Your life has changed. The visit to your mother in law's you didn't want to make may have saved your life. You weren't there to get washed away as your possessions did. Now you are concerned about your loved ones, your friends, and neighbors. It went from being concerned about the remodeling to how do I get this mud out of my house? From being mad at your relative to being so thankful he is alive. From being unhappy with your cats aggravating you to being devastated because they are dead; not just dead but mangled up.

I can't imagine seeing someone walk into the water to go get a vehicle, yelling at him while knowing he can't hear you and he would ignore you if he did, and then see this person washed away, hoping he might make it but knowing that he won't. So many emotions. In a few hours, some people have experienced every emotion known to them; and maybe a few they never had before.

I think; this is the worst flood I have ever seem. I'm sad and overwhelmed by all the devastation and death while being elated and excited about being here and being able to help someone. Glad to see people I have worked with before. Wanting to talk to people and encourage them as I'm scared I won't say the right thing. Man, it is an emotional roller coaster just coming here and volunteering. Think what it's like to live through it. I can't imagine. I don't want to imagine; and I hope I never have to experience it. The good thing about some of these emotions is; the bad ones go away or at least abate if we share them. The good ones grow when we share them. We get a chance to do both.

Such a conflict between positive and negative emotions. Seems like it fits the area and people. And as a matter of fact, it fits the volunteers too. When we question one of the volunteers about the tee shirt, he says he does triathlons (swimming, running, and bicycling), but he hates bicycling, while enjoying the other two. He mentions how beautiful eastern Kentucky is looking at the lakes, and then he sees how devastated and ugly it is where the flood washed cars and houses into the creeks.

The people here fit this also. So many of them are trying to be independent and self-sufficient while at the same time due to poverty and injuries or disabilities they depend on checks to help them live. And even if they don't get any assistance themselves, if their friends and neighbors didn't, they know there would not be enough money in the area for everyone to live in a normal way. Organizations like CAP seem to be needed here to get some people on a subsistence level. There are people here who don't feel anything like that. They are out to get anything they can from anyone they can. After a disaster, police have to be here to keep people from looting the places of the people who are trying to rebuild.

We stop at one of the places where they are trying to clean up and rebuild. They were trying to remodel before the flood, and they were at the wife's mother when it happened. When we stop, it's afternoon. Both of them are working like dogs and are exhausted and depressed. We ask, "Do you need any help; or do you have someone handling it?" The lady looks at us kind of confused. Well that is the way I take it at the time, but it was more like, "Are you guys crazy asking us such a thing or are you teasing us?" They were removing a hard wood floor which isn't very easy when there are only two of you and you haven't done it before. There usually isn't any reason to remove a floor. Most people install them instead.

I say, "we will knock this out in a short time." I can see my lead isn't agreeing. Hey, we are fresh and we have plenty of tools and muscle. We start and I can see at first the homeowners are a little concerned we might tear up more stuff or cut too deep with our saw as we cut the hardwood into smaller sections to aid in removing it.

We do get about half of it removed by quitting time and I can see the homeowners are encouraged. The next day we come back and finish by noon. Now we have two local volunteers helping us. The Baptist church has come by with dinners cooked by the Church of God so we take some and eat before they leave. The lady there went from confusion and depression to more hopeful and positive. She also has to have some medical tests to determine if she has cancer or not and the group prayed about that last night.

It seems there are a lot more problems in people's lives than just a natural disaster. Natural disasters come up on them sudden and sometimes in the night where you didn't have to worry about them until they came. The other disasters (poor health, bad relationships) come slowly where you can see them coming and have fear of the future which causes more problems.

Well, we didn't solve their personal disasters but we showed them there is light at the end of the tunnel, there is hope they can rebuild, doctors can help relieve their health problems, and there are people in the world who will care for others. People are not wanting to take from them but are there to help.

This is the good thing about natural disasters. They give people an opportunity to see a need and to give assistance. Too bad we can't see the needs of people in our ordinary life and then assist them. Well, I guess this is something we just have to be more discerning about. As we grow in the Lord, we get better. Hey, maybe that is a reason some of us don't grow and we are satisfied just to say, "how are you doing?" and when we get the response of "Fine" we go on about our business.

Most people are not "Fine" they may be "OK" but we all have some kind or problem a brother could help us by being encouraging. My goal is to see the problems and to share mine with others so they can encourage me as I encourage others.

Everything Wants to Live

October 14, 2015

South Carolina

It is raining in South Carolina (a bunch). Rebecca calls her 84-year mom and asks if she is okay. She says, "Well it is raining and wet but creek isn't that high; everything is fine." Well, it would have been, but there was a dam on up the creek and it broke. Water flows down (and fast) and floods the place. Mom wakes up as water comes into house. Maybe she woke up as her refrigerator falls over. Who knows? but she wakes up.

Water is rising fast and she decides to leave. She grabs her purse and also her three-legged dog. She tries to open front door, but waist high water puts too much force on the door to keep an 84-year-old lady from opening it. She goes into living room, raises the window, climbs out and decides to swim with her dog. Water is running too fast. A broken dam runs out fast and rises fast. There is a wrought iron railing that goes to the roof eave and the lady hangs on to that to keep from washing off.

She can't hang onto her dog so he gets washed away. Water is rising fast and will get over the top of the eaves pretty soon. The lady has to do something else. Up the street there are some people with a boat and they are on a mission to get people out. They credit the lady with having good lungs because they hear her yelling, "HELP, HELP, HELP."

These people are local and have their fishing boat and know the neighborhood so they know there are elderly ladies on the street. Only problem is, it is pitch dark. It is a rainy dark night. Did I mention there is a flood? The most feeble lady lives across the street so they take the boat over there and can't find anyone. The boat motor is running; rain is falling and they are yelling back and forth asking each other. "DO YOU SEE ANYONE?".

Across the street, the 84-year-old lady is holding onto the railing as the water is rising she continues to yell (maybe even louder as water is rising) "HELP, HELP!!" The guys finally locate the sound and come to her. She relates she heard the guy say, "pick her up like a little girl, she is small" The guy tells her, "hold on tight." She says, "I held on to his neck as tight as I could" He said, "don't worry I've got you." I feel he is saying that because "tight as she can" is probably choking him.

They take her to dry ground where an ambulance is waiting. The fire department is also waiting and their mission and job is to save people. They confiscate the boat and take off. Problem is, they are not used to the boat and they wreck it. They don't manage to rescue anyone. Fortunately, no one in this neighborhood died. They tried to confiscate another boat but the owner was a South Carolina fisherman and he didn't go with people who had just wrecked a boat to take his, so he went on a mission alone. Don't know if he rescued anyone, but he still had his boat intact.

Now maybe I can do a little something to help get the lady's house in better shape so I'm helping muck it out. As we are mucking out, we have to remove the ceiling because water got into ceiling which was plywood and there is blown-in insulation in the attic. When we do that, the nastiest stuff drops and splats on to the floor. It splashes onto the volunteers and it stinks. We are told to leave before we get it all shoveled out because the stench is so bad. The worst stuff I have ever seem came out of that ceiling.

Later, I'm in the kitchen and I see some mud in the window. It isn't very deep but there is some stuff sprouting out of the mud. It doesn't seem deep enough and I would like to know what kind of seed this is. I almost would like to transplant it but it is probably something noxious; some kind of weed.

This proves to me; everything wants to live. The lady wanted to live, the dog wanted to live and he fought a valiant fight swimming with his three little legs. The plant wants to live. People wondered how this lady got out the window. She didn't have to think too hard but now she is thinking about her dog and having survivor guilt about her dog dying.

Plants will die and not worry but it will continue trying to live and grow. We may think we are superior as humans but the same drive to live in the plant, is in us. Maybe it is not as strong. Sometimes we seem to have a drive to destroy ourselves and it seems we don't have the drive to grow. At least not beyond a certain spot. A plant has the desire to grow to its potential. Seems like we humans may not have that.

So, today the lady is having a medical procedure to do something with her blood. Remove some of it and replace (or maybe not). It is something she has done regularly to live a better and longer life. Her friends are taking her to the procedure as her daughter from Atlanta handles what she can to get her Mom's life to a new normal. Mom says she will not live in the house again if it can be repaired. Everything is up in air and there is confusion and indecision everywhere. But people are still living and life goes on. Relationships are renewed. New friends are made while working together to help others. Out of every disaster there is rebirth of some kind or other. Rebirth of hope, relationships, plants and more.

So, pray for Ms. Fila, for Rebecca, for South Carolina, for relationships to be reborn, for volunteers to stay strong, for the world for anything and everything. JUST PRAY.

Be a Conduit for Hope

May 2012

On the Gulf Coast

I'm going to do the devotion for the group this morning. First, I'm going to Tato Nut to get doughnuts. My devotion is about something I learned yesterday at the Community Health Conference. Life goes on. Whether we do anything of not. Life goes on. The best we can do is be a conduit for hope while life does its work.

Intervention only works when people have hope. It will work, so our job is to give them hope. On the way I see a turtle walking across the road. He would have made it anyway, but I helped him up on the curb. I wouldn't have seen him if it had not been for a lady slowing down and parking. In front of the doughnut shop was a young lady reading a book with the title, "What To Do After You Believe" She seemed interesting (and she was pretty) so I started sharing stuff I had learned yesterday.

She thanked me and she showed me what she had written on her wrist, "Greater is he who is in me, than he who is in the world." She reads this to people and says they look at her funny and ask, "do really believe this?" She says, "Of course because Jesus is in me." So now you see my dilemma.

"Be careful what you pick up, you may not be able to get rid of it." Or how a 71-year marriage got started

Our crew leader said we were going to work on a house where the couple was around 90 years old. As it came out the wife, Mary, was 88 and the husband, Allan, was 90. They had been married for 71 years and had lived in this house for 51 years. It was a full gut out, which means everything is taken out to the ceiling. In this case the ceiling was coming out too. I sort of think this is easier because we don't have to decide where to quit and we don't have to cut any sheetrock

When we get there, one of the daughters and one son and his wife are there. The daughter informs us her father can't hear very well and he's legally blind. She introduces us to him. He has told his son and daughter what part of the house he doesn't want us to bother which consists of the bathrooms and part of the kitchen. We talk awhile and he says he is going to mow the lawn. He has a riding lawnmower and he gets on it and takes off. It is a big area he is mowing, more like a pasture than a lawn.

A person who is 90 is going to have had some experiences in their life. We all have experiences. Maybe the most interesting thing is this 71-year marriage. Mary wasn't feeling so well so they took her back to a fifth wheel trailer they were staying in, but at the end of the day they went and got her. By then her husband had finally quit mowing and they lead her in to sit beside him. I notice he reaches over and holds her hand. Holding hands after 71 years seems pretty romantic. Mary tells us how Allan fought in the Battle of the Bulge. She didn't know him when he was in the Army.

As it came out, she was she was in Shreveport visiting her sister who was much older than her. Her niece was her age and they were at the bus station watching the soldiers come in and they were acting silly. When a sailor walked by, her niece would take off after him and she would grab her and pull her back. When an Army guy walked by, she would take off after him and her niece would grab her and pull her back. They are having fun doing this and people are laughing at them and then Allan comes up on the scene and he starts talking to them.

Back then soldiers got preferential treatment on Greyhound. He told her she could ride with him as his wife. She said, "That was November first wasn't it" He says, "December 12th". Well he may have misunderstood what she was saying, because they got married on December 12th. I commented, "You didn't wait long after you met each other." She said, "No it wasn't long." He said, "You have to be careful what you pick up, you may not be able to get rid of it." They had four kids. Allan worked in every state except three, Wyoming, Utah, and Hawaii.

Mary told me, "He didn't want to fly or go by boat anywhere after he had been to the war." He said jobs were plentiful then so he could basically go anywhere he wanted to work (I never did ask him what he did; one can just talk so much). Before school was out, he would pick three states he could go to and then let his children pick where they wanted to go. While he worked, they went sightseeing and then on the weekends he could go with them. Mary said, "It was a good thing they liked camping. That is pretty much what they did during the summer because it would be too expensive to get a motel." Well it worked out, the brothers and sisters seemed to get along with each other and their parents very well.

Walk through the Hood

May 1, 2015

I drop my vehicle off at 'Long Haired Rick's." I tell him I was wrong about which wheel had a bad break. It was the passenger side instead of the driver's side. (which would mean I should have done what the guy in West Virginia told me which was to replace both calipers). He teases me about not bringing it in yesterday. I pick up my computer and some fruit in a bag and walk up the street. As I'm walking, I can stand on a spot and see four houses we worked on, a church we attended night watch on New Year's Eve 2006, and a house where we moved a schizophrenic lady who had lived there 42 years. There are stories for each one of these houses. If I went into it, I would have a few chapters in a book.

I've walked by another house and some businesses which would make a few more chapters. I walk up the railroad tracks until I get to a clearing that leads to the OS parking lot. Walk by a sign, "Best Barbecue on the Coast." Pleasant's, which is actually two businesses, owned by brothers and the other businesses is a tire repair shop. Another story about how a lady ran into their building on a Sunday morning after she smashed into a building across the street. (Am I going to get this story told about today because of so many memories?).

I walk on past the place where I first met Willie Mills and prayed with him on the street when I was with Evelyn Huff who went on to help his wife get her kitchen fixed. Did this prayer affect that? I walk past his house where the 2nd time I saw him (well at least the 2nd time we prayed) he took me back to a bush he called the burning bush because he had a light in it and we prayed while the ladies with me walked on. I see the bush is not there and wonder if there is some significance to that. As I walk past I look at the window installed in the kitchen that had no outside light before and think of the story of how Evelyn acquired the window.

As I walk up the street thinking of other houses we worked on, I meet a guy in a black car that could be a police car. I see he has a poster in the passenger seat saying, *"FO FO GILRICH for Mayor of Biloxi."* I wave and walk on. I walk by some more houses with stories and come to *Buzzy's Breakfast.* In November of 2005 it was a coffee shop and we stayed in tent in a field next to the shop. I walk over and look at field that seems too small to have held the tents, porta johns and shower trailer.

Think about eating there, but I have oysters Rockefeller from the Bay View Gourmet on my mind so I continue on. Eat on the deck and watch ladies in convertibles drive by and think how nice it is to be rich. The meal was delicious. There may not have been enough oysters, but it tasted and looked beautiful. I can see why people take pictures of the food and put them on Facebook. Rick called and said, "Your caliper is bad and it should be about 100 dollars to fix." I guess 100 dollars is cheap to get in and out of a mechanic's shop. I walk back inside after I eat on the outside chance, I may see someone I know and I walk by the kitchen to give my compliments to the chef (first time I have ever done this)

I walk back down the street and a black car pulls up and stops. The guys ask me if I'm homeless. I didn't understand what he was saying so I asked, "What?" He asks again "Are you homeless?" I say, "No." I don't know if he is buying this or not because he tells me, "You can get a good meal over to the soup kitchen." I tell him, "I thought about that yesterday." I did as a matter of fact.

We should hang out with homeless folks when we can to get a feel for what is going on. I ask him, "Are you Fo?" and he tells me, "He's my cousin and I can 't vote for him because he lives in the next county. I start to tell him I'm here staying at his cousin's camp, but he drives away. I guess he has done his good deed for the day, guiding a person to a meal.

I guess it is hard to tell rich people from poor people because we kind of dress the same. It's just that the poor walk in the hood instead of driving through it."

Will it Rain in Heaven?

"the rain falls on the righteous and the unrighteous." Ecclesiastes 9(5.45)

I wake up this morning and hear the rain. I like that. Then I start feeling a little guilty thinking about the homeless who may not be able to get out of the rain. Then I remember being at Lake Jocassee in South Carolina when it started raining and we had to get in the tent. It seemed to be a bad deal we had been rained out. But as I sat there hearing the rain hitting the tent and see the drops fall into the lake, I realized it was the best part of the trip. Just sitting there, not having to do anything, having a conversation with someone next to you which is not going to be interrupted by someone who runs up on the dock asking where the bait is.

As I'm thinking about all of this the thought comes into my mind" Will it rain in heaven? This gets followed by, "Will there be seasons?" I know I just hear about the sun shining all the time but I would hate to think I can't get to see the moon, the autumn when the leaves turn, and the winter when it snows. Can there be anything more peaceful than snow falling at night in the moon light? The Bible says, "the rain falls on the righteous", so if we are righteous will we still get rain in heaven?

Too many questions with no answers; I have to get back to other thoughts. My muscles have some pain and stiffness. I'm thankful because now I know which ones I should exercise. We don't know how important it is for us to have pain. It gives us an indication of what we need to improve on. Otherwise we would never fix anything.

Is This What It Feels Like to be a Minority?

May 12, 2012

Okay so much to say, so little time. Yesterday I decided to walk up the street where I am working. The first time I was here I was lost, it was a dead-end street, signs everywhere saying NO TRESPASSING, pit bulls barking at me, no good place to turn around, and everybody looking me because I was the only white person around. I was thinking, "Is this what it feels like to be a minority?" Then I thought, "I'm sure it is not, because besides being slightly uncomfortable, I'm okay. I don't think anyone is going to let his pit bull loose or shoot me."

I would much rather be white in a black neighborhood than black in a white neighborhood." Then again, we never know what it feels like to be in another person's shoes., I don't make it to the end which is the third house. At the second house a pit bull is barking at me. He is tied and I don't feel threatened. As I come back, I notice the house I'm at has a pit bull too; but it isn't barking.

It is going to be an exciting day

March 8, 2016

Another first before daylight. I am going to put on my pants and I have a pain in my leg, followed by pains running up and down my leg and then feeling like my leg is cramping. It is stinging like it could be a wasp, but it is not in one place. It is like something is running up my leg stinging it. I want to take my pants off, but I'm in the dark and don't want to turn on the lights and afraid to run into the lighted area and take off my pants because women may be there.

I take my pants off in the dark and put on another pair and carry the stingy ones out in the light. I look down the pants leg and don't see anything. I could turn them wrong side out, but I don't want to stick my hand in a place that has hurt me. I finally get the leg and poke it in a little so I can keep my shin against the outside of my jeans. I do find a wasp. I carry it outside and kill it. I was glad to know what it was.

I didn't have to kill it because it was scared and stung me out of fear, and I knew what it was, so I killed it out of vengeance. I was still kind of confused how it could hurt my entire leg. Then I took a shower and saw three whelps on my leg and felt there was one more I couldn't see, so I believe it stung me four times. So that was a first. First time I got stung before daylight. First time when I was putting pants on. First time I have been stung four times in a day.

It is going to be an exciting day. I go to the dismissal service to see the student volunteers off. A lot of hugging going on as friendships are going to be broken up. A week ago, most of these people didn't know each other and now they have bonded together for what in some cases may be lifelong friendships. Some of them have resulted in marriages in years past.

Life is Amazing

April 28, 2017

All one has to do it to go to where there are a few people at a flea market to realize how amazing life is. I go to Pickens Flea Market and I see these people and every one of them is unique. Then I walk and hear all kinds of conversations. I see a tattooed guy telling someone how well a sweeper works. Never in my life would I have picked this guy for a sweeper salesman. I smell all kinds of smells. I smell cedar where someone is trying to sell two-inch-thick cedar planks. I hear him tell the reason he is there and has them. His brother in law told him if he cut them into two-inch planks he would buy them and make benches. Now he has a garage full of them and the brother in law hasn't mentioned buying any of them.

Not everything one says is always true. I smell perfumes as I walk by a stand and I see a lot of ladies listening to a lady tell how her mother was a cosmetologist and she is giving them pointers about how to wear makeup.

She looks like she has done a good job on her face and I think how women want to look different on different occasion. She would look over made up if she was shopping the flea market instead of selling cosmetics. Seems like from these two encounters, I could get into some deep philosophy.

I smell food cooking and see a lady who is Mennonite (long dress, hair covering,) selling hamburgers, pork steaks, etc. This seems weird to me because I always think of them selling stuff related to good health. Why do I think this? Is it because they are always slim? Maybe, but as I think about this they are usually selling doughnuts and cakes so I don't think that would be as healthy as a hamburger.

Hispanics are selling fruit I don't even know what it is. (bigger than a coconut and it is green). I see another Hispanic woman selling birds. Some ladies are trying to ask her what kind of stuff she used to put in the bird house as a nest, but she can't understand them.

By the stand they are playing mountain music. It is packed with people who have various instruments. There are at least twenty. The one guy I see there all the time is dressed in a stereotypical outfit of the hillbilly hat and bib overalls. He has worn the hat a bunch because of the sweat marks on it. He has a beard and mustache. He plays the tub with a broom handle with a string tied to the top of the broom handle and the other end in the bottom of the tub.

As I look at him, I'm wondering is he as hillbilly as he looks; or is this is business suit? Just before that, I saw a guy with the widest mustache I had ever seen. It was about three inches wide as it came down his face. Appeared to be more of a beard than a mustache.

I could go on forever, but the point is, I was just in a little corner of South Carolina on a few acres of land, and saw so many unique people, smelled so many smells, heard so many conversations, saw so many colors, and shapes, wondered at how did someone find the stuff they had and how would one every use it all? I had to fight the desire to buy tools I may never use; and wouldn't be able to find if I needed them. I saw people in wheelchairs and was thankful I could walk without that. I saw people on oxygen and was thankful I don't need an oxygen tank. Thoughts, smells, tastes (I did eat a fried apple pie), sounds and feeling the sun on my face. I was almost on sensory and emotional overload. And this was just a little taste of life.

LIFE IS TRULY AMAZING.

Let's access our resources
December 3, 2016

Someone mentioned about not having enough financial resources for their old age; especially if they got sick. I have a friend who said, "the reason people are in poverty is they don't know how to access their resources." That made me wonder if this means sometimes we get in 'spiritual poverty' without knowing it because we are not accessing our spiritual resources. As Christians, we have been given various gifts so we can live a better and peaceful life and to share them to help others. We have been given the gift of faith. Actually, this isn't even a gift which has to be accessed.

The Bible says, "everyone has been given a measure of faith." One's measure may be small, but it is a part of us, and any part we use gets stronger as we use it. Some of the other gifts we have access to are 'the gift of healing (we can use this to heal others or ourselves), the gift of wisdom to make wise decisions about our health and how to interact with others, the gift of knowledge to know what to do in certain situations, the gift of discernment to see if things are as they appear. And the list goes on.

We have the Holy Spirit to guide us and comfort us and to counsel us. Of course, He is only a guide, a comforter, and a counselor. He is not a dictator. He does not make us do things. We have to listen and ask Him to guide us. We have to allow the Holy Spirit to work in our lives, but He is always there to be accessed.

In the early church, everyone pooled their resources and there was enough for all. Everyone who was cared for. Seems like as we work together we will be able to take care of each other. (and we will be stronger than the sum of our parts). The Bible talks about the seed sower and the person who has the talents. So, we all have both of these. Where did we get them? Well, the Lord gave them to us. For what? To use in the Kingdom of God for an increase. So, if we want an increase, we have to sow. If we want to keep our talents and have them to get stronger, we have to use them

An example in my life. I was offered a van. I almost didn't accept it, but the owner told me the Lord told him to give it to me. It had over 180,000 miles and it appeared the transmission was about to go out. I drove it until it had over 300, 000 miles and was in very bad shape. Someone told me he thought I had done enough for the Lord so I should slow down. He was concerned I would break down somewhere. He was right. I was on a mission and broke down on the interstate. I started walking, but a cold wind can take pride out of you, so I went back and started calling people to help me.

For a few days, I allowed others to share their food with me. I also mentioned on social media that I was stranded. Someone was moved and offered me another van with an almost new transmission and tires. It was kind of irony because the guy who warned me and the guy who gave me the van were both from Michigan. If I had not used the older van until it was used up, I would not have got the newer one. If I don't use the one I have now, I will not get anything else to use either. The Lord doesn't keep giving us stuff figuring we will use it sooner or later. He gives us something, and when we use it he gives us something better.

So, let's access our resources so we won't get into poverty. Let us live as the King's kids that we are. The Lord can give us peace beyond understanding. Just one more thing we can share with others. One thing is, we have limited resources when it comes to finances, but we are not limited on love, compassion, peace, joy, and we won't be limited on our finances if we use them for the Kingdom. So, whatever we do, the one thing the Lord told us more than anything else, was "Fear not." So quit worrying. It is not the end of the world; and if it is, we know where we are going.

CHAPTER THREE

FOUR LETTER WORDS

Positive or Negative?

When we have a choice, which do we choose? It would seem we would choose the positive but in real life we usually don't; at least when we are talking about something. Now I know there are more positive things happening then negative, but it is a good thing I do, otherwise I would not think there is anything positive from listening to conversations. We even label words bad that should have no negative connotations. We talk about four letter words being bad. I try to think what would make a four letter word bad. Word is good. Sometimes we say, "good word" when a preacher preaches. We call the Bible, The Word of God. That definitely is Good,which is another four letter word.

The letter four seems to be good. It is usually used as an example of a proven fact (just as two plus two is four). So I tried to think of some bad four letter words. Well shit, hell and damn came to mind. I don't see that except for hell these are such bad words. Then I did think of some bad four letter words, Fear, Hate, Envy, Evil, Sick, Jail, Need, Want, Hard, Prey, Cold, and Hurt were all I could think of, but I'm sure there are others.

The first one, Fear, causes most of the others to happen. Seems kind of weird because fear in not a real thing. It is a thought that so many times isn't even true. The letters can stand for False Expectations Appearing Real. In my life at least most of these expectations never happened. So we are in fear of things that don't happen; of people we perceive as enemies that have never done anything to us. This Fear generates Hate. Hate causes us to do Evil things. This makes us Sick and gets us in jail and causes us to have needs and wants and then we are hurt and hurt other people. So if we could just do away with this Fear, everybody would be so much better off. It hurts the people who fear and who are feared. That probably is the reason

Jesus said 'Fear not" more than anything else. He loves us and doesn't want us to be in fear or to hurt others because we fear them.

If we could do away with Fear, we would knock out a bunch of those other bad four letter words. We need a good four letter work to knock out fear. What do we have? Love, Hope, Good, Glad, Calm, Rest, Easy, Well, Kind, Lord, Have, Holy, Book, Heal, Care, Tend, Pray, Free, Gain, Heat, Cool and probably a lot 'more' but the first one was probably enough. Love overrides everything else and we know there is more love. "For God so Loved the World" so to show it He created Mothers who love their children. That is all of us again. "1 John 4:18 "....perfect love casteth out fear". So love definitely trumps fear.

Then we also all have hope. At least according to the poet, "hope springs eternal from the human breast." So let's put our trust in the Lord and let Him guide us. He gives us His Work in the Holy Bible about how to do Live a Good Life if we just Obey it. Even when he uses a word that isn't especially thought of as good, He says, "My yoke is light", meaning it is Easy to do His Will. If we don't always know his Will, we can Pray directly to the Lord. This will Free us from Fear so we can be Calm and be Kind to everyone by showing them we Care.

Envy

This is definitely a four-letter word. Is it bad? It seems to be, but can a word be bad? Is a person bad when they envy someone? Well I would say, we are actually supposed to envy others. How else can we see they have gifts and skills we would like to have. We see someone who speaks well, or knows scripture and we think, "Man I would really like to do that." The good thing about wanting something is, it gives us a goal. If we were content with where we are and what we have we would never grow. If we see something someone is doing and we feel envy (desire that we could do it as well), this may show us this thing is one of the desires of our heart.

If it is, we know the Bible says, "the Lord will give you the desires of your heart." Of course He will, He is the one who put them in there in the first place. He put the desire in there, and He gave us the talent to obtain our desire. The problem is, even though we have talent, it takes a lot of work to perfect it. Naturally, the more we practice, the better we get. We will not get any better if we don't work at it.

If we see a person who can recite scripture, or sing, and we feel envious, then we should start working on that skill. If we are envious of how someone else does something, this should be the person we approach to help us learn it. It wouldn't make any sense to go to anyone else. The reason you were envious was because they were good. If you want to be as good as them, you wouldn't go to a person who isn't good to find information about how to be good.

I know the word 'envy' has got a bad rap. It seems the Bible says, 'to not envy', but when I look up these scriptures, it tells us to not envy the evildoer. We are not to envy people who are not using their talents to help others. For one thing we know what is going to happen to them. The Lord blesses people who bless others. If we use our talent to help others, our talent will get stronger and we will grow and have more to share.

And it seems as when they had envy in their heart, the just was jealous of the other person who had a talent or was better liked, or whatever. They didn't want to obtain the talent. They wanted to kill the person who had the talent. They weren't just envious; they had a spirit of envy. Is this where the 'green eyed monster' comes in. This is when it takes over and makes a person 'green with envy'. We know one of the Ten Commandments says, to not covet stuff. Don't covet anything of your neighbor's. It is one of the "ten big ones," so it is very bad to covet. Yet One Corinthians, tells us, "earnestly covet the best gifts.'

So, it isn't the covet or envy that is the problem. It is when we want to take something away from someone. It is when the guy has a gift and we want to take it. If he can sing well and he can teach us to sing, then there are two people who can sing. They can harmonize or go out and sing to two different groups. Acquiring skills does not take away from another person who has this skill.

If the Jews who were envious of Jesus and plotted his death, had said, "man we are envious of how he gets these big crowds. Maybe we should see how he does it and then we can get big crowds too." We know why they didn't do that. They didn't want to change the way they were doing things. They were preaching it is the law which gives people salvation and if one doesn't adhere to the law they are lost.

Jesus said, salvation is a free gift. When one receives it, he will want to uphold the law. The Lord gave us gifts so we could live life to the fullest; to make our life richer; not poorer. It seems like it was almost the same thing, except now the people were going to obey the law out of love instead of fear. It seems like a win to me for the Jews. Well they would rather kill Jesus than change.

It is the same with any of us. If we are envious of someone's gift, we are going to have to change to acquire it. We are going to have to read the Bible more, study more, and mainly practice more. It seems for some reason we are usually envious of people we don't like, so the hardest part may be to get over that and ask the person to give us tips on how to do better. The problem may be, you don't like the person and you are not as envious of the gift as you are jealous he has it. You don't want it; you just don't want him to have it. So 'envy' may help you realize you don't have the love for this person you should have.

Fine "Fine as a frog hair."

Another good four-letter word. When one is fine they are good. Sometimes it describes something more than good. He is "looking fine." Sometimes it seems to be beyond description. How are your today? "Fine as a frog hair." But then again there is "fine tooth comb." Takes thin hair to go through that. So fine hair doesn't especially mean good; just the thickness of it. When one is discussing something and another says "fine," it usually means they see your point and it is a good one.

On the other hand, when one is arguing with a woman and all at once she says, "FINE THEN." Don't take it that she was saying, "everything is fine." She is saying the argument is over until she can find a way to retaliate. Fine is a good word but one needs to know the context. When you ask someone how they are doing and they say, "I'm doing fine." It could mean they are doing exceptionally well or they are barely surviving and they are just being polite. You need to hear the excitement in their voice to see if it is really fine or not.

I guess this means you have to be really paying attention in a conversation to know what a person is really trying to say (or not trying to say). I guess this is why it says in the Bible, "He who has ears, let him hear." It means; pay more attention to more than the words. Listen to the heart and the true meaning.

Fear
Unflappable

Definitely a bad four-letter word. It paralyzes us. It makes us see things that are not true. The list seems to go forever of what it does. I know I'm supposed to write about fear; and then I was in fear about writing it. No one will want to see it, no one will read it, I won't say the right thing, and again the list goes on. Well if I am supposed to write it, most of these things won't matter. How can I say the wrong thing?

We all have fears. It isn't like I will offend someone. And there are a lot more reasons I will write too much than the other way around. One could talk about fear forever; and most of us spend too much time talking about it. Fear of the state of the nation, of the world, of the future, and the list goes on forever. So, because I am so egocentric (like everyone else) I will talk about mine.

Most people I know commend me on my faith, about me not worrying no matter what. When I was at the CAP volunteer house, we were doing a devotion describing each house mate in one word; and of the words they described me as was 'unflappable'. The 'we can do this no matter what has happened' attitude. It doesn't matter what has happened, everything will be okay. I quote Romans 8:28 almost constantly and I believe it. ALL THINGS DO WORK TOGETHER FOR GOOD.

The problem is, I know they "work together'" for good. I know they are not good individually. It is just later in life one can see things we may have considered bad ended up working together for a good result. And like I have told people they work together for good, but it could have been 'better' if we had made better decisions. If I say something stupid to someone and they hit me in the nose, it will teach me not to say things like that and therefore I can teach others to not do that and not do it to a bigger guy. It works to keep me from getting hurt worse than I may have, but I also could have learned seeing someone else get hit and avoided some pain, the getting hit in the nose was not a good thing even though it all worked together for good.

So those are my fears; the things happening in the middle. My van is broken down in Texas. I'm in Louisiana so I'm not far away.

Fear?
"God has not given us the spirit of fear"

Oct 2017

Is this true? Are the things we have fear of unreal? Think of the things you had fears about. Did they come true? Or at least when you were in fear of them? The things we have fears of are probably real. The expectations of them are what isn't real. I'm amazed at what people fear. I'm even more amazed when one is trying to show people their fear is unfounded, they seem to look for more reasons it isn't. And if by some wild circumstance we prove to them it isn't a justified fear, they just see something else to be in fear about. Maybe people like to be in fear. Maybe it justifies their inaction because it is almost always something that keeps things from moving on.

I can't go witness because somebody will be mean to me. I can't reach out because I will be rebuked. We can't start a soup kitchen because people will be taking advantage of it and won't work because they have food and will steal from people in the area where the soup kitchen is, and it will give them an entitlement outlook. The fear of all the things that could happen just grows and grows until we are justified in not doing what should have been done. None of the stuff happened which we were afraid of because we didn't do anything.

Now of course we hear all kinds of stories about how successful soup kitchens and mission trips were for the ones who had the nerve to do them. We hear about some person's life being changed. We hear about the recipient who got a new lease on life; and we hear about the giver who thought they were giving a blessing but actually received a blessing. We all grow when we try to do the right thing. We learn things about others and ourselves when we step out.

Fear keeps us from this. It doesn't let us step out because of what "might happen". Well what will happen is… everyone grows. That small step may lead to a lifelong journey. And one thing for sure, when we step out we grow. It is the only way we can grow. II Timothy 1:7 "*For God has*

not given us the spirit of fear; but of power and of love and of a sound mind". It seems fear is a spirit. It keeps us from using the power the Lord has given us. It keeps us from loving; and it keeps us from thinking straight. Obviously, we know all of this is true. Fear basically paralyzes us.

So, are there not legit concerns? Of course, and plenty of them. We can work with a concern. If I have a concern a soup kitchen might not work because of the location, I can work on putting it somewhere else or work on educating the people who may oppose it. The main thing is not to let a concern which can be addressed turn into a fear that stops us in our tracks.

Should we not fear evil? Well a friend of mine wrote a book called "Fear No Evil" so I say he would say not. Should we be concerned about it? Of course; and address it in any circumstance we may encounter it. What can be the evil in doing good? Well, one may be doing it for show or gain. Be aware, as much as everything can be worked for good, it can also we worked for bad. Be vigilant. Be in prayer about all things. Continue doing good.

Fear
Still on the Fear Thing

I'm still on the fear thing this morning. As we used to say, "it is only a thing" Implying it is just 'one' thing. It will pass. Things will pass if we keep moving. If we stand still, they may envelop us. The best way to get out of a bad situation is to move out. So why don't we move? Is it because we are afraid to make a decision? Or is it because it is work? This morning I remember on the Seinfeld show, Jerry said, "the number one fear is talking in front of people and the number two is death."

Therefore, the rationale is; a person would rather be in the box than the one doing the eulogy. Well of course this doesn't make any sense; except the one in the box doesn't have to decide and he isn't having to do any work. I don't think either one of these are the things we are scared of most anyway. I think we are scared of what people will think of us. The guy speaking already decided to do it. He already worked on what he was going to say. But now he has to say it to people who are going to judge what he says.

I make decisions every day. Many times a day. Should I turn left, or right? Should I go here or there? What am I going to eat? Well it isn't hard for me to make these decisions because I know whatever I do, it will be fine in the long run. But could I make them so easily if someone was with me? If they were saying, "Why are you going that way". Now I have to explain and justify. "Surely you are going to eat that." Now not only do I have to justify, now I feel I'm being judged. So, is this the fear? Fear of judgment by man? Sadly, actually it is.

I don't think I have ever been afraid of dying. But I have thought of it at various times when I was in danger because of a dumb decision I have made. If I die, people are going to say, "How dumb can he be to crawl under a car with the jack no better than that?" As the jack is moving and I'm scrambling to get out the fear of being crushed and dying fast and was overcome by how dumb people would think I was. The ironic thing is the people I was worried about would do dumber things. Not only that, most of them were people I didn't care about what they thought about me anyway. Now there is some irony. Our biggest fear is what people who we don't like us will think of us.

I am thinking one of our greatest fears may be; we are scared of our loved ones being disappointed in us. It still isn't as great as the first because if it was, we would make different decisions. For example, we may take a drink (or two or three, or more) because we don't want our friends to think we are prudes, but we know our loved ones will be disappointed we were drinking. The list goes on. There are thousands of examples. Most of our major decisions may have been influenced by what we thought people were thinking.

Home
Grateful we have a home

July 2018

Next to love, home may be the best four-letter word there is. We hear, "Home, Sweet Home," and "Home is where the Heart Is." Going home seems like such a great thing. We sing about it in church when we are referring to passing leaving this life and going to heaven. One reason we talk about how good it is 'be home' is it implies we can really be ourselves.

We can scratch where it itches, put on our sweats, don't have to wear makeup. We can be ourselves and be relaxed.

We are always welcomed because home is a place where our loved ones are. Home is where our family is. We say we have a "church home." We are in a place where people know us, know our flaws, and still love us and try to help us. Home is where we get comforted and nurtured. Home is the first place we ever know about and the place we want to go to in the end.

On the other hand, there is nothing sadder than hearing someone saying, "I can never go home again". When we say someone is homeless it implies they have no permanent residence. They have no family. Basically, when we hear of someone being homeless, it implies they have no hope. It seems to say they have no family. They have no one who cares for them. They may have someone somewhere who does care for them, but due to circumstances can't do anything for them.

I'm thinking of the millions of people in the world in refugee camps who can't go home. And if they can go home, their home as they know it has been destroyed. Makes the saying, "one can never go home again" true because so many times what we considered home (the place we were born and raised) has been altered so much it can never be the same.

All of this is very sad. And there is not really anything we can do about it; except we can have compassion for people who are homeless due to whatever reason, whether it be for bad decisions or circumstances beyond their control. We can pray about what should our role be in this, because we are our brother's keeper. Every homeless person is created in the image of God just as the rest of us are. Jesus saw the multitude and he had compassion. So as followers of Jesus we should have compassion for people.

Mainly, I think we should be grateful; grateful we have a home. We should appreciate our family members, our church home, our neighbors who are a part of our home because when we talk of going home, we are not just talking about a house with blood relatives, we are talking about friends and neighbors. So, tell your loved ones you love them. Don't take anyone or anything for granted. Circumstances can change in a minute and when we lose a loved one, all at once our home wasn't what it once was. So be grateful we have a home and family and make friends with people so our family can increase. Most homeless people and refugees did not ever think they were going to be homeless.

The same thing could happen to anyone of us due to political and economic conditions we have no control over. So be thankful. Tell someone you love them. Do a random act of kindness. Buy a homeless person a meal. Talk to them. Pray for the refugees. Have compassion and be grateful. Being grateful is good because the more grateful we are the happier we are.

Kink
What about the kinks in our life?

Kink is a four-letter word. I have never heard of it being bad. Maybe that is the problem. We have certain words and things we think are bad and we ignore things that seem to be inconsequential. I have never heard anyone be concerned about 'kink.' I have heard people talk about someone being kinky and usually meant they were perverted. How does kink become kinky? We have a kink in the plans and that slows everything up. So maybe this is what is meant by 'the devil is in the details'. They more details one has in a plan, the more complicated and the more chances for it to go wrong. The kink is in the middle somewhere and is hard to see; or to figure out.

I have been trying to get water out of a hose with a kink in it and of course very little water (if any) is coming though the hose. I get aggravated because I think someone may have turned it off and I go back to see if it is turned on. Then I check the nozzle and after finding out there isn't a problem on either end I go look for the kink. Usually of course I just try to pull it out, which sometimes just makes it worse. If a hose with a kink won't allow water to run, what about a chain. Well a chain is designed to pull something with link to link in a line. When one gets a kink in a chain, one of the links is twisted and there is too much pressure on the side of a link. This causes the link to break. One broken link in the middle of the chain makes it useless for what it was designed

We have referenced kinks in plans, hoses, and chains and realized a kink is bad in any of these. What about the kinks in our life? Well we have a kink in our back sometimes and may mean we have to work it out or we could break something or have pain when we try to move. I am not so concerned about the physical kinks because we can feel them. What about our spiritual or emotional kinks? What could they be? I know I have them. I know there is something inside of me that keeps the love from flowing as full as it could. I know I have some kind of thing inside my mind that might break if I pulled too hard. I just don't know what they are. This is scary when one thinks of it. We can fix a problem when we know the problem. When we don't then we continue on until the problem causes a failure. I don't want a failure. I want everything to work as well as possible; without a kink in it.

So how can I find this kink? The Bible has an answer for everything. Let's go there. John 7:38 Jesus says, "He that believeth on me, as the scripture hath said, out of his belly shall flow rivers of living water." In verse 37, He said, "If any man thirst, let him come onto me and drink". So as believers we have already 'come onto Jesus.' Did we drink? Maybe; maybe not. If we drink, we are not thirsty, but are rivers of water flowing out of our bellies? Are we satisfying others thirst? Or are we dry? Does just a little water flow out. Enough to see we do believe in Jesus to call Him our Savior, but not enough to flood over people with our enthusiasm of talking about Jesus. Not enough to cool hot tempers. Not enough to wash away people's fears.

So why not? We most likely have a kink in there somewhere. When Jesus says, 'he that believeth on me' does he mean we are to forgive everyone like He said? Of course he does. Is there someone we haven't forgiven? When He said, "Fear not", and we are living in fear of the economy, world situation or any other thing does that mean 'we believeth in Him. He says, He will never forsake us, so when we think we are all alone in a situation, are we still believing in Him? Any of these things (and so many more) could be kinks.

If the rivers of water are not flowing out of us we either have a kink or there is so much junk in us, not much water can get through. Water might be flowing good, and then one gets a kink because we get all twisted up. When one is at church and testifying, it seems the water is flowing good. We can go over and lay hands on people and pray for them. We can encourage them. It is when we get out in the world and are wandering around that the kinks of fear, unforgiveness, desires of the world, and whatever else may keep the 'living water' from flowing. Well the answer is simple. Just straighten out that hose. Get those kinks out. Get rid of the fear, or unforgiveness, or whatever got us in a knot.

Love
Let's make the choice to love everyone.

I am crossing a bridge over Lake Keowee, look to the right and the lake is a shiny light blue. I think this is so beautiful so I look to the left and imagine my surprise when I see the lake is a different color and doesn't look so smooth. How can one side be light and smooth and the other side be dark and rough? I know there actually could be a difference but I know in this instance there is not. It is the same lake, the same water and the same color, and the same texture. What makes me see the two sides differently? Well the sun was to the right of me so when I saw the water there I saw the light reflection off the water which may it looked lighter.

On the other side, the water was absorbing the light and it looked differently. In other words, one was when I was looking toward the light and the other was when I was looking away from the light. Water and light are so amazing to me. Depending at what angle the light hits and where one is standing, it seems things are changing as the day progresses. Now of course things are not changing. It is just my perception changing.

A drop of water doesn't change because the sun moves or a cloud passes over. It's just my perception. So, which is real? Are things light and bright or dark and gloomy? Well I guess it is up to me to decide. The absence of light doesn't have to mean something is gloomy. I get to decide. I can't change the things I see where I stand, but I can move to where I see things at a different angle. If I was in a boat to the left of that bridge everything to my right would look brighter.

We know in nature all the leaves of a tree and all the drops in a pond are the same, it is just our perception that makes them different. Why can't we apply that to people? As believers we believe leaves, water and people were all made by the Creator. People were made in His image and the other things were made for a purpose and each one of them produces its own kind. Gen. 1:12. An oak tree will produce acorns which makes more oak trees. No matter how the light shines an oak tree is an oak tree and was created for a purpose. In the case of humans, no matter how we look (and even act) we were made for a purpose (for a good purpose). The purpose was to take care of every living thing on the earth. (Gen 1:28).

If every person is created in the image of God and we have the same purpose (just different jobs which we are given different abilities to do) then it shouldn't be so hard to love everyone instead of fearing them just because they have a different skin coloring or they are from a different culture or they worship differently. No reason to fear them regardless because (II Tim 1:7) says, "we are not given a spirit of fear, but of power and love and a sound mind." So instead of fear, we should love everyone. Either one is choice, so why not choose love?

I am sure some people do not believe it is a choice of who they love. They seem to think they just kind of wandered through life and all at once there was a person sent to them by the Lord for them to love. Now it may be true the Lord sent someone to be a helpmate (some people say soul mate) but as far as who we want to love we make decisions about that. I have seen this happen more than once.

Here is an example. I used to go by the nursery at the hospital for whatever reason. Maybe a friend or relative had a baby. I would look at all of those babies laying there and I could not tell one from another. I couldn't even tell what sex they were. That is why they put name tags on their bassinets. The Jones kid's grandparents come by and look. They see Jones on the bassinet and they say, "oh, my gosh, how cute. He has his daddy's nose." Now there is no way I could even pick that baby out, much less his nose, but sometimes they are right and he grows us and has a nose like his dad.

All at once those grandparents love one baby more than all the rest put together. If something was to happen and all of the babies but one was going to die, and they got the choice of who to save, it would be their grandson. If they were given the choice of saving all of the babies but their grandson, they would pick their grandson to live and let the rest die. As parents we would all do this. We picked who to love and who not to. Or at least who to love most. We picked depending on what someone wrote on a tag. There have been babies switched at birth before and the parents loved the one they took home.

After we take the baby home, he may be fussy, but we still love him. He may grow up to be a criminal, but we still love him. And when we look at him through our perspective of love, it seems as the things he does are not as bad as the things some other kids do; even when they are the exact same thing. A group of boys get in trouble and our boy was urged into it by the others because our boy is not bad, which proves a couple of scriptures. Proverbs 10:12 "love covers all sin" and I Peter 4:8 "and love shall cover the multitude of sins"

If we look at people through the perspective of love they will look a lot better to us. We can look through a facade of meanness or whatever ugliness that would normally keep us from seeing the good inside and see they have a good heart. There was a reason when Jesus was on the cross, He could say, "Forgive them, because they know not what they do" He was looking at them with love; knowing they were created to do good things and later many of them would.

Let's make the choice to love everyone. It actually makes it a lot easier There was a reason Jesus told us to love our enemies. It wasn't just because he loved our enemies. It was because He loved us and wanted us to be filled with love and to be happy instead of being filled with hate and felling horrible. John 10:10., "I came to bring life; life more abundant." If we follow the teachings of Jesus which are to love everyone, we will have a more abundant life. So, let's live large. Let's love. Love everyone and all of God's creation. It wasn't just created for the Lord to enjoy; it was created for us to enjoy. Let's see the goodness in everything and love that goodness.

Pain
Don't dread pain just use it

Dec 5, 2016

I hear volunteers come in after work and say things like, "I'm going to be sore tomorrow" or "Where's the Tylenol?" I'm thinking, "why this negativity?" I speak of healing. I thank the Lord He will strengthen my body during the night. I'm thankful for a body designed to heal itself. A body that mends scratches, bruises, that makes new skin when some has been scraped off. I wake up in the night and as I feel whatever pain I may be having, I say, "Thank you Lord for healing me" "Thank you for strengthening my muscles" "Just Thank You for allowing me to be here, to be a part of this mission"

But then the Lord revealed to me there was more of a reason for pain than just to make us appreciative of the healing power of our body, and of Him. Pain is to show us there are parts of our body that need strengthening. There are muscles needing more exercise. There are parts of the body needing healing. Sometimes the body doesn't do this by itself. Sometimes we need help. A person who is more knowledgeable will tell us where to improve; and tell us what we need for our healing. Sometimes the pain shows us this is a job too big for us alone, we get more help, maybe more preparation before we tackle it. Maybe more protection. We didn't wear the protective equipment we should have.

This morning my nose is slightly stopped up. This is because I didn't wear my dust mask as I should have. My knee is skinned because I tripped because I was in a hurry and wasn't watching what I was doing. My body is healing, but I'm to learn from this so I don't go through the same pain again. If I don't learn this time, I will get another chance. The tests of life are painful and we keep getting them until we pass them. Of course, after we learn something we just graduate to a higher job; one that will bring more tests and more pain.

We are to get out of our comfort zone if we want to grow. Growing is not comfortable. There is stretching of muscles. There are emotions that are affected; that get more of a workout as we go through life and see death, divorces, and losses of jobs.

Yeah, this pain is not just from physical reasons. It is emotional and spiritual also. Our body consists of three parts. Spiritual, emotional, and physical. All of these have pain as they are stretched; as they get out of their comfort zones. Part of our job is to comfort others. When we have to comfort one who is hurt, we have to be prepared. We pray for knowledge, wisdom, discernment, strength to say and do the right thing. We get another person to go with us and help us. We are not in this alone. We need others to encourage us as we try (and fail) to comfort another. Just as we need someone to help us lift something too heavy for us, we need help in our emotional and spiritual endeavors.

Our physical job does not stop because of pain, or rain, or snow, and our spiritual and emotional tasks don't either. We just have to access the resources to do the task. This is exercise, planning, prayer, people, and equipment. Our boss won't give us a task that can't be accomplished, but He will give us one that will cause pain. There is no other way we can work to our maximum capacity that we were designed for without pain. I think examples would be runners, swimmers, and mountain climbers in the physical realm. In the emotional it would include counselors. In the spiritual, it would be pastors.

Don't dread pain. Just use it to see what to do to be more efficient in your tasks.

Pain
A Few More Pains and People May Start Feeling Sorry for Me

July 26, 2015

I wake us this morning, and my elbow is stiff, but working it will get it loosened up. Reminds me, if we don't keep working for the Lord we will get stiff and things will be harder to do and we won't want to do them. It gets harder to move things the longer they set, but as soon as we start moving again, the muscles start responding, God gives us something to do and the strength to do it. The problem is the longer we stay inactive, the weaker we get and the longer it takes us to get back to where we were.

Keep moving, work through the pain, ask for a healing and accept you are healed to do what the Lord is calling you to do. If you are in pain, realize there is a reason for it. It may be a warning not to do something again. It may be a notice you have worked longer than the Lord was asking you to and you have exceeded the manufacturer's (God) recommendations (law) for use of the body you have been given to use for God's glory. If you misuse it and don't maintain it, it will not last as long as it was designed to last.

Wow, I didn't know I was going to get into all I have written so far. Well I might as well continue. So, I wake up this morning and my eye is itching; probably from fiber glass insulation that got into them while I was removing insulation from under a trailer without wearing my goggles. I couldn't see because my goggles got fogged up, so I was trying to keep my eyes shut as I pulled the insulation down with all the flood mud that had all kinds of junk in it.

I'm amazed at how our eye works so well to flush that stuff out. I would blink a few times and most of it would get out. What didn't get out then got out during the night and it would be in the corner of my eye, so I could get it out without rubbing my eye. Some of it was in the eyelid, the tears moistened so it would stick and I could get it out later. Some of it caused my eye to itch to remind me to wear eye protection so my eye mechanism won't have to be over worked. It is designed to get dust out, but not that much.

I wake up this morning and my finger is itching where it was stung by a wasp. It is swelled a little, but not as much as it was. Shows me how the body heals itself after it has been injured. It shows me pain is there to tell me I have been injured. If I had not have felt pain when I first got stung I would have proceeded on into that wasp nest.

Pain warns us about things and shows us what to fix. If our body doesn't fix them on its own, and we have talked to the Lord about them and we are still in pain, we may need to go to a doctor and ask what he can do to fix them. He may be able to tell us something to avoid the pain again.

In personal relationships we should share the pain with others so they can help us alleviate it. A lot of the time the fix is simple. It is just that we can't see it from our perspective. We are looking from the inside; or we have fogged up goggles, and our friends can see a simple answer. A lot of times, it is, "get away from the thing that is causing you pain". The itch also reminds me to be more aware of where wasps nests may be anywhere and to wear protection when I may encounter them. I did and the wasp still stung me through my glove. That reminds me, we can be hurt regardless of personal protection so we should be aware and ask others (God and our coworkers) to watch out for us.

Wow this went into a deeper perspective than I intended. I could go on more, but this is enough. A few more pains and people may start feeling sorry for me. I am great and pain is good. It teaches us all kinds of stuff; mainly God's healing power.

This is the day the Lord has made and I will rejoice in it. I hope you will too.

Pain in the Big Toe

Lately I have really been concerned about statements I have heard Christians make. Most of them seem to be gloom and doom. I was confused because Rom 8:28 says "…We know All things work together for good." We are also told in Genesis 1; we were given dominion over everything. If we are given dominion (that means we dominate) over 'everything' and "All things 'work together' for good," what is the gripe? We should be rejoicing. Doesn't sound like anything but 'good news' to me. Before the Lord left, He told us our main objective was to share the "good news with everyone in the world." And what is this 'good news' besides what I just wrote? Well, Jesus is our Savior (John 3:16) who shows us how to have eternal life; abundant life, we can live in now (John 10:10) and He will always be with us (Mt 25:20). All the Lord wants us to do is to not worry and to share His love with everyone.

This sounds so simple and is. I can't see the problem these Christians have doing it. Well I couldn't until my toe started to hurt. I had a bunion and the doctors installed a screw and a pin to align my toe in 1993. Later the screw was removed but the pin is still in there. The pin moves sometimes and causes me pain. When I am in pain I can't think of much else. The pain is not excruciating and I can still do my job. I can walk and jump. The problem is when I am laying in bed it is hard for me to get to sleep. Sometimes I rub it and try to move my toe to get some relief.

At this time the pain in my toe has my undivided attention but I finally get to sleep. I miss sleep and can't function as well the next day. If it is still hurting I can't think as well. Now I know all things are still working together for good. But if it wasn't for this pain, they could be working together for better. I have nine toes not hurting. The toe is the only bone in my body that's hurting, all my joints (except for a little arthritis) are working well. I am blessed. There is only a small percentage of my body in pain. I can do all the things and do what the Lord has told me to do.

The problem is; my flesh is lazy. It doesn't want to do these things. It says, "Hey the toe is in pain. Don't you care about it? Let it rest. Maybe it will heal if you don't move it much," because this affects my mind also, it is coming up with excuses not to do what the Lord has told me to do. The ironic thing is, when I do what I'm supposed to do, I don't feel the pain in my toe and my mind is busy so it isn't making excuses and I am actually on an emotional high as I'm helping people.

I should not be so judgmental of Christians who are complaining. "Forgive them for they know not what they do." I have to do my job and give them love by showing them how they can get out of the complaining mode. Everyone has a sore toe. They either have something causing them physical or emotional pain. They have lost a loved one to death or divorce or something. They know they have a lot more to be thankful for than to be sad about, but the one they have lost is causing them pain. They have more loved ones around, but they can't focus on the good because of the pain.

They may even have spiritual pain because they have been hurt in church. They know there are other churches and the Lord still loves them, but the pain keeps them from focusing on the love of others. I will show them there is a way out of pain. The way is to follow Jesus; to put our trust in Him; to do what he told us to do, which is to help others. When we help others, we will feel their pain too which some way lessens ours. (I don't know how that works exactly. Maybe a subject for another post).

Let's not be distracted by our pains whether physical or emotional or spiritual. Let's try to stay focused on doing what the Lord has told us to do (feed the hungry, clothe the naked). Go volunteer to help in some way. The Lord has a plan for each one of us and He guides our steps so if we start, He will guide us to what He has qualified us to do. Mostly this is to show love.

We know we can all do that because He has given us all a heart. Well we can do it, if we ignore the pain we have and concentrate of helping others. We are not to totally ignore the pain. Look to the Lord for guidance of what we should do about the pain. If we have a thorn in our side that can be removed, we should remove it. Maybe I should get the pin taken out of my foot. Maybe get out of a toxic relationship; and the list goes on. The main thing is to do what we know to do and not concentrate on our pains or make excuses for staying in pain.

Poor vs Poverty

My thoughts and observations, not official definitions

What is the difference? It seems being poor is not having much. Poverty seems to be an attitude. My friend said, "it is not being able to assess one's resources." It seems that in being poor a person realizes he doesn't have much, but that he can get a job, work hard, and have a few breaks, and acquire some stuff. In other words when people are poor they can still have a dream. It seems that in poverty, people seem to have no hope. When people are poor they think they can do better. When a person is in poverty it seems, he thinks he can't do any better. When people are poor, they appreciate help as they strive to help themselves. In poverty it seems people think help is due them and they wait for someone to help them.

Rich
When does one have more than they need?

A four-letter word. Is it good or bad? Well I would imagine most of us wouldn't mind being rich. The problem is; Jesus said in Mt. 19:23 "it is hard for a rich man to enter the Kingdom of heaven." How can this be? Wouldn't a rich man be able to do all kinds of good things? He could build a homeless shelter. He could I guess if he had more than he needed. Maybe that's the problem. When does one have more than they need? I don't know if I have ever met such a person.

It seems the more one has, the more they need. And it makes sense. If someone gave me a boat, I would have to get a trailer to carry it and I would need a truck to pull the trailer and boat. So maybe this getting a boat wasn't the blessing it looked like. It didn't satisfy anything. In fact, it made me needier. Maybe this is the problem with getting stuff. If makes you need more.

If a person inherits a million dollars and a mansion, they hire someone to take care of it. They have to get tax lawyers to keep the government from getting most of it. They have to build a fence and get a security system to protect their stuff. Now can I trust anyone? Before when someone came to talk to me it was because they enjoyed my company, but now maybe they are coming by because they want my money. When I was poor, sometimes I said stuff I thought the Holy Spirit revealed to me and people sometimes were impressed with what I said. I don't know if they were agreeing with me because of a wise saying or they will always agree with a rich person. Stuff that was supposed to bring me security has made me more insecure.

I saw a little two-year-old girl yesterday who was happy because she had a key chain to jingle and she was looking at her reflection in a glass door at a parts shop. She was content. She was in the Kingdom of Heaven. She had not a care in the world. She knew her parents were going to take care of her. Therefore, the rich man cannot enter this Kingdom. He is not content with what he has and he is not trusting his heavenly Father to care for him. He is depending on his riches. He doesn't have enough to build a homeless shelter. He will if he can make more money and if it will give him a tax break. Before he was working in a shelter, but now he hasn't time. The riches have separated him from his poor brethren and the Lord. Yep, it would seem rich is not a good four-letter word.

Now if we can say we are rich because we are content and we know we have a rich Father who according to Philippians 4:19 *"And my God will shall supply all your need according to His riches.........*" then I guess we are rich. So maybe being rich is a state of mind (or a state of knowing who we are in Christ). In that case being rich is a good thing and we will already be in the Kingdom.

If we are not in the Kingdom what do we need to get rid of or acquire to get there? I guess getting rid of bitterness, worry, pride, envy (among a few) and reacquiring love, compassion, empathy, and contentment might do it. If not, it definitely would be a good start.

Walk
Walk in His steps

Oct 24, 2017

Another good four-letter word. It's time to go to the pharmacy. I don't have a vehicle so I can walk. That is a means of transportation we will always have. It is a good one because it is the first one the Lord gave us. At one time Adam got to walk with the Lord. Then he spoke to him. We don't get to do that like Adam did, but it should be our goal. To walk with the Lord.

We are spoken of highly when we "walk the talk." It means we do as we say. When we walk we get to hear, smell, and see things we wouldn't as we speed down the road in a vehicle. When we walk, we get good exercise anyone can do. We move more parts of our body than when sitting and help the internal organs that are not moving to be activated as they were designed. It gives our heart and lungs exercise. It slows down time and allows us to stop and look at things we wouldn't otherwise. It allows us to think of things we wouldn't also because we are distracted as much.

As I walked last night I noticed how beautiful the moon was. Was I on a moon walk? I know I wasn't doing the dance and I wasn't on the moon but maybe walking with one's head in the clouds (now how is that possible?) may also be considered a moon walk. When one is out of this world and in another world of peace and harmony as they contemplate how beautiful the moon is and how functional and how it all works in with controlling the tides and how amazing it can stay where it is circling the earth.

One thinks about this as they hear crickets and other night sounds; as they smell the honeysuckle and other night plants. So how much are these sounds and smells affecting our thoughts? Who knows? but I believe they make us think better. Being on a walk makes us think better and think of things we wouldn't think of otherwise. It gets our blood circulating to the brain more so we can think better. Hey, if I keep this up, I may stop drinking coffee. Naaaw. Maybe I will walk and drink coffee.

When one walks they have to make decisions they wouldn't otherwise. It makes one confront their fears. The dogs are down the street. The people are there arguing. Last night I saw a fight. I was across the street from it so I wasn't directly involved but I saw it so I felt as if I needed to do something. I knew in my mind there wasn't anything I could physically do because at least one of the people was out of control.

I prayed they would be calmed down. I'm pretty sure they didn't calm down, but it did calm me some and helped me accept what was going on. That is one more good thing about being on a walk. We can walk and pray (an even better four-letter word). We can meditate and try to "walk in Jesus steps." Or walk like Jesus. Hey, didn't He walk like everyone else. I think it means; do like He would have done. Walk means so much more than the act of taking a walk. It means living a certain lifestyle.

So "walk the talk." Walk in His steps. Walk in the Way. It is definitely a thing to be thankful for. After writing this, I may never be able to just walk without purpose and contemplation again.

Weed
Grow deep roots and stand up

July 2018

This is a four-letter work word for people who have flower gardens. This morning a few of us went to pray about the drug situation in the county and we got there before the person who opens the church. We saw he had pulled some weeds but there were more to pull so we figured we would pull some while we waited (plus the doughnut shop wasn't open. That was our first choice).

As we are pulling them, I notice they have long deep roots. I got a message from this. Sometimes we are like a weed and are not in a place where others want us to be. As Christians this can be almost anywhere (an office meeting or any public forum where it may not be appreciated when one is espousing Christian values). Well we may be as unwanted as the weed, but if we have deep roots it will be hard to get rid of us.

Be rooted in the word, in our faith, in patience, in love, and in all things, that make us strong. The deeper the root, the more varied nutrients the weed can get and this allows it to grow taller and stronger. The deeper it is, the more the little rootlets branch off it. The deeper we get into these things that make us grow, the stronger we will get; the taller we will get so we will be noticed more and it will be harder to dislodge us from wherever we are. I also noticed as the weed gets taller, it puts out flowers also.

If it survives long enough people look upon it as a flower instead of a weed. They notice it has beauty (and as the caretaker there mentioned, all those weeds are good for something if we just know what it is). If we stand and grow, we will show our beauty and people will see our function. Then people won't be so quick to try to get rid of us. They will realize we are strong, beautiful, vibrant, and not afraid to speak our truth and we were put in their midst for a reason.

Let's be like a weed. Grow deep roots and stand up and not be ashamed. Put out a lot of seed. Put out the flowers to show we have beauty.

Wish or Want?
Turn wishes to wants

Many times, I hear people say they want to be healed or they want to do more. In my case I said, "I want to be more organized." I was lying. I didn't want to be organized; I just wished I was. So now I want to, so I'm getting more organized. What makes the difference? Well if we want to do something, we start working on it. If we want to be healed, we do what it takes to be healed. We read up on what our condition is and try the cures recommended. We take our meds, eat right, exercise, free our minds of things hindering our healing (this may be bitterness, unforgiveness, anxiety.)

Our mind may have more to do with our health than anything. And our mind has more to do with our wants and wishes than anything else. We can blame our unfulfilled wishes on our circumstances but if we turn these wishes to wants we will do what it takes to obtain these wants in spite of our circumstances.

Let's say we want to have a million dollars. We can wish we had a million and go down and buy a lottery ticket and wish the number wins; or one can go to the library and check out some books about people who make a million from being poor and read about habits of successful people and then start putting these habits and ideas into action.

One may not ever get a million dollars no matter how hard they work; and they may never have perfect health, but we will be healthier and wealthier than we are and we will be happier realizing we at least did our part to accomplish our goals.

CHAPTER FOUR

SPIRITUAL REFLECTIONS

Love is Essential to Our Existence

I talked with a person who had done something hurtful because they thought they were not loved. We seem to do hurtful things to ourselves and others when we think we are not loved. So, what makes us think we are not loved? The root cause seems to be we think we are not worthy. What is ironic about this is; this is the only time true love can be shown. If someone is worthy because they have done some great deed we can show admiration or respect or whatever, but the thing we are showing is not love. Love is when we serve someone who can do nothing for us. If it took worth, there would be no way a baby would be worthy of anyone's love.

A baby can do nothing. In fact, it does less than nothing. It poops and throws up on the person who is holding it. The person holding it cleans it up and the baby smiles to show it accepts the love it was shown. Then we are so happy she smiled; we send pictures to everyone we can think of. The love we send to the baby nourishes it. If it doesn't get love it dies. There was an experiment done once where babies were fed, changed, but were not held and they died. Love is essential to our existence. There is nothing worse than rejection. Fortunately, most babies are not rejected. They are shown love by everyone who meets them and they bask in it. They are held in the air and they don't worry about falling because they are held up by love.

But everything grows, and to grow, the hand of protection has to be withdrawn. It is withdrawn so one can stand on their feet, so they can walk, and run and ride a bicycle. Then the person gets hurt, but the ones who love them pick them up and kiss their "boo boos" and they still know they are loved. They still know they are loved for themselves. Later they are told how well they can run, ride the bicycle, do well in school and they may start to think they are loved because of their accomplishments. They accomplish more and more and get more accolades and they bask in this admiration and they think they are loved because of this.

Finally, they reach their peak. They lose a race or don't do so well on a test. The people who love them tell them it doesn't make any difference, but they cannot believe this. What about all the people who were cheering for them? If it didn't make any difference, they would still be cheering. So, they don't accept this love from the ones who love them. This makes the ones who love them sad, and they cannot smile when they come around. When they don't smile it proves to the one who lost they don't love them either. They think they are not smiling because the person isn't worthy. They don't realize it is because they are sad that the person they love is not accepting their love.

Then something happens and the person who is loved gets hurt, handicapped, and maybe old. The ones who love them come around and feed them and pet them and then the person knows they are loved again. They appreciate and smile as they are laying there incapacitated. The person feeding them sees their smile showing their love is accepted and acknowledged and they are glad.

I guess this proves the scripture, "in our weakness is when we are the strongest." In our weakness people come around to show their love and support. Before we were doing it on our own. Now we have our friends to support us. So as weak as we may be, we can accomplish more working in a group knowing we love each other.

There Are a Lot of Angels

April 28, 2015

Christian Appalachian Project's Workfest is over and CAP is having a breakfast for employees and volunteers at the Cracker Barrel in Berea, Kentucky. Doesn't seem to be everyone, but I'm involved in it (maybe I'm not supposed to be there, but I come anyway). The food is good and we fellowship some and then we leave. I'm one of the last ones leaving because I have been talking to a few people.

Our group walks out and there is a black woman sitting in a chair on the porch. She is short (her legs seemed to be barely touching the floor) and broad (about half as wide as tall) and wearing sunglasses She says something to us but I don't know what it was, but I do know it was something about the Lord blessing us so we stop and talk. She quotes scripture after scripture and tells us the Lord has sent her to a town in Ohio. He has given her a message to give them. It is Romans 13:1 which says, everyone must obey state authorities because no authority exists without God's permission and the existing authority has been put there by God. (maybe she was supposed to take that message to Baltimore instead of Ohio). She won't tell us what town she is from or her name. All of this seems mystic, but it is making sense to me.

The head of the housing department for CAP asks what we can do for her. She says, "You can pray for healing in my body." He asks, "Is there is anything else?" She says, "Well it takes money to go places." I tell her, "We are going to do more than just pray, we are going to lay hands on you and pray." We do and I get very emotional as I pray. I give her 20 dollars. I don't know if anyone else gives her anything or not. Seems weird to me we are so stingy. We seem to be concerned someone is trying to get something for nothing and yet we have just walked out of a nice restaurant where we enjoyed a free meal, had good fellowship and had been given the gas to get there and I assure the employees were getting paid.

We are told to give to anyone who asks. As Christians we say we have been given all we have by the Lord. It just seems we would be more generous. Maybe we would if we realized the undeserved blessings we have received. If we thought of them, we couldn't keep from sharing. I know this makes me so excited and I want to share the good news with others while I'm doing whatever I can to help them.

As we are walking away the housing manager smiles and says, "just another day in the life of a volunteer." One of the volunteers says she has to get on her way home. I ask her where she is going and she says in kind of a sheepish voice (I don't know what a sheepish voice is but it seems to fit) "Ohio." I move my head back toward the lady and say, "the Lord may want you to take her". I know she isn't because of fear, or not wanting to be inconvenience. I'm upset about this, but I'm not upset with the volunteer being fearful or selfish. I'm just upset she has an opportunity to listen to a person who is sold out to God talk for a few hours and she isn't seeing this as an opportunity. Maybe it isn't an opportunity for everyone, but I know

I was excited. If I hadn't been doing anything else (or even maybe if I had my vehicle there) I would have been volunteering to take her.

We get in the van to go back to the Jackson House and I say, "Someone got a healing when we prayed. I did, or she did. I hope we both did." I felt so good. A few days later I went to my regular doctor and my respiratory doctor and I felt so good both times I couldn't remember I was going to ask about a pain that keeps coming in my shoulder. It didn't hurt all the time but seems like something catches and I didn't know if I should tell them and let them x-ray it or not because I kept thinking it might wear off. Well it has been a month now I guess and it hasn't hurt once since then, so I got a healing for that.

I feel this lady was an angel. Now what kind of angel I can't say (or much care; well it would be nice if I knew she was a celestial angel). But an angel is a messenger, and she said she was going to give a town a message; and she definitely gave us one.

Later when we were in West Virginia I mentioned her to the person in charge of the Disaster Relief with CAP and she said she had seen that lady praying for someone when she came out of the restaurant also.

So now I'm in South Carolina helping someone put up some shelves. All at once she shows me a tract that says JESUS LOVES YOU. Then she says, "I was walking out to a store and this black lady reached in her purse and gave me this. It just seemed as if it was the only one she had and she just felt I needed it. I said, "Was she about this tall and this wide" as I move my hands to the dimensions that I remembered. She said, "yes" I said, "well you saw the same angel then" well it may not have been because this lady didn't have sunglasses.

I don't know what any of this means. Probably nothing to anyone else. Could be a coincidence. Could be anything. There are a lot of short black ladies. There are also a lot of angels. The important thing to me is it reminds me there are angels watching over us. It reminds me I'm to be generous and help whoever I can, whenever I can.

What do I Believe?
Lord, I believe, help my unbelief

I say I am a Christian and the Lord takes care of me, and He has a plan; a good plan. For me. So, if I believe this, why do I worry when things do not go the way I would like for them to go? Why does it bother me when the unexpected happens? Do I really believe he has a 'good' plan for me; or do I just think maybe it will work out for Him, but it may not be the best for me.

When a loved one dies, they go to Heaven, I learned about grief and I can counsel someone later to help them get through their grief, so of course all in all me losing a loved one wasn't so bad. But was it the best thing for me? Sure, I got stronger. Was getting stronger the best thing for me? I guess there is only one way to know. When one looks back, would they go through it again? If they would be willing to go through it again then it showed the pain was worth the gain and one became a better stronger person.

Well, what if we weren't willing to go through it again. Does that necessarily mean it still wasn't the best for us? There are instances we can see in our life when seeing the results show we are stronger and better, but if we had to do them over again, we still wouldn't do them. I can imagine something like losing a child and then starting a support group, which grew into something national and helped thousands of others and allowed us to handle grief better.

I believe if I had the choice of losing a child again or helping many people and for me to get stronger, I still would elect to keep my child and not be as strong nor help the other people. Then again, when I got older and my child would also be old, would I be sorry that I didn't allow my child to be sacrificed to help others. I got to spend more time with my child, but was it really worth it.

Our life is very short, so if I go through some pain for a short time to help others is this not really the best for me? I don't know. I don't even have an opinion about it. I do know I am glad I don't have to make decisions like this. I do know if I can believe the Lord has the best plan for me it makes it easier for me to get through life.

So, what do I believe? I guess I am like the guy in Mark 5:23-24 who was asking Jesus to heal his son, "Jesus said, if you can believe, all things are possible to him who believes. Immediately the father of the child cried out with tears, "Lord, I believe, help my unbelief" So as Christians we do believe. We just have to be helped in our unbelief.

Three Crosses

Jesus was on a cross between two thieves. One of them railed on him and asked Jesus why he didn't save all three of them. The other rebuked the first and said that Jesus didn't deserve His punishment but both of them did. He asked Jesus to remember him. Jesus said to the thief, "You will be with me in Paradise." But the thief didn't do anything to get to heaven. He couldn't do anything. If Jesus had said, "Whoever wants to go with me wave their hand", the thief couldn't have gone.

I told a preacher the other day that it seems as if we don't reject Jesus we will go to heaven. He seemed pained when I said this. If it is that easy, why would we need preachers? Well, it is that easy, but what did the thief really do? He rebuked the guy bullying the Lord. He did all he could do. That is what the Lord wants out of us; to do all we can do. But what more did the thief do, besides rebuke the other thief? He admitted he was guilty and that he deserved his punishment. He asked the Lord to remember him.

Do we admit to the Lord we are guilty of anything? If we admit we might be guilty of something, do we admit we deserve the punishment? Usually we are saying, "why is this happening to me" "I don't deserve this" and "Lord deliver me" If we admit we may have done something wrong then it was because of our circumstances, our friends, or our family, or our job, or our culture or our government. We have a dozen (or more) excuses. Then we whine that what we are enduring is unfair, because we haven't done anything someone else hasn't done.

Then instead of asking the Lord to remember us, strengthen us, teach us and use us as we are on the cross (the situation of our own making due to our own bad decisions we made on our own without consulting with the Lord), we say, "GET ME OUT OF THIS." In our situation we have the opportunity to encourage others, but instead we want to just get out of the situation. Why? If we have not learned it is our doing, we will be right back in it. If we continue blaming our situations on others we will always be victims and we will never be able to get off the cross; or at least to stay off.

That day, two people had an encounter with Christ. One of them rebuked him and the other defended him. One of them was blessed and the other one wasn't. Both of them were in the same situation and had the same opportunity to do whatever. Do we ever have an encounter with Christ and if we do how do we handle it?

Every time we see someone on a cross (in a bad situation) we have the same opportunity as the thief to uplift the person. Jesus said, "when you did it for the least of these you did it for me" When we see 'the least of these' in a bad situation, we are having an encounter with Jesus. Do we rebuke them or help them? Unfortunately, we sometimes rebuke them because they have done something to be in their situation; and if we don't rebuke we usually don't help.

If the Holy Spirit brings it to our attention when we didn't help in the situation, we have a dozen reasons why we didn't. We were on the way to church; our kids needed something. We probably should be more like the thief and admit our shortcomings, quit making excuses, and accept our punishment (life), and ask the Lord to remember us. It may be the only way we will get off that cross. Are we on a cross? If we are not moving and stuck in a situation, I guess we are. And if we are not, what can we do to help someone who is on a cross?

Woman at the Well; His First Evangelist

I've just been to Ashland, Mississippi to help clean up after a tornado. I wanted to write about it but it seems to be hard to get it all in. This always seems to be a problem. Too much stuff to tell. Too many experiences. Some funny. Some sad. Too many meaningful conversations I would like to share. One reason I want to write about mission trips is so others will see the need and the joy in serving. There are not enough people who go on these trips.

Instead of being able to write about it, I keep thinking about the "woman at the well" and it seems this tells us what we should do and when we should do it and who should do it. We all know about the Woman at the Well. (if you don't, you can read about her in John 4:4-42) How she met Jesus unexpectedly. How she had to come to the well in the middle of the day when it was hot because she couldn't come in the cool of the morning when the other women did because she had been married five times and now she was living with a guy. Then she was to have been considered living in sin. (and it wouldn't be looked on so favorably now).

No self-respecting woman would want to be around her. And we know she wouldn't fit in a group of them. She is amazed Jesus knows about her marital situation (or lack of it) and doesn't condemn her for it. A rabbi, a prophet, the Christ; and He doesn't come unglued when he finds she is living in sin. He talks to her as an equal; not as some hussy out of a less than reputable culture.

He tells her what He can give her if she will accept it. She does; and runs with it. She immediately goes to the village where the guys are hanging out and tells them she has just met the Christ. She left her jug at the well; she didn't confer with anyone; she didn't go back to her house and tell her live-in he couldn't live there anymore; she just ran and told people (who were probably going to look at her somewhat askance), the Good News. Some believed because of what she said; and others believed after they came to see him.

So, because one woman, who didn't have the best reputation, went to the people she knew (who hadn't been so friendly to her) and told them what she had seen and heard, there was revival in the area and a lot of people came to the Lord. She could have had a dozen excuses to not go tell the men. She was a woman, no one would believe her, she didn't have time because she was doing chores, she needed to get the sin out of her life, she needed to talk to her boyfriend first. It's a hot day. I'm sweaty. I need to take a shower first. Maybe I should study the scriptures more to make sure this lines up. Maybe I better ask the priest about this. It was a good thing she didn't think of all these things or she would have talked herself out of it.

One may have thought Jesus would not have been so happy a Samaritan woman, who was living in sin was the first person who told people, Jesus was The Christ. That seems to make her His first evangelist. I guess it shows Jesus is no respecter of persons, he wants to use you where you are at; and He wants to use you right now. He just wants you to share the love.

This is the main thing on mission trips. I'm amazed people we serve are so thankful. We usually don't do much they couldn't finally get done without us. But the main thing we do is to 'show up' and show them someone cares. We can all do this. Regardless of our finances, health, what problems (even including sin) we may have in our life, we can share the love.

Tell people the Good News. Be an encourager. Tell people things will get better. When we do this, not only do things get better in their lives; they get better in ours. When we share the love of Christ and tell people what He has done in our life we all become evangelists.

What We Can't See

I woke up this am thinking about condensation on the underside of metal. The underside is the place where we may be told not to worry about because no one can see it. The parts we can't see may be the most important parts. Look at the parts of our body we can't see. The lungs, liver, heart, they are the most important parts. The parts we can see are just a façade and have very little to do with the function of our body.

Just as the underside of our car is critical; if it rusts we are in big trouble. But if it gets a dent in the fender, the functions aren't damaged at all. The weird thing is this outward appearance is what everyone pays attention to; either complimenting or condemning depending on the appearance. Of course, this is not totally bad. I would like to know if my face is dirty; or if a taillight is busted on my car.

The problem with the things we can't see going bad is, they are killers. If we don't do anything to fix them we will die. This isn't just true in the physical, it is also true in the emotional and spiritual. If we have jealousy, envy, unforgiveness toward another we will get mentally sick. And whether it makes us sick or not, it will keep us from being focused on the good things of life.

We can't enjoy our life, family, and friends as much when we are eaten up with envy, jealousy and if keeps us from functioning as well as we could. Not only does this hurt us, but it hurts our family and friends and keeps them from functioning as well as they could because they are distracted by how we are acting or reacting.

The same thing happens in the church congregation. Because of bitterness or unforgiveness, not only can the individual not grow, the congregation cannot either. It just doesn't keep one from growing; it kills us. Unforgiveness hurts us physically, emotionally, and spiritually. Another problem is these things are usually hidden from ourselves. We don't see the water behind the wall or on the underside of the metal causing the rot or rust. We don't see damage to the liver or any other inward parts.

And then worse, if we happen to see it, we don't acknowledge it is such a big deal. What does a little moisture amount to? What if my lungs or liver aren't functioning up to 100%? I'm doing okay. What if I don't pray, read the Bible every day. I'm okay. Well it is a good thing, Jesus said, "Forgive them for they know not what they do." All these people He was asking to be forgiven didn't have any idea they even needed forgiving. This forgiveness didn't make any of them better. Let us see the problems in our life, physically, emotionally, spiritually and ask for forgiveness and then get to work on improving them.

See the J E S U S in ourselves and others

June 25, 2018

I'm at a friend's house and I see a rectangular piece of wood on a shelf that seems to have some weird indecipherable letters. I actually know what it is. The indecipherable letters are what was left over after other places had been carved out. The pieces carved out said J E S U S. Even though I knew the J E S U S part was what I was supposed to see, I just kept seeing the rest of the wood instead. Because I knew what I was supposed to see, I kept blinking until I saw it, but then it went away. Now that I have seen it, I blink a couple of times until I see it constantly (well almost). Now when I look at it I can see the J E S U S almost every time; and even when I don't, it will come up in a few seconds.

I imagine the people who live there always see J E S U S when they look at it. This made me think of people. I don't always see the J E S U S in people. I know it is in there because in Genesis 1:27 it says, "And God created man in His own image.........". John 14:9 Jesus says," .... he that hath seen me has seen the Father."

Jesus was a man like everyone else. No one could pick him out of a crowd, this means Godliness is in all of us. So why can't we see it? Probably because that is not what we are looking for. We seem to see what we want to see (a mother sees a perfect baby).

Sometimes we pay more attention to the little things than we do the big things. A wart is a little thing. It is usually just a small percentage of a person's whole face, but we will notice the wart more than any other feature. But when we love people we don't notice the warts or whatever distracts from their total beauty. When we love people, we look for internal beauty. When we look for it, we see it, because there is more good in any one than bad.

Everyone does good things for the people the love. Almost everyone will go out of their way to help others. Most of us hardly ever break the laws. We take care of our families. In general, almost all of us are much better than we are bad. So why do we look for the bad in people? Do we do it because we are afraid if we don't see the bad, then the person will take advantage of us? Or do we do it because we want to think we are better than other people? Why would we think that? I am made in the image of God, and everyone else is make in the image of God so we are all equal. Sometimes we don't act like we are created in His image. So how can we grow back into that image; and how can we help others do the same.

Philippians 4:8-9 says, "...whatsoever things are honest, just, pure.... lovely, ...of good report if there be any virtue or praise, think on these things. These things which you have learned and received and heard and seen, do and the God of peace shall be with you."

When we look for these things in ourselves and do them, and we look for them in others and encourage them we will see the J E S U S in ourselves and others.

Where do the Ashes Come From?

I went to an Ash Wednesday service and got ashes put on my forehead. I wondered where they came from. I find out that once a guy who was doing good for everyone came riding into town. A whole bunch of people who had heard about what he had done heard he was coming and wanted to honor him so they got some palm leaves to wave They were happy he was coming because of all the things they had heard he had done.

They knew the religious leaders didn't like this guy because he was telling people religions rituals weren't what it was all about. In fact he seemed to say that people who helped other people they didn't know were better people than the religious leaders. He was blessing and feeding poor people who didn't have any hope. So all of these hopeless people now had hope and wanted him to be their leader. These people were waving palm leaves and everything else they had to show their appreciation to Him.

They hoped he would run for supreme commander and make their country great again and get rid of the religious and political leaders who had been oppressing them. They wouldn't have to pay taxes to a corrupt government, or honor to hypocritical religious leaders. They wanted him to be king; a king that would take care them; free medical care because he could heal; free food because he had fed thousands with a few fish; free booze because he had made wine from water; who wouldn't want a leader like that. So they are yelling "Hosanna, Hosanna" which basically meant "Praise to you".

He agrees to be their leader. The kicker is when he tells them what he expects out of them. He tells them to forgive every one and to love people who hate them. Now this is pretty ridiculous. But then he gets more crazy. He tells them to give their stuff away, to wash peoples feet who are in a lower class then them, to not only pay taxes but not to gripe about it, when bums who you know won't pay you back ask you for something, he said to give it to them; and even more.

Good golly, who would want a leader like that? How would you call that leading? Then he tells them to be his followers, they must serve everyone. EVERYONE? Now that was the last straw. Serve everyone? People don't want to serve anyone, much less everyone. He wants us to pick up a cross and follow him. Yeah right. We will pick up a cross and nail him to it! Get our hopes up? Who does he think he is? God?

So they did what anyone else would probably do; get mad at the person who had got their hopes up. And we can't just say, "hey dude you were wrong in trying to change the status quo", we have to make an example of anyone who fights against the political and religious establishment. So they crucified him. Sounds harsh, but you have to nip ideas like in the bud. How would any merchants make any money if everyone is serving each other and not buying more stuff?. How could anyone sell weapons if no one has enemies? That kind of thinking could end wars. No one would be any better than anyone else. How could anyone have prestige, or say how proud they are to be from a certain country or family? So it was pretty much of a joint consensus this guy would have to go. They didn't want any remembrances of this guy; and they definitely didn't want others thinking they had been followers so they even burned the palm leaves they had been waving.

Well, he did get crucified and died, but wonders of wonders, a few days later, he came back to prove that he could give eternal life. Now the few followers; left were elated. They went from being in fear to fearless. How can one go wrong following a guy who can come back from the dead? Of course He still tells them the same thing about what they are supposed to do. He says they still have to serve everyone; and they will be persecuted. AND, He is going to leave again. But He tells them if they go to Jerusalem and pray, He will send them the Holy Ghost to live in them to guide, comfort, and strengthen them.

Well a ghost can't be killed, so they realize this means they are going to have eternal life, so they go and do this. A lot of the other people start feeling sorry they caused they guy to be crucified. They had heard about this 'ashes and sackcloth' thing so they go get these palm leaf ashes and put the symbol of the cross on their foreheads to show they are not ashamed of this guy who died on the cross and they are sorry for how they treated him and they vow they will change the way they treat people.

After that they build buildings and put a cross on the buildings to show they are followers of Christ. Now of course we are not going to give up all our stuff, forgive everyone, love everyone, and do all the other things Jesus told us to do so every year, some of us get ashes put on our heads and agree to repent. The problem with repenting is that we have to change the way we are doing something. If I was wanting to change, I probably would have already done it. It does make me think about things I should change and I may change some of them for a while. Of course I usually don't change too many things for long and I have to repent again. Fortunately, I don't have to put ashes on my forehead every time I repent because if I did, it would always be dirty and people would think I had a birth mark on my forehead.

None of us are going to give up all our stuff so some of us agree to give up something for 40 days. It usually is something that we know is bad for us anyway (sweets, tobacco, etc) and we may not even be able to make it 40 days. All of this makes us realize how far off we are from what Jesus told us to do so we become more thankful for grace and hopefully that makes us not be so judgmental to others. So while putting the ashes on our head and listening to someone telling us to repent doesn't really make us better people, but I think it does make up more aware of how much God loves us to put up with how we act most of the time.

This Is The Day Which The Lord Has Made. We Will Rejoice And Be Glad In It. Psalm 118:24

I said this so much when I was a volunteer with CAP that one day when a young lady couldn't find her scripture of the day, her roommate said, "why don't you use Jimbo's"

I say it a lot along with Rom 8:28"...all things work together for good...." and "...the joy of the Lord is your strength:" Neh 8:10. I say these things because I believe them and I want to encourage others. Of course I am encouraging myself when I say them. No matter how bad it seems things are we have these promises; or are they commands?

What if we don't live these statements? Is it a sin?. Well why wouldn't be living them? Why wouldn't we rejoice? Why wouldn't we be glad today? Well I'm sure there are kinds of reason. We go through deaths, divorces, job losses, family on drugs, and the list could go on forever. Of course these are things called 'life'. So everyone is going through them. This is the reason we should rejoice, knowing the Lord has created this day. So if he has created it, He is in charge of it. We are not in this by our self. We have the creator of the universe watching over us. We have the promise that 'all things work together for good' for us. So when things we consider bad are happening, we know these bad things will work out ok; not just ok, but good.

So again, if we are not rejoicing today, are we sinning? Well we are also created in the image of God and we are representatives of Christ if we are calling ourselves Christians so when we don't represent Him in a good light we are not doing the job very well. We are acting like we don't believe His promises and if we don't believe them, how can we think other people will. In a way I think that may be Christian's worst sin. Acting like we don't have a joyful life.

I talked to a guy yesterday about asking people in the church how they were doing and so many times I heard the response of, "I'm just hanging on." He said he was raised in the church and he heard that comment more than anything else. You would think the response would be "I'm walking in the victory" Before I was a Christian I thought they were the most sad, jealous, judgmental people in the world. I don't remember seeing anyone of them smile at me as I was staggering in as they were going to church. They seemed to be jealous I was having fun and they were telling me I was going to hell for doing the things I did.

Well I didn't enjoy my life so well, hangovers, getting in jail, messed up relationships, but it seemed I was enjoying it more than the Christians. In my life I can remember only meeting a half dozen people who seemed to be enjoying their life as Christians. Most everyone seemed to be Christians because they didn't want to go to hell. So I couldn't see the advantage of their life. Finally the Lord moved on me. I actually was in a church where the people (including the preacher) were having a good time. Later I found out there were a lot of churches like that, but at the time, I was wondering if I was in a real church because I didn't equate fun with Christianity.

So yes, I think 'not rejoicing' may be our worse sin. Jesus told us to spread the gospel to the world. The gospel is the 'good news'. The good news is we are loved unconditionally. Jesus died for us and He has a better life for us. If we are trying to share this with others and we are acting unhappy I doubt too many people are going to believe it. My wife asked me once why I didn't believe and I told her I thought it was because I didn't believe the Christians believed.

This is the Day the Lord has made, Let's Rejoice and be Glad in it so we can show people we believe the Good News. The Joy of the Lord is My Strength I am not just holding on and you don't have to either. All Things Do work out for Good for those who Love the Lord, so you don't have to worry about diseases or the elections or anything else in life. The Bible has the answers to these problems. So read it and live it. Then we can show people it works and they can see why we are rejoicing.

"Do we want to be the one? Do we want to be made whole?"

If we start acting like Christ, most religious people will get nervous and not want to associate with us. I've been asking "what is the church supposed to be?" Is it just a building where believers get together for a few hours a week, sing some songs, hear a message, and then go back to their normal life?

We heard a good sermon today about the ten lepers. Nine were religious and couldn't acknowledge they were healed until a priest told them they were. One was grateful and worshipped the one who healed him. So not only was he healed, he was made whole. The pastor asked, "Do we want to be the one. Do we want to be made whole?" Then follow Christ and work with Him to free the captives, give sight to the blind, feed the poor and go help in disasters.

God is Greater Than Anyone Could Ever Tell About or Imagine

I woke up this morning in the Mt. Vernon, Kentucky volunteer house thinking about how many things went on yesterday. Wanting to write about them in a concise way and realize there is just too many. As concise as I could be I would never be able to get them into a few paragraphs.

I met people who have influenced my life. Met new people. Worked with guy who will be 83 today. Met people who volunteered here in the 60's where they met other people and got married and went out to have a life serving God as a couple while raising a family.

I went on a hike after standing in the rain for a long time. Heard stories about volunteer life. Saw the wonders of the Lord. Amazed at how He has worked in their lives. Amazed at how He works in nature. Amazed at how He works in my life. More amazed at how he works in so many Christians lives and they never notice it; or if the notice it they don't let anyone else know about it. They seem to be fixated on how bad things are.

I went downstairs this morning and wondered if I missed a flood. The floor is wet and now my socks are wet. No one around to tell me what is going on; and I can't find the coffee. Maybe the gloom and doom people are right. Maybe all the goodness I saw yesterday was an illusion. I'm sunburned, hurting from work, have all kinds of ailments, I'm old. No one listens to what I say; and definitely no one pays any attention to it and it is a gloomy day. No one wanted me to stay here and now the place is flooded and I can't find any coffee. Can it get any worse than this?

Now why in the world would I want the reality of that last sentence or two to be true? My reality is; people love me; I get to hear more stories than I can ever share. I just got some good rest in a comfortable bed. The day is cool and enjoyable. I'll get to see more people. I will find some coffee and good food. Life is Good and God is Great. Life is "gooder" than I can ever describe and God is Greater than anyone could ever tell about or imagine.

This is a Great World and We Can Make It Better

I saw someone post, "The world gets scarier every day." Naturally, I don't agree with that. Especially since the implication is the world already is a scary place. I definitely disagree. Of course, there are things to be scared of, but there always have been. There have always been tornadoes, volcanoes, and earthquakes. These should be less scary now because we know these are natural phenomena and people used to think they were gods being upset. Do you think we have something to be scared of now? Just think if you had been a virgin about to be sacrificed to appease some god's anger. No wonder morals went out the door a long time ago.

What seems to be making us scared is our technology. Something bad happens anywhere in the world and we know it almost immediately. And even though it happened miles away, we get scared it could happen to us. Technology should make us feel much safer. It used to be if a woman broke down somewhere at night she might be in danger; and even if she wasn't she was going to have to walk somewhere in the dark which would lead to some discomfort and there definitely would be a fear of walking into a ditch or getting dog bit.

Now the woman just calls someone on her cell phone and they come and get her. Hey, we even have cars that call as soon as something unusual happens. It used to be if we had a heart attack there was a good chance we would die. Now they do heart transplants on a regular basis. It is almost an outpatient procedure. They clean out arteries so blood can flow better. We live longer than we have for a while.

I can remember when a woman got asked how many children she had and she would reply with, "Five; living". It was common for children to die at birth or soon after. I have seen gravestones that showed five children who had died before they were two years old. I assume the mother had some who lived in between the ones who died, but I don't know.

We know violence has always been around. The first child born in this world killed the second child who was born in this world. At the time he wiped out one fourth of the population. We talk about people not taking responsibility now, but the first human blamed the second human and the Creator for his transgression. Adam was supposed to be in control anyway. And we are too. We were given dominion over the earth, so if it is in bad shape, let's do what we can to get it in better shape.

I know the mass killings in Las Vegas are a big deal to the people affected, but in the big scope of things it is pretty small. In Myanmar there have been hundreds of thousands of people who have fled Bangladesh because of persecution. There are natural disasters affecting millions of people. There have always been acts of violence and there always will be.

The Bible says, "There is nothing new under the sun." I know I would rather be living now than anytime I could think of. In times past there was a holocaust, a black plague, the inquisition, slavery, genocide of the native Americans, San Francisco earthquake. Black towns being wiped out by whites. Massacres. More things than we can even imagine. Now when these things happen we have the technology to do something about them. The media warns us about natural disasters about to happen; places to avoid because of wrecks or shooting, or hostage situations.

In our Christian life, nothing has changed. We still are to get up and admire sunrises and sunsets and all of God's handiwork. We are to go tell people the good news we have a Savior; and they do too. We have nothing to fear, because Jesus said, when we go to the end of the earth doing this, he will always be with us. We have quite a responsibility because we have been given dominion over the earth; we are our brother's keeper; we have been given the task of feeding the hungry, clothing the naked, visiting the sick and imprisoned. It is a daunting task, but the Joy of the Lord is our strength, He will never forsake us, the Lord is our shepherd and we will not want.

Hey, how could it get any better? Well it can't. Not in this world without natural bodies. Maybe in Heaven it might get better, but then what would we have to do? Here we have plenty of things to do and being fearful is not one of them. We are here to spread peace and joy. Don't get distracted by things going on and let the world steal your joy. This is a great world and we can make it better.

Wasting time: Is that a sin?

May 5, 2015

Wasting time. Is that a sin? And how do we waste time? Well we waste time anytime we are not doing what the Lord created us to do. When we are angry at someone; when we do not forgive someone, when we spend time thinking what we should say to another criticizing what they did that we didn't agree with. Anytime we don't have positive thoughts and actions we are wasting time and griping.

It is good to see the problem, but how can we be part of the solution. Just telling someone they are messing up doesn't help anyone. It just wastes time and usually makes the other person waste time being angry with us. Feelings are hurt and they don't want to associate with us, which is wasting time again, when we could be working together accomplishing something instead of both of us not being productive.

So how do I get better. Well it isn't usually so much what we say; but how we say it, so when we see a problem if we speak in love and a soft voice this usually keeps the person from responding in anger. Most of us do try to defend our actions. That is a waste of time and breath. The person who may be bringing up the problem or gripe isn't asking why we are doing something; they are saying they are not happy.

What can I do to make them happy? Well, thank them for bringing the problem up. Then ask them if they have a solution? Tell them you will get back with them to address it. The point is to not attack a fellow creation of the Lord. This is wasting time again. We know He didn't create us to fight and gossip. Wow, so many ways to waste time. They are all sin; or the results of sin. Thank God for Grace.

So how do I get out of this wasting time? Well identifying it is a start. I never thought of being upset with anyone as wasting time before. The instance I realized it was when it caused three of us to waste time. I was critical of something someone did. Their feelings were hurt and they went off to do something that could have waited and they spent longer than they should because they weren't ready to come back and interface with me. They also had to think of a reason for this to tell me why they went to do something else.

Another guy came to help me who should have also been doing something else. He probably wasn't so happy about this either. So, it continues. I am always saying; if you do a good deed it is like dropping a rock in water; the riffles go out and keep going so the one little good deed may be multiplied. It works the same for harsh words or unforgiveness, or whatever negative thing we may do or say. When a rock is dropped into the pool the riffles go off in the same way influencing more people than we may imagine.

We are human and we make mistakes. Of course we do and how do we correct them? By developing habits. Doing good things over and over and over. Sooner or later we don't have to think; it will be second nature. If you went to ask forgiveness of whoever you got mad at and spoke harshly to, it would be an incentive for not doing it again. I always forgive whoever talks badly to me, but I hardly ever ask forgiveness from anyone. If I practice more it will teach me more humility; and it will get them to forgive me sooner so they can get on with their life and not be wasting time being upset with me.

Vines are Like Sin

August 20, 2015

I'm asked to cut some trees down that are blocking a view. Seems like a small job. The trees are tall but skinny. The trouble is there are a lot of vines intertwined between the trees. I have to cut some of them to get to the trees. The good thing about them is they are intertwined in a way so when I cut the trees they will not fall on the power line, but back toward the lane on the other side. After I get into them, I cut them down and they fall on the lane. Now I need to get them cut up and out of the lane before a car comes. Should be simple except for all those vines. As I cut something loose, more vines come dragging out and finally we have stuff pulled out everywhere. I have to go back on the other side and cut those vines that are big as my wrist.

As I'm doing this, I'm realizing these vines are like sin. They look good and smell good and are not so bad when they are in their place. There is nothing wrong with honeysuckle and morning glories when they are not choking something out. There is nothing wrong with wanting a better life for your family until you do something that hinders others. There is nothing bad about wanting a better ride to church until you get tore up because your car got scratched. So here is the trouble with sin and vines. They are pretty and neat until they interfere with what the Lord has designed for your life. He has designed a tree to grow a certain way; and it is just not up. It is to leaf out and spread out to be a haven for birds.

When the vines get on it, they keep it from filling out. They don't always keep it from growing up. It grows taller than it would because it is not filling out. Sometimes we do that. We get in the Spirit and get some revelation, but we don't flesh out by studying the Bible more; or praying more and we grow faster upward than our support system can stand. That is what happens to the tree. It isn't getting rooted or spread out like it should. We and the trees grow as we are designed. Roots hold us firm. Branches fill out to embrace people and birds; and grow in all the ways we were designed to grow.

As the tree is to get subsistence from the air, sun, and soil, we are to get subsistence from various ways, prayer, reading the Bible, associating with other Christians, eating right, and sleeping enough. If any of these things get neglected, we do not grow as we could and we are designed. Sin and vines keep us from this and cause us to grow crooked and hindered. After a tree or we get crooked, we can straighten up but the effects of the crook are there forever.

Sin is Bad for Us

Sin is anything that is bad for us. God gave us a book of instructions telling us what to do (or not to do) so as to avoid things that are bad for us. These instructions are for our benefit; not to make things hard on us; but to help us live better, happier, more productive lives.

Is Trust Like Faith?

April 10, 2015

Is trust like faith? I don't know. To trust someone, do you have to have faith in them? Jesus trusted Judas to take care of the finances, but I don't think he thought Judas was trustworthy. I guess we can trust without having faith. Maybe the key is to trust without worrying about the outcome. I will trust this will be a nice day; knowing it may rain, or there may be an accident, or some disaster may befall me. I don't have faith those things won't happen to me. I know they will sooner or later, but I trust every day will be good. Why wouldn't it? It is a day Got created; it will be good.

There may be a lot of bad things happening in a good day. Because I trust, I believe Romans 8:28, "All things work together for good to those who love the Lord." There are a lot of other promises in the Bible I trust in. The main one which is repeated more than any other is, "Fear not". Trust keeps us from fearing.

Jesus trusted a young girl to take care of him while he was an infant (and even before when He was in her womb). He trusted Judas. He trusted the disciples to spread the word; and He is trusting us now to give people the salvation message. Does he have faith we all will do that? Of course not. He knows some of us won't; and none of us will do it every chance we get.

He told us to tell every creature; and to go to the ends of the world. This means to tell everyone, everywhere. So far, I haven't met (or heard) or anyone who does this. Just because we don't do it doesn't mean He doesn't trust us to do it. If we trust in people it doesn't mean we are gullible. We are just following Jesus example. It may mean most things that happen won't make much difference. If we trust will we get betrayed? YES, and we will get betrayed if we don't trust. The only difference is; we won't allow these people to be friends. Can we say, "we are friends" to people we don't trust? We won't enjoy life as much because we will be watching for them to betray us.

So, do what the Lord says. "Don't worry." Things are going to happen regardless, so just deal with them when they happen. When Judas led the soldiers to Jesus in the garden, Jesus said, "Hello friend" He didn't rant on him. He asked him a question, about why Judas was betraying him with a kiss. We can trust someone and still convict them with our response.

Did Judas trust Jesus? He had faith Jesus could overthrow the Romans. He had faith Jesus was the son of God. His faith probably made him act as he did. He didn't trust Jesus would do what he and the other Jews wanted. This same lack of trust caused the crowd to yell, "Crucify Him"

Do we trust the Lord to do what He tells us to do, regardless of the consequences? How do we show our trust? If we have trust, we follow his commandments and forgive everyone and not worry about what they are going to do or what is going to happen to us. We have faith to believe He will take care of us. We have faith to believe He will come and get us and He is preparing a place for us. Let's trust Him and do his commandments.

No Excuses If We Want to Grow

Wake up this am thinking about gardening. I guess I did; I may have been thinking about anything. I remember seeing a family on Friday night setting plants as I was on my way to an Elder Retreat at Camp Aldersgate in Fitchburg, Kentucky. As I passed them and saw all their family involved, I thought about how our family used to do that. My dad worked long hours but it stayed daylight late in the summer so when he came home we went out in the garden to work. I was small but he cut a hoe handle down short enough for me to use.

Every spring, he got someone to come and plow and harrow the garden. Before he did that, we had to clear everything and have a big fire to burn what we had cleared. It seemed back then almost everyone had gardens. I can still remember how good a 'mater' out of the garden tasted. Put it on some 'light bread' and it was better and if we had some mayonnaise; that was heaven. Of course, we didn't have light bread all the time and mayonnaise hardly ever.

Before we planted the big garden, we had a lettuce bed. It had lettuce, radishes, and onions. That was pretty good too. We could take vinegar and grease to put on the lettuce, onions, and radishes for a salad. Now it would be vinegar and oil I guess, but I don't remember cooking oil then (it was lard) and if it had been we wouldn't have bought it anyway. Why would you buy cooking oil when you could melt lard down?

Now hardly anyone has a garden. There are various reasons for this. We don't have time. It is too much trouble. It is too expensive. The poor people have food stamps and don't need to. Plenty of reasons not to and not many to do it. Well, that is true in anything. I don't have time to write what I think the Lord has given me to write. If I wrote it, I wouldn't have time to edit it. No one reads it. It would be better for me to forward something.

We always have reasons for not doing things and the main one seems to be time but we seem to have time to do what we want to do. We may not have time to visit our relatives in the nursing home, but if we get free tickets to a Reds game we manage to get there and I've heard of people who never miss a UK game on TV. Most of us spend plenty of time on Facebook. It is hard to use the time thing as an excuse. Why make an excuse anyway?

I know everyone should be involved in gardening. Every family, every church and every civic minded organization and if I say everyone, this has to include me. Well I have no excuse, but the reason I'm not going to is because I don't want to and that would have to be the reason anyone else doesn't do things too. Any reason we want to use is fine, but make sure it's not an excuse. Sometimes it is difficult for us to see when a response is an excuse instead of a reason. It is both, but an excuse seems to get us off the hook, and the reason means we may have to change something.

For instance, I'm almost always late. My excuse is I was stuck in traffic. The real reason was I didn't start early enough. I was usually talking and I wanted to stay and talk to someone as long as I could until I just had enough time to get to where I'm going. If the traffic is bad I will be late. I will continue being late unless I change and leave early enough to maneuver through the traffic. I probably won't change because I usually think the conversation I'm in is more important than being right on time.

So, the question to me would be, "Well in that case, do I mind telling the person I was supposed to meet, I considered the conversation with another person more important than meeting them on time?" As a matter of fact, I don't have a problem with that. I don't say they are less important, but I did feel it was important to keep talking to the person I was talking to. If I didn't feel the conversation was important, I probably shouldn't have gotten into it to start with.

There have been times I should have called the person (or more likely a church) where I was going and say I wasn't going to make it because I was involved in a conversation with another person. But I didn't because I would have rather gone to the meeting (and been late) than continuing listening to the person I was in a conversation with. I don't think it's a bad thing. It's best to see the reason and not the excuse; because there should be no excuses if I want to grow.

Speaking of growing, I should get back to the gardening. I think it is healthier to eat food out of the garden, cheaper, promotes bonding of children, grandchildren, and friends, allows people to learn, promotes health by getting exercise, one gets more vitamin D from the sun, and it allows us to have food to share with others. The list goes on. I've heard people in the church say, "There will be a time when no one can buy or sell without a mark." Christians shouldn't have to worry about this because there should be enough of us knowing how to do various things. We can help each do what it takes to survive.

I'm going to promote gardening to as many people as I can. I'm not going to raise a garden myself because I'm too lazy and I would rather do something else with my time. I will help someone who asks if I don't want to do something else at the time. I can't use the excuse; I don't have a place, because I could raise a few plants in my van. The Gestalt Gardener raises stuff in his truck.

Man this 'no excuse' stuff is great. If someone asks me why I didn't meet them or why I was late to church. I can say "I was doing something I considered more important at the time" and then the other person doesn't have to come up with a solution to tell me how to avoid this happening to me again. They don't have to be sorry for me because I was stuck in traffic or whatever the situation was. They don't have to tell me I could or should have been somewhere.

I may ask them for prayer or guidance in the situation; this will show them I consider them important. I just I considered the situation I was in more important at the time.

Asking the Lord to Move on a Situation

Jan 12, 2016

I hear people praying for God to move on various situations. I assume the implication is He is not moving in these situations and He should be or He is not aware of the situation. I would hate to think He isn't aware of the situation. It would mean he isn't all knowing. I would also hate to presume He is not doing something He should be doing. This would imply He either doesn't care or He doesn't know He is supposed to handle the situation.

Ah, maybe that is it! He thinks we are supposed to handle the situation. He has moved on us to see it. He may have already moved on others to be receptive of what we do or say. The point is; He didn't come here to walk around with the disciples to show them what He could do so when they saw a problem, they could call on Him to fix it. He came to teach them to do what He wanted them to do. He sent the Word in the form of the Bible to give us instructions to do His work.

In chapter 4 of Mark, He slept through a storm to allow the disciples to handle it. They panicked and woke Him up. They didn't just wake Him up, they accused Him of not caring if they perished or not. He arose, rebuked the wind, and then chastised the disciples for being afraid and not having faith they could get through the storm. Later in Luke 9, when there were five thousand people to feed, Jesus told the disciples to feed them. They immediately told Him they didn't have enough and they would have to go buy food. He told them to take what they had (five loaves and two fish) and feed the people.

It seems the point is to use whatever you have to help as many people as you can right then at the time. To not say, "I don't have enough" or "first I need to go get something, or I need to get better prepared." He doesn't want excuses and procrastination to get in the picture. We are all guilty of this so He does give us second (and third and more) chances to serve Him, but the quicker we can get over our fear and go, the happier we will be.

In Luke 9, Jesus sent the twelve out to preach and heal. He sent them out with no money and told them to stay wherever anyone allowed them. They preached and healed everywhere. Then in chapter 10, Jesus turned it up a notch and sent seventy people out two by two and told them to not take any money and to go barefoot. I guess he didn't want them to kick any rocks or to run off. He sent them out as lambs among wolves. He told them, "the harvest is great but the laborers are few: pray ye therefore the Lord of the harvest, he would send forth laborers into his harvest." Luke 10:2.

So that is the prayer He wants us to pray (as we are already working in the situation); He will move others to come out and work in the harvest. This is how He is moving; by telling us to not worry but to go with what we have to help. Hey, we can take our wallets and wear shoes. We can even drive our cars.

The seventy people come back; and they are happy; just as everyone who has been on a mission trip is. They told Him (like He didn't know), "even the demons are subject to us through Your Name." and He said, "I beheld Satan as lightning fell from heaven. Behold I give you power to tread on serpents and scorpions, and over all the power of the enemy; and nothing shall by any means hurt you." Luke 10:18-19.

Later the disciples ask Him to teach them to pray. He told them to pray to the Father, for the Father to show them His will to help them allow His Kingdom to be here on earth as it is in heaven. To ask for their daily requirements (food, patience) and to forgive their sins (implying they sin daily) and to help them realize they are to forgive others and to show them what might tempt them so they can stay out of evil. (this is a paraphrase of the Lord's prayer)

The point is; we are to do what we know to do; to ask the Lord, what He would have us do, to ask Him to provide what we need to do His will, to ask Him to forgive us for our shortcomings; to not be afraid, because He has given us all power. He has given us the Holy Spirit to guide and comfort us.

We don't need to ask him to move in the situation. Ask Him What He would have us do in the situation we are aware of. If we are aware of it, he has already given us what we need to help. Just go and show the people in the situation… our love.

It is very hard not to be afraid and to have faith but we have some faith and the way to get more is to step out. We will never know if we have power to tread on snakes and scorpions unless we do it. The first time is hardest. The first time we walk into a bunch of people and tell them Jesus loves them it is a lot scarier than the second time. If we continue doing it, it will become second nature (well actually first nature).

Wherever we see a need, we are to do what we can about it. We will be amazed at the results.

Body of Christ? or Maybe Just Parts

Nov 29, 2016

I woke up this morning thinking about things Christians seem to disagree about. Evolution seems to be one. Well are we not supposed to be evolving. Surely, we are not where we are supposed to be. Before Jesus left, He said we would be able to do the things He did; and even greater. Well I don't see more people being raised from the dead. I don't see more lepers cleansed. I don't see more people getting fed. I don't see more people getting healed. I do see these things happening; I just don't see a gradual increase. It seems we are plagued with homelessness, with drug addictions, with more people taking meds, with more worries, etc. etc. and if anything, that is getting worse; especially in the US.

So, what is the problem? Is it the Church doesn't know the problem or is ineffective in doing what Jesus said? Do we think when Jesus said, "the thing I do, you will do, even greater," it was just a prophecy it would come to pass, or was it a command? Like when your parents tell you, "You WILL clean your room", or "you WILL get your homework before you go out to play." Maybe that is the problem. Maybe we think the Lord is coming to clean our room, to do our work while we play.

Maybe we think we are just supposed to go out and celebrate on Sunday by singing a few songs and listening to a message to make us feel good, and then throwing in some money so we can have electricity and heat in the building we celebrate in. Maybe when we say, "Come Lord Jesus, come quickly", we think He is coming to tell us, "well done good and faithful servant." Well I have got to think this is wrong. Usually when parents come to get their children it is because they are in detention; or in jail; or at the babysitters. Adult children don't have to have their parents come and get them. Even spouses don't come and get another spouse until their day of work is done.

I think we might as well be saying things we have seen on TV like, "Calgon take me away" or "Beam me up Scotty." I don't think the Lord is coming to get us until we have done the job He gave us, "feed the hungry," "go to Judea, Samaria, and to the ends of the earth, telling people the God News." I have never heard of a boss who comes and gives a person a raise or promotion who wasn't working; who was only looking to see when the Boss was coming. So, we must be working; to be doing what we were put here to do.

There are congregations and individuals who do some of these things. They feed, house, cloth, they minister to the addicts and broken hearted. There are individual congregations who do each individual thing. The problem is; we are supposed to be the Body of Christ; not the parts of Christ. We have plenty of congregations who see there is a problem, hear there is a problem; and even talk about it.

I hear all the time about how bad the world has gotten. This means someone has seen a need (or listened to TV and just heard and seen the worst of humanity). Many times, we see the worst and instead of giving us incentive to do the things Jesus told us to do, we get scared and huddle in a church building. We tell each other how bad the world is and how much power Satan has. We are glad we are like the Pharisee and know everything and not like the poor drug addict who has to go down to the mission church to get some food.

Sadly, we may also be glad we are not the mission church that has to deal with these undesirables. We are glad we only have people in our congregation who look and think like us. The problem is we are not just a congregation. We are a part of the Body of Christ. If we realize we could work as effective as our bodies do. Otherwise we will be a Frankenstein body; or worse; not even a part of The Body.

We are part of the church. We are to work together; to pray for each other; to support each other; and to do what we were designed to do as the part we are. The liver doesn't do the heart's job (and better yet it doesn't criticize what the heart does) but if they didn't work together our body would be in bad shape. That is why the Body of Christ isn't in as good as shape as it should be. Maybe it hasn't evolved to where kidneys, lungs, and lips work together. Maybe we are still in the embryonic stage. So, let's evolve. Grow from babies, to children, to adults who work together to obtain a common goal.

Forgive Everyone

We all know we are supposed to forgive everyone. It says it in the scripture, if you don't forgive, you won't be forgiven. To me this is a scary statement. I knew I hadn't forgiven everyone. Now I still haven't forgiven everyone either, but I'm not concerned about being forgiven.

I know the Lord loves me and most of the stuff I have asked forgiveness for was stuff that didn't amount to diddly anyway. It was basically getting in the candy jar stuff. It was not resisting temptation and I realized I shouldn't be doing it; partly because I had a stomachache or other consequences I didn't like dealing with later. We ask forgiveness and we are given forgiveness (at least most of the time). It isn't hard to forgive because we know it isn't personal.

Someone steals my money, or tries to go with my wife, or even backbites me because he wants a position in the workplace (or even in the church) I may be about to get. None of these were personal. The person would have wanted money no matter who had it; or he would have wanted the woman no matter who she was married to, and they would have wanted the position regardless of whoever was trying to get it. They may even have a twinge of guilt about those things because they are your friend and hated to take advantage of your friendship, but you just happen to have what they want; or more importantly sometimes, you have what they think they need, so any action on their part to get it is justified in their mind.

"Hey, I have to feed my family." So we realize these things are not personal and the Lord was right when he said, 'Forgive them, for they know not what they do." If they knew money wasn't enough to help them get out of their situation and I would have loaned it to them anyway, or the woman wasn't as nice as they thought and they wouldn't be happy with her anyway, or the job is hard and has a lot of responsibilities they couldn't handle anyway, they wouldn't have done the things to get them anyway.

It isn't hard to forgive these things. Sometimes we forgive with a sense of superiority. We are better than them, so we should be the better person and forgive. This is a pride thing we are in trouble for then. Man, this life is more complicated than I used to think.

But the things people do to be this are personal when I see there is no benefit to them. When they vote against me because I voted however I did. When they get stuff they think I deserved, but I didn't get it. I have problems forgiving those kinds of things. Why do I have problems doing this? Because most of I don't realize I am upset about this. And if I realize I'm upset, I don't see there is something I should forgive about. I just harbor this inside of me deep.

We know it isn't personal and maybe it's even harder because we would like to think someone cares one way or the other. When someone comes in and always goes over and talks to the prettier or outspoken person, do we hold that against them. Of course we do; we just don't admit it. This is the reason for sibling rivalry. We don't forgive the sibling or the parent when the parent gives the sibling something we should have gotten.

My dad always blesses my brother more than me. But we know if we were the better we would so we say we have or it didn't bother us anyway. Sometimes this manifests in ways harmful to us and others. We act out to get attention and of course the attention is negative then we resent our sibling and our parent more.

Well, we know sibling rivalry but what about caretakers or being parents or someone who is in charge at a business or church? Do we hold it against the people we are caring for? We have a special needs child who we are very appreciative of, but do we hold it against them sometimes because of us not being able to do something? We have a mother in the nursing home who we love to visit, but do we hold it against her because of how much money it takes to care for her or the time I could be doing something else.

At work here, I am going to the boss for better working conditions and no one is appreciating it and as a matter of fact they are griping. My family does the same, I bust my butt and they are complaining we don't have enough money to go on vacation. Well if they wouldn't waste so much money on wanting game boys, or shopping, or whatever we would have money. If I was single again, I would have money. If my Mom wasn't in the nursing home. If she had taken better care of herself she wouldn't have been there.

Sometimes we resent people who didn't take better care of themselves or if they had acted better they wouldn't be in the situation they are in. We resent this. We love them and we want to do what we can to help, but we are still resenting this takes our time and money. We know we are not supposed to do this so we deny that we are. Therefore, we don't ask forgiveness for feeling this way.

Grace and Consequences Work Together

May 25, 2018 ·

Grace is unmerited favor. Consequences are the results of any act. I don't think there is actually any versus here; more an and. Grace keeps the consequences from being as bad as they could. I do something dumb on Thursday and instead of getting killed or a broken bone I get a cut resulting in stitches. I don't get disabled where I can't go to the Mankind Elder retreat on Friday, but I can't do the high rope course on Saturday.

Grace gives me a body that will heal itself, gives me blood to flow and clean out the wound and then coagulate so no more blood than necessary flows out. Grace allows pain to show me I have an injury and keeps the pain down enough so I can function enough to drive to where I can get sewed up. Consequences cause me pain and keep me from doing what I had planned. Grace keeps me from being injured much worse and consequences show me I could have done things better. Grace and consequences work together because it wouldn't be much grace that didn't allow things to happen so I could learn from them.

If grace didn't allow a dumb act to be punished then we would continue doing these dumb acts. We would keep doing dumber acts until they really hurt someone who wasn't covered by grace. So, when parents protect their children from the consequences of their acts they are not really showing love. They are keeping the child from learning about consequences.

Forgiveness as Christ Forgives

August 30, 2015

I heard someone say something about forgiving someone after they were sure what the person had done. I guess the implication was; depending on what the perceived offense was they would determine if they could forgive or if the person was worthy of forgiving. If it was too bad of an offense they couldn't forgive and it seemed as if the person who had committed the sin needed to ask for forgiveness. I guess this was like if the person hit them accidentally they would forgive but not if it was on purpose. Or if they stole ten dollars, but not a thousand. As I thought on this I wonder how we as Christians have got this so perverted. If we are followers of Christ this should mean we are to be Christ like. None of us are, but we are to strive for this.

When it came to forgiveness, Peter asked Jesus if we were supposed to forgive seven times and Jesus responded, "seven times seventy," which means indefinitely. Later when Christ was on the cross, He said, "Forgive them, for they know not what they do" Is He saying, these people didn't know what they did, when they deliberately yelled "Crucify Him" and drove nails into His hands? He was saying, these people don't know what is best for them. And that is what happens in our life.

If we knew what was best for us, we would not do things to offend others. Jesus tells us: if we don't forgive we won't be forgiven. It seems pretty scary but I have to believe it is for us. We have to forgive so, we can get on with our life. If we don't forgive, we can't have peace. He promises us "peace beyond understanding." We can't have this peace with unforgiveness in our heart.

It is not about people asking us to forgive them. We are to forgive them immediately. If they don't know if they have done something to offend us they definitely won't ask to be forgiven for it. If we walk in the spirit as we are told, then we won't take offense at these things anyway Plus we can't forgive sins anyway, so if we love as we are supposed to, we pray for them. It is fine to tell them we have been offended, but also ask them to forgive us for getting offended. We are told to "reason together" so we should be able to discuss these so-called offenses.

Our offenses are what we should be concerned with. Jesus said, if we go to the altar to give a gift and we realize a "brother has ought against us" (*Sermon on the Mount, Matthew 5*), we go ask our brother for forgiveness. I'm not sure what ought means, but I am pretty sure it means if he has anything against us. So, it would be even if what we did was not wrong and even if the person was in the wrong being upset with us, we are to go to them to try to get it rectified.

It seems so against our nature to forgive; especially when it is something that truly hurts us or causes us a lot of discomfort. But if we could realize people who are doing things to hurt us have problems so much worse than us and they need Christ in their lives and we may be the ones who are supposed to be representing Christ, maybe we can be more understanding and look at this as an opportunity to witness. Like if someone steals from us to buy drugs it means they have an addiction so strong it is causing them to do things very detrimental to them.

It isn't just the drugs hurting them. The things they are doing to get the drugs are hurting them more. They are losing friends; getting into jail. This is messing up their life forever beyond the effects to their body. So instead of being mad at them, we should feel sorry for them and pray for them and pray for guidance there is some way we can help them. We are told if anybody asks us for anything, we are to give it to them (and even more) so if they steal, I guess that would be the same. We are also supposed to depend on the Lord for our provision so what can someone steal that the Lord can't supply to us?

It gets down to this, as Christians we are to forgive as Christ did (immediately) and to see what we can do to help this person who did what we perceived as wrong. The only person who needs to ask for forgiveness is us. Ask forgiveness of the Lord for not representing Him better. If we do that, it isn't so much He will forgive us, (He already has); but He will guide us to show His love better. Okay, I know this is hard, and I'm sure I'm the worst offender. There are a lot of things I haven't forgiven people for and that hinders me. It doesn't do anything to them. I doubt any CEOs are losing sleep because I haven't forgiven them for sending jobs to China or for polluting the air and water.

If I have offended anyone, forgive me so you can move on. If it is something you think I should change, inform me (try not to be too harsh).

I do apologize for not quoting scripture. I don't have the best concordance and I don't have scripture memorized like some people do. I think this is supposed to get out to someone (probably me).

Love in Christ,

Jim

Failure: Light at the End of the Tunnel

Oct 7, 2017

A guy did devotion the other morning and he talked about how he had been reminiscing about his life and realized there were so many things he had not accomplished that he thought he should. The word came to him. FAILURE. Now he knew this wasn't true because he had accomplished a lot of stuff, but while he knew it in his head he could not get it into his heart. Every morning when he first woke up he would hear the word FAILURE. Of course, he wasn't and he finally overcame that, but the point of the devotion was; we all deal with self-doubts and need to be encouraged.

We realize we are not alone and the quickest way to get over this is to talk to people who will pray with us and encourage us. We had a time of prayer after this. As I was leaving the devotion, I overheard him tell someone, "When I was in that dark place of FAILURE I fought if for a while but it was very draining to fight and after a while I realized it was easier to just accept I was a FAILURE and to quit fighting." Especially when he had to fight each day.

As he was saying this, it struck a chord in me. I then realized why so many people stay in the situation they are. It is easier. That makes me feel a little more compassion for them instead of just being aggravated about them not moving on from the situation or condition they are in. For one thing, when one is in any situation, it is easy to stay than it is to move. It takes energy and planning to move. It doesn't take anything to stay.

After a while one doesn't feel so bad about the situation they are in. Of course, the main reason people stay is they can't see a way out. It takes too much effort to just get out for a while and then it will still come back to them they are a FAILURE.

While on the one hand this revelation gives me more compassion for people who are in a bad situation, it makes me grieve when it is harder for me to help them out. How do you tell a person who has been deserted by her husband, her father has just died, has small kids to take care of and her house is destroyed, and every relationship she has been in has been bad …if she keeps on keeping on things will get better?

She cannot see the light at the end of the tunnel. She knows she is at the end of her rope. While she may be able to hold on, that is going to be the best she can do. She can't climb up. The best she can do is to try to tie a knot so she can't fall any further.

I am depressed because I don't know the answer so I'm looking at my life to see why I am where I am. Maybe there is an answer there. I was born poor and weak. I had a double hernia that caused me to wear a truss for years. I knew I would always be poor, but I refused to believe I would always be weak; and even if I was I would do all I could do. I might not lift, but I can climb.

Because I was small, light, and had long arms I could climb higher than anyone else. I guess this gave me some confidence. Because I was weak and in bed a lot it made me want to read so even when I couldn't read I pretended I could. I guess when you pretend to do something, it makes it easier to learn to do it.

Walking Through the Storms; or rebuking them

This is the day the Lord has made. Let us rejoice in it. This is a life changing day. If our life isn't changed today then we have not lived it to the fullest. All nature changes every day. It is either growing or dying; either way is changing. Do we want to grow or die? Do we want to live in curiosity and embrace this change or do we want to fear it?

The choice is ours. Jesus said the kingdom of heaven is at hand. That means it is here. It is reality. He said He is the Way. He said we could do greater things than He had done. If we walk in His way of being compassionate, generous, forgiving, we will feed more people than we thought possible with what we have; we will touch more people who will healed than we thought was possible. We will do better than walking on water; we will walk above the storms. As we walk above the storms we will feel compassion for the people who are in the storms; the ones who are hunkered down waiting for the storms to pass. And we will tell them how to avoid that by walking through the storm.

Storms will always come. The quicker we can walk through them, the quicker we can get on with what we were doing before the storm. We can rebuke the storm. We can say, this is not a storm. This is just some wind to make us deepen our root to get stronger; some water to wash stuff away, some lighting to admire the awesomeness of nature. This isn't an unusual event; it is reality. It is a challenge and an opportunity to help others who think it is a storm.

We all have the storms of life. Our children are in bad relationships, they are on drugs, our loved ones are going through divorces, our friends are dying, the list goes on forever. This is life. But we are here to show them we have a right relationship with the Lord and they can to. We are here to show we have a life more exciting than drugs. We are the light in the storm. The light to show the way. To show us sickness can be cured and the death of the body is just a transition to eternal life.

We can show people who think they are dying, it isn't about dying, but it is about living until our body gives up the ghost. All of these storms are learning opportunities for us. To learn how to show more compassion; to find the right words to speak to the next person who is going through a storm; to just grow in our faith. To help show others (and ourselves) the Lord really is always with us.

Whatever the storm, our job stays the same; to feed the hungry, clothe the naked, visit the sick and imprisoned, and to tell everyone the 'good news'. The kingdom of heaven is at hand; let's walk in it.

Living Life to the Fullest

April 21, 2015

While I'm on an adventure (broke down and can't go anywhere if the Lord or a kindhearted person doesn't intervene), I interface with a guy who shares with me his thoughts about what the Lord wants. He says, "All the

Lord wants is for us to live life to the fullest." I'm thinking 'man, this is profound'. It makes so much sense. Why else would He have created us in the way He did if He didn't want us to live to the fullest potential? Maybe him sharing this with me is better than him fixing my vehicle so I can get moving again.

I share this at Bible study last night and someone seems to think people could take this the wrong way. Most of us seem to be able to take the scriptures the wrong way. But maybe they don't take them the wrong way. They just seem to ignore them. Especially the red writing where He tells us to forgive everyone, feed the hungry, clothe the naked, visit the sick and imprisoned, tell people the good news, don't worry about tomorrow or today either. If anyone asks anything of you, give it to them.

I'm trying to think of scriptures that verify God wants us to live life to the fullest. I'm trying to think of some that don't because all those I can think of I agree with. When Jesus says, "Be anxious for nothing" I would say these words are not contradicting living life to the fullest. When he says, if anyone asks anything of you, just do it (and more). This is not contradicting to show; anything you can ask of me; the Lord will give me the strength and means to do it.

We have been created to serve, so if we don't serve, we are not living life to the fullest. That would be like a plate on the wall. A plate is made to have food on it and be pretty so you can enjoy the beauty as you enjoy the function of the plate. A plate on the wall is not living to its fullest. If we are just looking pretty in church, we are not living to our fullest.

We are created to live in community; so if we are not living to build the community up, we are not living our fullest. Paul gives us a lot of instructions about how we are supposed to live with each other. None of this contradicts with us living to the fullest. We are given dietary laws so we can eat healthy.

Like anything else, the problem may be to define what 'living to the fullest' means. I would say living to the fullest would be to live as we were designed to, physically, emotionally, and spiritually. The Bible is the instruction book for us. If we are living to our capacity in body, mind, and spirit, I would say this is living to the fullest. The Designer has created us to serve and enjoy life as we serve and then He has given us an instruction manual to follow so we can serve and enjoy this life.

Yep, there is no doubt we are to live our lives to the fullest. Is that what we want our children to do? Why? Is it because we have been created in the image of God; and this is what He wants for His children?

One Never Knows How Much Effect a Comment Might Have

April 30, 2017

I went to church this morning. Got there before service but Bible study was going on. I walked in and guy said to me, "I was thinking of you this morning." He had been wondering if his pastor had told me about their tent revival. He hadn't. I said, "Well he was probably thinking I talked so much he wouldn't get a chance to preach." The pastor seemed to be kind of embarrassed he hadn't told me it was going on. The guy who mentioned this commented, "You said something last tent revival that really stuck with me."

Naturally, I didn't remember much of anything I said a year ago. He reminded me the comment I made was "I don't know why when we see someone broke down we don't stop because the Lord didn't tell us to. It would seem we should be saying, "Lord, I'm stopping to help these people. If there is any danger, warn me and I won't stop.'" He said, "Since then I've stopped and helped a bunch of people."

I guess besides my comment helping him to not be so afraid to stop, it also allowed people to get help who may not have gotten help. One never knows how much effect a comment might make on people.

Return Evil with Good

King Herod had John the Baptist's head cut off because John had preached against Herod being in an adulterous relationship. Well, John had a cousin, Jesus who happened to be the Son of God. Because Jesus was the Son of God, He had all power. Jesus had emotions like the rest of us so He was sad Herod had cut his cousin's head off. So "He called His disciples together and gave them power over all devils and to cure disease. And he sent them to preach the kingdom of God and to heal the sick" Luke 9:1-2.

He also told them to not take anything for their trouble. To just stay where someone lets you stay. Stay there for a short time and move on, talk to whoever will listen and if they don't listen, don't worry about, just "shake the dust" off their feet and move on. So, they did. They preached the gospel and healed everywhere. Herod heard about this and was perplexed. Why would Jesus and His disciples heal people and cast out demons at a time like this.

Didn't they realize John had been beheaded. Shouldn't they have been at the palace protesting this injustice? Shouldn't they have been standing up for God and His Prophets? Well Jesus had preached about that. He said, "return evil with good," so that is what they were doing.

If we are to be followers of Christ, this is what we are to do. Do you know anyone who has a demon or who is sick? If you do, go to them and help them. If you don't, ask a person if they know someone who you might go minister to. Most everyone I seem to come in contact with has both. Drug addictions, trapped in bad relationships, depressed, obese, demons of pride, envy, guilt, fear, the list is endless.

We have the answer. We have the Gospel (the good news). We are to share this answer with whoever is oppressed or depressed. When we do that, the news media will be perplexed. The politicians will be perplexed. And Satan will be depressed. And a lot of people will be happy and free. I know it is a lot harder than posting stuff on Facebook, but it truly will be worth it. And if the scripture is correct it is really what Jesus wants us to do.

Affirmation: Accept That You Are Loved

Feb 12, 2015

Last night I was in a Bible study and the teacher said, "When I read the Bible I get better." Now I know this may not make sense to a non-believer, but it spoke to my heart and the work affirmation came to me. I shared this with the class. When we read the Bible, we see that God created us in His image. That should make us realize we are good. Then after He created us, He said 'very good'. Later He sent His Son because in John 3:16, He affirms He loves all of us. In Psalm 139:14. "I am fearfully and wonderfully made." There are so many others and of course we have also messed up and sinned and not taken care of the wonderful body we have been given. In Romans 5:20, "where sin abounded, grace did much more abound."

We are made wonderfully in the image of God and He loves us" Why wouldn't He? He created us and everybody loves what they make. An artist loves his paintings. He doesn't always love what we do; just as we don't always love what our loved ones do. But He promises us He will never forsake us and His Love is Eternal. True Love is Eternal. We get affirmations all the times we are loved. Sometimes we are the ones who have trouble accepting this; so, if we have problems, then others do also. When I volunteered with Christian Appalachian Project we wrote affirmations to each other and it made one feel good to realize others appreciated what you did.

The challenge of the day is to accept you are loved and are a good person. Then pass on to other people they are loved and appreciated. If each one of us does this to one other person, the world will be a better place. If we do it to two it will be a much better place so do your part. Tell someone (or two or three and so on) they are appreciated. I appreciate the smile the waitress gives me at the restaurant. I can tell her and then show her with a good tip. The list is endless so it will be hard for us to fail unless we try.

Sermon on a Dandelion: How Can I Not Get Excited When I am Talking About God's Creation?

Eastern Kentucky
Spring 2018

A while back I noticed a bunch of dandelions in someone's yard. I wondered why there were so many and what are they good for. It seemed there are a lot of them and they are pretty useless. Most people call them a weed. The thought came to me, if a preacher can't tell me why God created the dandelion then I probably shouldn't listen to him when he says, "he knows the mind of God." I mean if one doesn't know why God created something as simple as a dandelion, how would they know why He created something more complex; like man?

Well, we know there are a lot of dandelions and we know God is good and He created everything and it was all good; so obviously the dandelion is good.

The first thing I think of when I hear dandelion is 'dandelion wine.' I've never tasted it or even seen it. Maybe I think of it because of a song. But this makes me think of the first miracle Jesus did which was to turn water into wine. The dandelion is also one of the first flowers to show up in the Spring. It springs up fast and is sign of renewal. It reminds me of the resurrection.

I have also heard of dandelion greens. This means we can eat the dandelion for nourishment; and it is one of the first greens to come up so it is the one which can nourish us first in the spring.

Then I saw an article saying the dandelion flower was the first plant where bees get honey from. The dandelion nourishes bees so they can have strength to live until other flowers bloom. We know how important bees are. If it wasn't for bees there would not be much pollination and we would be in big trouble. There was a scare a few years ago (and may still be) about so many bees dying.

Then I go to the nursing home to see my brother and I see two little girls picking dandelions to make garlands and bracelets. They remind me of flower girls in a wedding and it all seems to come together. The dandelion can provide, wine, food, and flowers for a wedding banquet. A wedding where two people cleave together to become as one. The children are having a good time and I think of the scripture, "lest we become as little children we cannot enter in the Kingdom of Heaven." They are playing and they are in the kingdom now.

I think of how the seeds come out in a ball and kids get so much enjoyment of blowing the seeds off of the stem and as the blow off I'm thinking how the dandelion answered one of the first commandments humans were given, "be fruitful and multiply"

I know enough about why God created the dandelion, but of course I don't know the whole reason. I know yellow is one of my favorite colors, but I don't think he just made it for me. I was aiming to be content with what I know, but then I finally looked up the dandelion on the internet and I found out it is good for so many things (diabetes, liver, cancer, acne, to just name a few). Wow, does God make everything a multitasker? I believe He does. It just shows God's provision and how he uses something we consider a weed to do all kinds of things.

That should make us me more appreciative of His creation and realize when we had man tend the garden He meant every plant He created. (or course this also means things like poison ivy so we should try to find out what these weeds are good for.) And when He said all seed-bearing fruit is good for meat (Genesis 1:29), did he just mean fruit or anything that produces seed? It produces seeds because God wants it to reproduce. If He wants it to reproduce it has to be for more of a reason than to aggravate people. We couldn't say God was good if he made stuff bad for us.

There are over 200 sub-species of the dandelion, which shows us God wants variety in everything. I knew he wanted variety in humans; I just never realized He wanted it in plant life. Each sub-specie does something a little different. He has a different job for each one of us.

I didn't go into the things about the roots being used to break up the soil. The dandelion grows where some other plants don't want to grow. It absorbs energy from the sun. It shuts when it gets cold to protect itself and then opens to absorb the warmth of the sun. There is a lesson here. It seems to go on for ever and ever. I should quit before I get too excited talking about the dandelion.

HOW CAN I NOT GET EXCITED WHEN I AM TALKING ABOUT GOD'S CREATION?

Such a beautiful day, we only need to open our eyes

It has rained which causes the vegetation to glisten. There is only a little water in the road but I can see the reflection of objects in it. Water is so amazing. light can shine through a rain drop and the drop breaks up the light so we see rainbows. How amazing is that? Well pretty amazing. it is more sensational than I would have thought. If one didn't know about it they could be charged admittance to see a rainbow; or a sunset; or a sunrise; or the moon. the list goes on forever. and we don't have to pay anything. we only have to open our eyes; which of course is another amazing thing.

There is a Reason We are Given a Gift

Someone mentioned about how many Christians are sick and I said I would hate to preach it; but I would say most of us are sick because we are not doing what the Lord tells us. This makes people think I am saying they are sinning and they start denying it. First off, I would say I am as guilty as anyone else. And if we worry, we are not doing what the Lord says, if we are upset about what someone said, we are walking in the flesh instead of the spirit. If we have bitterness, we have not forgiven someone. If we are sad about the circumstances we are in, then we are not trusting the Lord is going to do what He said He would; or we are not happy with His timing. The list goes on.

This does not mean we are bad people, it just means we are human and we are walking in the flesh more than the spirit. The good news is; when we see we are having any of these emotions we can check ourselves, repent, and ask the Lord to help us get back in the spirit; to accept the gift of peace He has given us; to accept all of the gifts He has given us.

Is it a sin to not accept a gift? I wouldn't say that; but there is a reason we are given a gift; it is to use it to help ourselves and others. It is a gift and we don't get it taken away from us if we don't use it, but the giver is definitely grieved if we are unhappy and sick, when we could be sharing and having a good time in the kingdom.

He Has Never Failed Me Yet
"All things work together for good."

July 2018

The other night, Pastor Story of Harvest Time preached on Romans 5:3-5 which says, we "glory in tribulation" because tribulation gives us patience (or endurance) in our life and from patience we get experience (or character) and the experience gives us hope. And hope makes us not ashamed because the love of God is in us and is poured out by the Holy Spirit.

I am reading and studying this to see how it applies to my life. Well, "glory in tribulation" might seem weird. Why would we glory in it? One thing is sure, we are going to have tribulations so we might as well glory in them. We are going to get through them and while we are doing that, we will be learning things and building character. This gives us hope we can make it through the next tribulation and not only make it through, but we can help others make it through their trials and tribulations.

All of this means when I am riding around exploring things and get stuck in the National Forest, miles from anywhere, I can glory in the experience. I'm going to get patience and endurance knowing I am not going to get to where I was going when as planned; and I'm going to have to walk a few miles to get somewhere to call for help. If I have a cell phone I have to wait a long time and figure out how I am going to pay for the wrecker. It may take a lot of patience to even tell them how to get to where I am stuck. I may need some fortitude to put up with them telling me how dumb I was to get stuck where I did. Someone will ask, "what were you doing up in there anyway?"

One time I didn't have a cell phone so I had to walk and find a house with a phone and then had to listen to my brother in law give me a rough time for getting stuck. The next day my nephew borrowed a truck and he, my brother in law and I had to go back and pull the vehicle out. Before I got stuck I had driven over something that broke a brake line so it was somewhat of a trial driving back over the forest service road to get it to a garage.

It seems weird but I was pretty much glorying while this was going on. While I was walking up the forest service road, it started getting dark and I realized I had taken a wrong turn at the tee. I had to turn around and as I did the scripture in Rom 8:28 came to me, "All things work together for good." I didn't know how it was going to but believed it would.

When I got to a house and made a call to my sister, my brother in law answered saying, "I just walked in the house from being out hunting." If I had not turned the wrong way at the tee, I would have gotten to the phone earlier and when I called no one would have been there to answer. GLORY. It worked out perfectly. Of course, getting stuck wasn't such a good thing. The scripture doesn't say "all things are good." It says, "all things work together for good"

I get patience and experience from these things. I know the Bible calls them trials and tribulations but I call them adventures and I can glory in them. Because of these experiences I learn to carry a jack and tools. Well somewhat, but sometimes I don't have them or can't find the tools, even if I have them. In that case I know I can use something around the area. I can get a tree limb and a rock to make lever and fulcrum to pry the vehicle out.

I have hope the Lord will provide even when I didn't prepare well enough. One reason I have this hope is, it has always happened before. He has never failed me yet. I will get through whatever I'm going through and then I can share the experience with others.

This experience gives me an opportunity to witness for the Lord. Sometimes I can witness as I'm going through the trial (or adventure) and sometimes I can testify about it later. Either way, "Life is an Adventure." And the trials are learning and strengthening experiences. The Lord wants us to live life to the fullest. John 10:10, Jesus says, "The thief came to kill and steal, but I came to bring life; life more abundant."

Even through these trials, we can live life to the fullest. We can enjoy nature as we are walking down a dark road. We can meditate on the scriptures as we are waiting on the wrecker. We can realize we are getting more patience by these delays. We are being strengthened by these walks. Best of all we are getting to meet new people we would have never got to meet if it hadn't been for the trial.

Our Spiritual Eyes

June 26, 2018

I have glaucoma. The eye doctor ran a test on me where a white dot moved across a screen. He said to hit a button when I saw the dot and to stop hitting it when I didn't. I'm hitting the button and all at once the dot disappeared. Directly it came back in sight but it was to the right of where it had been before. I hit the button again. It appeared to me I could see the dot very well. Well, until it disappeared and then when it came back on, I could see it clearly again. Then I'm told the dot didn't disappear. It had just gone past a part of my eye that was blind.

My whole eye is not blind, I only have a blind spot. This means when I stop at a stop sign and look up the road and I don't see a car there still may be one there. It may just be in my blind spot. I have to wait a second until the car could pass through that blind spot. I can also turn my head so the blind spot will be at a different place and I can see the area I couldn't see before.

The good thing about this is now I know there is a blind spot, I will be more cautious. I will look twice and turn my head as I'm looking so I can get a wider view. This made me think of my spiritual eyes. Do I have glaucoma in them? Are there blind spots? Are there sins in my life I don't see? Is this what Jesus was talking about in Matthew: 6:3-5, when He said we could see a speck in our brother's eye, but we can't see a log in our eye. Our vision is good when it comes to seeing other's sins, but we have a blind spot when it comes to our sins.

Maybe we have a blind spot when it comes to the letter of the law. Matthew 23:23 "tithing on mint and herbs but neglecting the weightier matters of the law; justice and mercy and faith" We clearly see the letter of the law but we are blind to the intent of the law. Maybe we can see clearly the bad things we do, but we don't see the good things. Maybe we are blind in the love department. We can be critical, but we can't be encouraging. We can see the problems, but we can't see the solutions.

How do we know if we have glaucoma of our spiritual eyes? Well, are we looking with love? If not, we have a blind spot. When we see someone with a problem, do we have compassion. If we are critical to others we are not looking through the love part of our eyes. Maybe spiritual glaucoma is seeing with our eyes and mind, and not seeing with our heart. *Matthew. 9:36,* "But when He saw the multitudes He was moved with compassion toward them because they were weary and scattered like sheep having no shepherd."

If we don't have spiritual glaucoma we will see the need instead of the wrong. We will see people need a shepherd. They should get answer to their problem instead of having the problem pointed out.

Purpose of Life

May 2015

I wake up this morning in a comfortable four poster bed. The sun is shining and I see more various colors of green than I can distinguish. Birds are singing. The sky is a beautiful blue. It is changing as I lay here enjoying it. All the colors are changing. How can this be? Can something besides a chameleon change colors? If things can, then what are their true colors. Does anything have a color or is it just a reflection?

I saw the same view last night under moonlight and it was different. The moon was white and bright. We know the moon is not white. Well it may be. I don't think we know what color it is. We know at night we are not seeing the light of the moon. We are seeing the light of the sun being reflected off of the moon. All the colors we think we see, are the light of the sun reflected off of the objects we see. Depending on the brightness; or whether it is a cloudy day, our perceptions of these objects change. Kind of weird, isn't it? Makes sense when we say, "I never saw it in that light before"

I know when I see the tree in the dark (or don't see it and bump into it) and when I see it in the brightest light (and anything in between), it is still the same tree. It is a creation of God's to do a certain purpose. The purpose doesn't change because of the light or our perception of it. So it is with us. Each person has a purpose ordained by God. Our purpose (or at least one of them) is to help a person recognize his own purpose and to encourage him. If we can realize the light we see in a person in has no bearing on what his purpose is, then we would be a lot less judgmental about their appearance and more likely to help them fulfill their purpose.

What is their purpose? The same as ours. To follow the instructions of Jesus to live a good life. To feed the hungry, visit the sick and imprisoned, clothe the naked, and tell people the good news. This is an awesome responsibility for one person and one more reason to see the purpose in others, so they can help. It isn't just up to the preachers to tell the good news. It isn't just up to the Salvation Army to feed and clothe. It is up to all of us to do our part. All trees are not the same. Some of them put out food for birds and some put out food for animals. Some of them put our materials for housing. Some of the plants put out material for clothing and some of them supply food for the hungry.

We are not in this alone. Even the plants help us feed the hungry and clothe the naked. If it wasn't for them we could not do it. It shows us all God's creations are valuable. None of them can do what needs to be done on its own. We are all in this together. All the humans, all the animals, all the plants; all of creation. We can respect each other and all creation or we cannot. We have free choice. But if we respect each other, we can accomplish our purpose so much better and we will be so much happier. Jesus said, "I came to bring life; life more abundantly" the first part of that quote is "the enemy came to steal, kill, and destroy."

If we follow the instructions of Jesus, we will live an abundant life. If we don't, we will be destroyed. Seems pretty simple. Live life to the fullest using the resources God gave us. Be happy. Be anxious for nothing. Realize the Lord has provided for us. He has given us every resource we need to live our life to the fullest. Utilize these resources. Ask the lord what they are and how to use them and He will guide us in the best use of them. Sounds simple; and it is, but it is so easy to get distracted.

All we have to remember is, the enemy came to kill, steal, and destroy and the Lord came to bring abundant life. If anything we say or do kills someone's joy, we know it is not of the Lord. Say and do things to encourage people to be the person God created them to be and we will be following the instructions of Jesus.

Who cares about a little bent over bush?

Wimberly, Texas

In Wimberly, Texas cleaning up after the Blanco River flooded. At one of the houses I see a little bush that has a bunch of debris in it and it is bowed down to the ground where the water washed over it. For some reason I start to take the debris out of the limbs. I don't know why I did this because it seems there was a lot more important things to do. Who cares about a little bush that is all bent over? Well maybe God does. It is one of His creations. And as it came out, He used it to speak to me. As I'm taking the debris out, I notice some new bright green leaves growing out and it comes to me "when sin abounds; grace abounds more" and I'm thinking that the flood was like sin or the cares of the world rushing over people but when things happen to stress a plant or people there is the potential for new growth.

When things flood over us it makes us aware there are things we need to do. We need to get regenerated. But sometimes the storms bend us over until the dirt and debris cover out heads so we can't see and can't get up.

That is when we need someone to uncover our heads so we can see. After we are bowed over like that for a while we don't realize we are able to straighten up; and probably we can't by ourselves. We know we are alive and it seems all we will ever be is what we are now. We need someone to come over and lift us up and to tell us there is still growth in us.

Sometimes a storm can push us to grow stronger roots so we can weather the next one, but sometimes the storm pulls our roots out of the ground and exposes them so we are so weak we may not make it through another storm. So someone has to come to encourage us and help us get rooted again. When I tried to straighten that bush up it still fell down because of how much it had been bent. I looked around for a stick to prop it up but didn't see anything. Sometimes we need a prop to keep us straight. We need someone to stand by us and uphold us until we get our strength and focus back. That bush will grow toward the light, but it wouldn't be so crooked and it would grow quicker if it had a prop to keep it up. That is like us, we may still grow toward the Light, but we may have a few crooks and not look so good or grow so fast due to these crooks. So if we can we need to help our brothers straighten up and sometimes we need help straightening up also.

As I cleaned the debris out of that bush it looked a lot better, but I noticed there was still quite a bit of smaller stuff that was harder to get out because it was wrapped around each little branch and as I was pulling it out I would break a branch every now and then. It made me think of how sin can get intertwined in our lives until it seems to be a part of us. We may be cleaned up the big stuff. We quit a lot of things when we became Christians, but these little things, our anger, doubts, envy, etc can keep us from looking as good, and growing as well as we could. Sometimes we consider this part of our personality and part of us has to be pruned to get rid of these things that are hindering us. Usually we don't realize they are hindering us so we need a friend (or a sermon by a pastor) to tell us this.

So I pulled some more of the smaller debris out of that bush and it looked better, but then I could see smaller stuff that I hadn't noticed before. So that is the way it is in our life also. As we clean up something, we notice something else that needs to be cleaned up. Well hopefully we do.

If we notice it and clean it up that is sanctification and it will be a lifelong job. If we don't notice it we won't and we will quit growing. Well we may still be growing; we just won't grow as fast as we could and we won't look as much like Jesus as we could. These smaller things weren't so hard to get out but there were a lot of them so I finally gave up. Well fortunately my lead called me to go tear out a floor. I had already got a devotion out of the bush and I didn't need to clean out every little piece of junk on the bush. And we don't have to clean up every little piece of stuff in our life either to survive, but if we want to thrive and be sanctified we need to keep working on them.

These are things that probably wouldn't be considered sin. They are things like spending too much time on the computer or spending too much money on videos or eating more healthy. At first glance these seem to be very minor things, but when one considers that any time wasted is time the Lord gave us and our bodies are temples and tools to serve Him it seems that everything we do is very important. We need friends and pastors who will tell us about these things. We may have a pretty smile but when we get a piece of spinach stuck between our teeth it takes away from the smile and we would never notice it if it wasn't for someone telling us. So we shouldn't be quick to be offended when someone tells us what we can do to improve our appearance.

Jimbo with friend and editor, Keith Gilbertson at home in Biloxi, Mississippi. Jimbo showed us how to duct tape a refrigerator.

Prayers with families and workers before starting the cleanup, after and sometimes during.

Hands joined in prayer with volunteers and family in Biloxi Mississippi after Katrina 2005

L-R Keith Gilbertson, Tonya (Sam's daughter), Jimbo, Sam Jackson the homeowner, Biloxi, Mississippi 2005

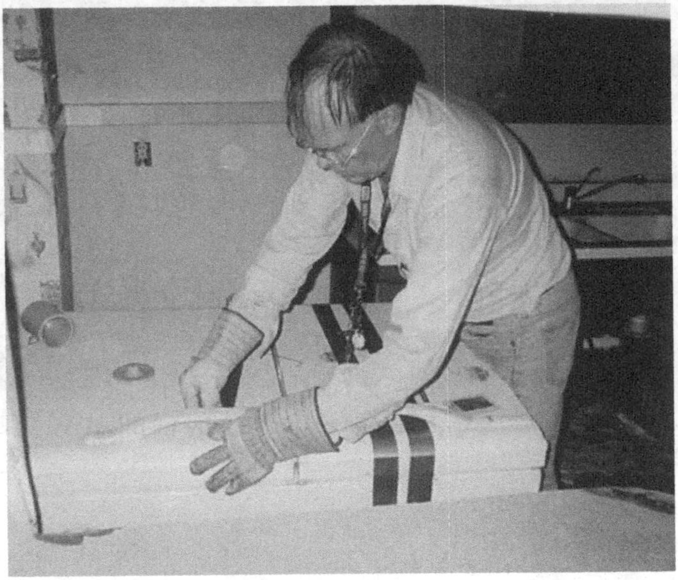

Jimbo taping up refrigerator to keep it from spilling rotted food when moved.

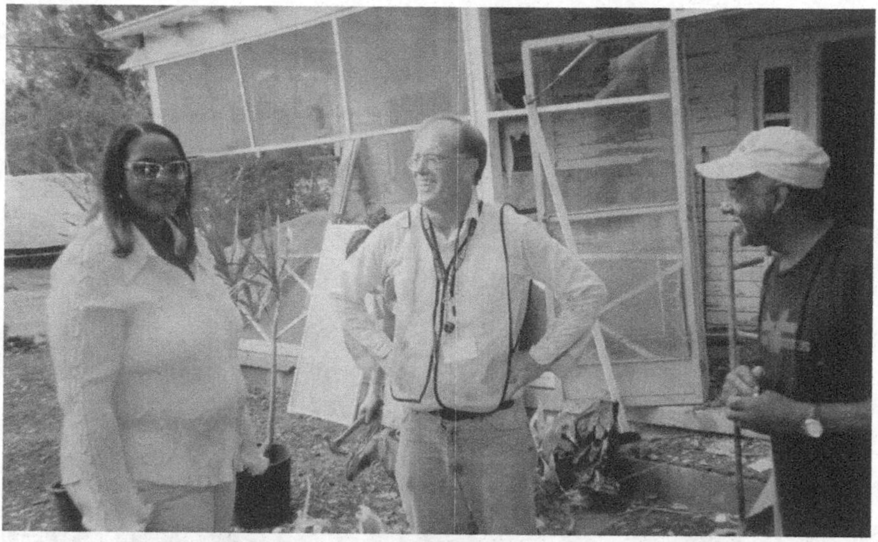

Jimbo telling stories with the Jackson family

Jimbo with three Trish, Parthena and Keith, Christian Appalachian Project volunteers Biloxi 2005

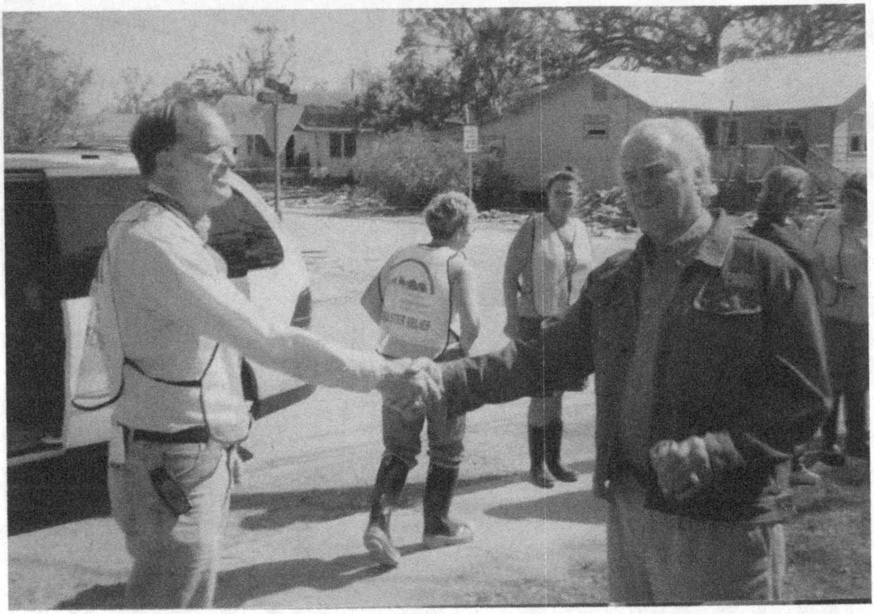

Mutual thanks from homeowner and volunteers who were able to :Go and Serve

Return two years later. Folks moved in. With homeowners, Jimbo and Mike Stephens

On Mr. Alley's porch with Jimbo and Keith Gilbertson. House much closer to moving in. Progress

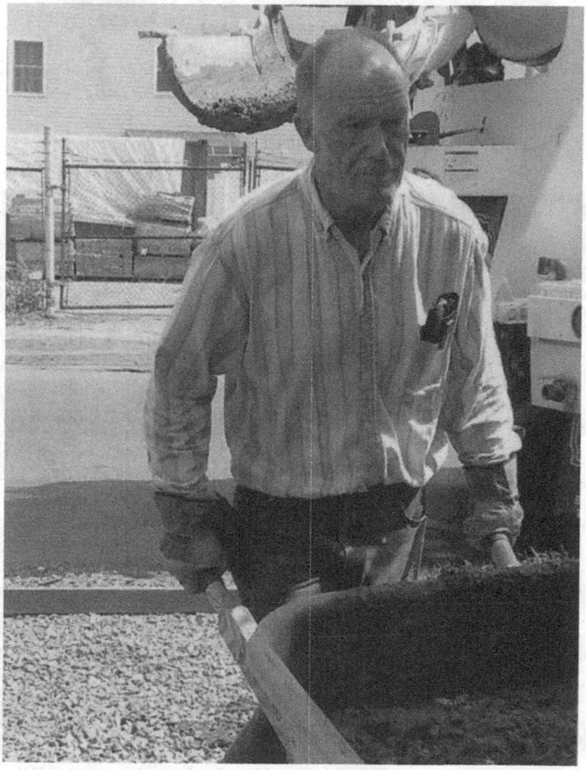

Author doing concrete work at another site. Rebuilding

Jimbo leading prayer again.

A group of volunteers with Jimbo on Mr. Jackson's porch. Biloxi, Mississippi 2005

CHAPTER FIVE

BEFORE I BECAME A CHRISTIAN

How Trying to get Close to a Red Headed Waitress is Like Trying to Get Close to God

July 2018

I hear people talk about the devil attacking them. I am confused about this and then I thought about a certain time of my life. I was fixated on red headed women. When I lived in Missouri, there was a red headed topless waitress in a bar I frequented occasionally. Of course, I frequented it more when she worked. I was enamored with her red hair and white shins (and a few more attributes). Well naturally if a woman looks good enough to be a topless waitress, she has a boyfriend and/or other admirers.

When I came around in my funky hat, with a beard and glasses, I got some snide remarks as I walked up close to the waitress. Some of them may have even been threatening. I acted like I didn't hear them, because I was focused on being close to the lady. If I had acknowledged the remarks it would have taken time from me looking at the lady. I wouldn't have gotten as close to her as quick as I did. My main objective was to get as close to her for as long a time as I could so I couldn't be distracted by snide remarks or threats. I knew if I got hit when I was in the bar, the guy who hit me would be thrown out. I also knew if I was nice to the lady, she would not especially appreciate it if other people were mean to me.

So, if we want to get as near to the Lord as we can and stay as long as we can, why would we allow the devil to distract us? The devil doesn't just attack us when we are trying to get close to the Lord, sometimes he attacks us when the Lord has sent us to do something. This would probably be the main time he would attack us. He can't separate us from the love of God, but he doesn't want us to be effective in winning souls. If he can distract us when we do this he accomplishes his goal. He has the people (just like the boyfriend had the waitress) and he wants to keep them.

We know he can't hurt us unless the Lord lets him so we should not have any fear. We know he is trying to distract us so we have to keep focused on what we are doing. If we are trying to win souls it means we are showing them we know of a better life. We are talking to them without judging and we are showing love. This should scare the devil because he is not showing love. He is condemning them by telling them no one loves then and no one will ever love them because of the bad things they have done'

If we truly want to win souls let's ignore the devil, get as close to these people as we can and stay around then as long as we can show love to them. Isn't this what Jesus did? He was getting gossiped about for hanging out with the "wine bibbers." (Luke 7:34) He had compassion on the people. He healed them and fed them. These were the lepers, the blind, the deaf and other undesirables. They had been told they were in their condition because of their sins. Jesus said this was not so and they were blessed.

We have the opportunity to do the same thing if we truly have compassion for them. If we are just going to talk to them for a few minutes to try to get them to come to our church so we can have a bigger crowd, they will see through that. If one loves a person they want to be around them as much as possible. We shouldn't go if we don't love people. If we don't want them to be our friends, then why would we want them to be in our church.

Let's be friends to people first. Show them we are interested in them because we love them. Why would we not love them? They are God's creation, aren't they? This is what we have to share. Everyone is God's creation and he loves every one of us. He can do this because his love is immeasurable and ours can be too because we are just showing His love through us.

His love flows out of Him just as the heat and light of the sun flows out. I can stand in the sun and feel the heat. If another person comes up, he feels as much heat as I do and I don't feel any less. If a million people come around, they will still feel the same amount of heat. None of us take any away from anyone else. The same amount of love flows into all of us.

We Get to be Nice Guys If We Live Long Enough

May 2018

While I was at the cemetery Sunday, I saw a grave of a guy I had an encounter with. The gravestone had a date of birth, but not of his death. He was older than me so I kind of figured he had died. The lady with me said, "He has to be buried somewhere else because I know he died." As we were leaving, I saw another head stone with his name on it with a birth date and a date of death. I only talked to this guy twice. The first time was when he worked at *The Bridge.* I told a guy to drop me off there and I would play some poker. I had never been there in a poker game before, but I had stopped there bunches of time to buy beer.

I knocked on the door and when the guy didn't recognize me as a regular poker player, he started to shut the door. I was too fast for him and I got my foot in the door before he could shut it. He looked at me and asked me how old I was. I said, "24". He said, "Then you should be old enough to know when to leave." I got the message and got my foot out of the door and walked up to the truck stop. A few months later he killed a guy in a poker game there. The guy who was killed ran a piece of equipment at the dam where I worked. He had got it stuck behind our lab and after his death, no one seemed to want to move it, so it set there for about a week.

The guy didn't do any time for killing the other guy because it was ruled self-defense. He may have killed a couple of other people but he never was charged with their murders. Later he came up to my house and he was talking to my landlord. He asked if there were any women around. I said my sister was and he moved out of the line of sight from the front window and he raised up his shirt. I thought he was about to use the bathroom and I was about to call him down even though I was pretty scared.

He pulled out a bottle of whiskey and took a drink. He didn't think it was gentlemanly to take a drink in front of a woman. I thought at the time, how odd he isn't bothered killing someone but he didn't want to take a drink in front of a woman. Well, we all have our codes.

Later one of my brother in laws was telling me about meeting a great guy. When he told me who it was, I said, "Well not everyone would agree he is a great guy." Of course, not everyone would agree I am a nice guy either. I think if we are fortunate enough to get to a certain age, most of us become nice guys. I'm sure he took up for his buddies and I did think his brother was a nice guy. Well, later *The Bridge* went out of business and then got blown up with what the police said was three cases of dynamite. My landlord said he did not hear that much dynamite was used.

I never got to play poker at *The Bridge*. The only other guy who I knew who did, got pistol whipped once while his brother had to watch. Both he and his brother had pistols, but it didn't seem to bother the guy pistol whipping him. He challenged them to pull their guns out to see if they could get him before he killed them both. The guy getting pistol whipped, Ben, said his brother, Jay, was afraid to pull his gun because the guy would have shot Ben.

When Ben was relaying this story, I said, "Man I would have hated to have been in Jay's place.". Ben said, "Hey I was the one getting whipped". I said, "I know, but I believe I would rather get beat than see my brother beaten and me not able to do anything about it." I never got killed or pistol whipped so I think I am ahead of the game. Ben is dead also, but I did get to pray with him on the street in front of the pool room.

The moral of these two stories is, (if there is one) we get to be nice guys if we live long enough. So, just hang on and pray for people and keep encouraging them.

Weird memories of my 1968 Pontiac... as I drive

Jan 23, 2018

I see a narrow underpass under a railroad and the thought of my 1968 Pontiac comes to me. When I bought it in 1973 both sides were scraped up. The seller said her husband bought it new and he drove it home drunk. He had to drive under an underpass and scraped one side. This made him mad and he backed up and came charging through again. This time he tore up the other side. Then her present husband, Scottie, looked at me as I sat in the back seat and he said, "the last owner died where you are sitting." I asked, "How?" Scottie says, "His brother shot him." I remember then about him getting killed at the bootlegger's place on Hwy 60 near

Morehead, Kentucky. That ended the bootlegging business. Now they sell tombstones there.

Scottie and his wife are smiling at me and I'm wondering who is the craziest. Scottie for marrying a woman whose previous husband was killed by his brother over her, or me for wanting to buy the car. I had just gotten out of the hospital after being in a wreck near the underpass at Salt Lick. I had hit a tree and busted everything in the car, (motor, radiator, alternator battery, drive shaft). except the head lights. I hit the steering wheel so hard it bent into my pancreas causing me to have quite a bit of pain.

I wanted to get a car that ran so fast so if I had another wreck I wouldn't feel any pain. Scottie said the car would run 140 miles an hour. I drove it and couldn't get 120 out of it. He said it could use a tune up and the tires weren't very good. I guess the tire part was to warn me not to drive too fast. I laughed and said, "I don't think there is much weight on the tires."

What is weird about this memory is I had a dream last night about some kind of prototype of a 1968 Pontiac. Sometimes when I'm remembering things, I'd like to write about them but I don't think anyone would believe them; it is hard for me to believe they happened and I was there. But a few minutes after I had this memory, I was in a restaurant hearing stories about miracles a lot stranger than this.

Working in Pea Sticks, Kentucky

"I don't believe I would have worked if it hadn't been for me wanting to drink and gamble."

East Baton Rouge, Louisiana

Tomorrow is Sunday and the restaurant next to us is closed so I'm looking for a place to eat breakfast. I guess this proves I'm from the south. Even when we have just eaten, we are thinking, "what am I goin' eat next?" I had seen a restaurant on our way to work in East Baton Rouge, so I went to check it out. It had a sign about "good times even with that dern storm." It was referring to the flood last year. I saw debris alongside the road as I drove on US190. It was a French, Cajun, whatever, restaurant but it wasn't open on Saturday and Sunny (*their spelling*). After I drove past the third McDonald's, I decided to go back. I still wasn't in Baton Rouge, but I was getting close.

The moon is almost full and is beautiful. The van is running well. I was tempted to just keep driving to Texas. It was a night like this when I drove across a bunch of Texas when I went to Oklahoma after the tornado. Well my meds are at the church and I promised to work here next week, and I really do want to see the people I met in the Sunday school class last week, so I guess I will go back. After I looked at how far Corpus Christ is from here versus Kentucky, I almost rethought it. If my van had been running earlier I would be heading to Texas now. Well it isn't like there isn't going to be stuff to do there for a while (many years)

What kind of bummed me out was; the restaurant on the corner of the building, James Grill and Coffee Shop, is going to close on Monday because it is Labor Day. I had forgotten. I almost always forget holidays when I'm on a mission. As I'm driving down the road I'm hearing songs about working like "Sixteen Tons." I'm thinking about how there have been discussions about the minimum wage being raised; and it seems a lot of people are against it because they don't think it should be a 'living wage" for some reason. There were songs about sharecropping, mining, waitress and one line I heard was about a lady walking from the diner after she had worked her shift "with both hands in her pockets, but one on a knife" because she knew she might get mugged. Another one was about a lady who had six kids and her husband had died in the mine.

It makes me think about how my ex-wife told me about when they lived in Cabin Creek, West Virginia and her dad worked in the coal mine. When the whistle blew it meant a cave-in and all the women walked down to the mine to wait. When the surviving miners came out, the wives walked home with them and fixed them supper. The women whose husbands didn't come out had thirty days to get moved out of the company houses or to get another coal mining husband.

Naturally one thought runs into another and I thought about what I've done during my life. I lived in Pea Sticks, Kentucky (Bath County) and it was poor, (tar paper shacks). If you didn't have a regular job, you worked for the farmers when they needed you. The pay was usually four dollars a day and dinner (if you didn't eat too much). Dinner would usually be at

Estill Warren's store where you could get a bologna and cheese on crackers for fifteen cents, an Ale-8 for a nickel and a candy bar for a nickel. Maybe instead of the bologna and cheese you could get a can of beanie-weenies, but if your lunch got to be more than forty cents, the farmer would be upset. That wasn't so bad because you did get dinner.

What you didn't want to happen was for the farmer to come up there at dinner and ask for help, because then you only got two dollars for a half day and no dinner. Worse than not getting dinner was the second half of the day is longer. The first half stops at noon and never started before seven, so that was five hours max. the second half went to dark if all the work didn't get done, so it could be eight o'clock from one o'clock (seven hours). Usually the work was in tobacco or hauling hay.

Some things like setting tobacco paid more. Setting tobacco paid six dollars a day, but suckering didn't and it also made me sick. One has to walk through the tobacco when it is fairly tall and pull the suckers off. These are smaller leaves growing along the bigger leaves and they are pulled because they are useless and they take nutrients away from the bigger leaves, keeping them from getting as big as they could. The tobacco is wet from the dew and the nicotine smell is strong. The one time I tried to do that, I got sick. I would come out of the field into the fresh air and I would be okay. Then I'd walk back in and throw up. After three or four times of this, I figured it wasn't worth the four dollars; and the farmer wasn't going to pay me anyway for walking into the field, puking, walking outside for a few minutes, and then going back and repeating this same thing.

Because of this my reputation as a worker wasn't good. Everyone knew I would rather sit across from the store and play 'tonk' or shoot dice. Well of course I did, but everyone there was a better 'tonk' player than me and the same went for the dice, so I had to work to get money to do that. We could haul in hay, so one day Rube (a farmer) and Eddie, a drinking buddy of mine, came up during dinner and asked me to go haul hay. I wasn't so fond of that deal, but I could sure use two dollars so I went.

Rube had an elevator (which is more like a conveyor) so it was easier. We rode a wagon out into the field, loaded it with bales of hay, drove over to the barn and put the bales on the elevator which took them to the loft. One person put them on the elevator as another carried them to him, while another guy in the barn stacked the hay as it came off the elevator. It was always hot when doing this, and Rube was such a hard worker, he didn't know what a break meant. I don't think any of the farmers did, but Rube was a little bit more gung-ho.

His wife did have mercy on us so she came out with some homemade ice cream. It was so good, most because it was cold. Rube let us eat it, but we had to stand on the wagon while we did. If we got off we might get lazy and goof off five or ten minutes. Well, I wasn't as strong as Eddie, so on the last load I couldn't get the bales up to the elevator. As the load gets smaller, one has to lift a bale higher to get it on the elevator. Eddie told me to get in the loft and stack. After a while I couldn't get them stacked either, because the stack kept getting taller, so I was just kicking them over to the stack as they came off the elevator.

So, the wagon gets unloaded and all the hay is in and it is getting dark. Rube gives me two dollars and Eddie four, and maybe he thanked us, but I doubt it. He turns around and walks into the house and we start walking back to the store, which was a couple of miles away. As we are walking, Eddie says, "You did better than I thought, I didn't think you would make it." I replied, "Well you won't see it again." I was so tired and it was amazing to me I was walking. We hadn't got too far, before Mozel, Rube's wife, pulled up and offered us a ride to the store. She was a life saver. If it hadn't been for the ice cream and ride, I'm not sure I would have made it.

Rube wasn't so bad. That was just the way it was. He contracted to build a barn and work on a slaughterhouse in Lexington, Kentucky (which was about 50 miles away). He gave us a dollar an hour but he didn't buy our lunch.. He did provide a ride there and back for free. It was a little over an hour away so we could sleep on the way over and back.

We usually only worked 32 hours a week because we'd be off a day for some reason or other. We basically got thirty-two dollars for four days work. That was a lot better than sixteen dollars for four days. Minimum wage was a dollar and a quarter an hour, but I don't guess there was a job in the county that paid it. We had to go to the next county to get minimum wage.

The farmers in the next county paid a dollar an hour to set tobacco and they worked us nine hours a day so it beat the six we got in Pea Sticks. We had to spend a couple of dollars for gas, but if four of you went, it would only be fifty cents each. You also had to buy your lunch. I think the best thing was, when we worked in Montgomery county, the farmer, Mr. Gatewood, acted like he appreciated us; and would actually ask us if we wanted to do something different when he came to get us to do something else. When he did that, we were pulling tobacco plants which means you are on your hands and knees in the sun. It would be hard to see why anyone wouldn't be ready to do something else, but one guy wanted to stay there and pull plants and Mr. Gatewood let him

I don't believe I would have worked if it hadn't been for me wanting to drink and gamble. I think I would have just bummed around and hunted and fished or married some woman who worked in a sewing factory in Mt. Sterling for minimum wage. I don't think the last one was an option. All the women who worked there were already married. This was the reason they had to work.

Back in St Francisville

Sept 4, 2017

Was aiming to drive up to St. Francisville tomorrow, but figured I might as well get it out of the way today. As most things my plans change as I do things. First off, I looked a Google Maps and saw the fastest way was to go on the interstate, but the closest way was to go Highway 190 to Highway 61. This takes me through Baton Rouge and a lot of stop lights. That would be okay, but North LA 16 runs by the church so why don't I just go north and then west and I'll run into 61 somewhere and I'll miss the lights and take a county drive. I end up going through Clinton which I had been twice before and the last time, I got a speeding ticket so I'm careful and don't speed this time.

I'm kind of hungry and I looking for a country diner where they might have seafood, or jambalaya or gumbo, or something Cajun. I don't see any but I do see a drive-in in Jackson. I smelled the food and turned around. It is a small historical place and I kind of wanted to look around anyway. I pull in behind the drive-in and walk around, but decide, it is just too much hamburger stuff. I do see they have "Po Boys," but they don't have an oyster "Po Boy" so I get back in the van and go on.

I get to St. Francisville and don't see a thing familiar except the IGA grocery. I get on a road going out of town and see it ends in a mile or so. I realize this is the Old Ferry Road I had seen on Google Maps. When I first saw this name for the road it made me sad, because when I lived in St. Francisville, I would drive out that road and ride the ferry across the Mississippi River and then wait for the ferry to go back and would ride it back. It seems sad a road you drove on is now call the 'old' road.

When I get to the end at the Mississippi, I see there is an Oyster Bar there. Good, I'll go in and get some oysters. It is a bar where one drinks and when I walk in people say hello. I say, "Hello" also and get a soft drink and watch some people play darts. I walk outside to the bayou that runs into the Mississippi and think how this one looks just like the one near the River Bend Nuclear plant where I worked. When one walked down the bayou there would be an alligator sliding into the bayou after you had walked past him. You kind of got scared thinking he could have bitten you when you walked by.

I go back in the bar and see they are cooking. Some lady brought potato salad, so they are having a potluck. I was kind of tempted to stay and eat but decided to move on. There are always interesting dramas going on and one can hear all the news around. As I was walking out, one of the ladies said something about not having any deodorant and then looked at me and said, "you weren't supposed to have heard us". She had been on the phone with some guy who was supposed to come out. I guess he said he didn't know if he had enough gas to get there or not. She told him if he didn't have enough gas to not come. I guess he said he was coming anyway, because she was griping to another lady saying, "If he runs out of gas I will have to go get him and I don't have a spare." I notice people who hang out in bars seem to get mad at their friends for making dumb decisions; but they still bail them out.

When leaving, I notice there is a road across from the bar that runs out on a levee, so I decide to check it out. It has some pretty big ruts but if I'm careful, I won't get stuck. At a big one, I get out and check it out before plunging into it. I'm pretty sure I can get across it, but the road pretty much dead ends there anyway. While looking down the mighty Mississippi' I think about just a few weeks ago when I crossed at the confluence of the Mississippi and the Ohio and how it doesn't seem any bigger here.

I drive back to St. Francisville and see the Episcopal Church. Now I don't remember, but it was built in 1848 so it was there when I lived there. I get out and walk around in the cemetery. There are big oaks with Spanish moss hanging from them and it just seems like a place where there should be a mystery. I walk around and notice there are some memorials and even a couple of crypts. I keep wondering why I can't remember this. Surely, I had gone there before but nothing jogs my memory.

As I leave, I see there is a building where a Jewish synagogue was started in 1901 and next to it is a building where the first telephone operator was moved from Bayou Sara back in the 30's. So much history and I remember walking around in the town admiring those old buildings and still nothing is coming back to me. Of course, I only lived there for a few months over 40 years ago.

As I am driving on I see a Lebanese restaurant that says it is open seven days a week. Maybe I'll check it out. Across from it is the Magnolia Restaurant. A lady I worked with last week mentioned it to me. I couldn't remember it, or any restaurant. We always rode the ferry over to New Roads and ate there. I drive on around because I wanted to check out the nuclear plant and drive by where I lived. I've even forgotten the name of the street but I figure how to get there. I drive by slowly and see they have added a room where the carport used to be.

Then I realize they had to because when we went out to look at the house, we had actually gone into the carport and found an unlocked window and I climbed in. Just one more thing in my life I could have been put in jail for. It was weird because some friends of ours had gotten us to move there from Mississippi and the wife was driving us around and she said she knew this house had been empty and she was the one who encouraged us to break in. The house had some pretty neat antique furniture so we walked next door and asked if they knew the owners. They referred us to someone else who had the owner call us. The next day she did.

Her name was Guy and she had to drive up from New Orleans. She told me on the phone it was a residential area. She said it like it was supposed to mean something. Back then, I had long hair and a beard so I figured she might not rent to me anyway. When I met her there, she said she had misplaced the key and had to climb in the side window. I almost said I had done the same thing the day before so I knew how everything looked.

She informed me the residents there before got drunk and into fights outside the house and the neighbors complained so they had to move. I told her, "I don't drink so I won't be a problem." She also told me her husband worked for the FBI and the next-door neighbor was a retired head of the DEA. I asked her, "Does this mean I can't grow any marijuana?" She said, "Well if you do, you better grow it on the other side of the house".

I met the guy later and he was like a Mr. Wilson type guy. My daughter was only two but she was like a Dennis the Menace and they got along fine. I'm sure he knew I smoked but he liked my daughter so I didn't figure he would turn me in. We lived there for eleven months because I remember them getting her an Easter basket because I wasn't going in for holidays.

We Can Show People We Have Peace in the Storm

July 7, 2015

I wake up this morning at 4:45. Need to go to bathroom. Figure I can make it without putting on my clothes. Wrong. I hear people walking. I guess cooks have come in. I run back through the maze to my room to get clothes. Go back to lay down and sleep because I have only been in bed three hours. I can't sleep because I keep thinking about last night's service and my thoughts and hurry to write them down.

The evangelist started off saying he couldn't go to certain places because he was anointed and his spirit didn't agree with the spirit in the casinos and bars. The spirit was moving. He mentioned earlier about different people having different gifts and talents and callings. Everyone has a unique calling and every church has one also, so we shouldn't be in competition. We are all part of the Body. We are to use the gifts we are given.

Sister Hootnanny is asked to sing and she says, "Well I don't know." He said, "If I had Sister Hootnanny's gift I would sing whether someone asked me or not." About this time, I got a message in my heart to prophesy to Sister Darlene she would sing in Walmart. She won't want to because of her flesh; because she is not comfortable, because she will look foolish. These reasons are from the devil. And they are lies. As soon as she hits her first note she will be comfortable. She won't look foolish. She will look like a lady who can sing well. People will be moved.

But to get back to the part where we feel we can't go certain places. Our spirits don't agree with the spirit of evil, but we are given all power, so our spirit will overcome. I needed to come back last night, but I mentioned to Brother Tony Miller, "we should go to Walmart right now. We should go out and witness; when we are fired up by the message."

We should go to these places we don't agree with. We should go to the drug dealer and tell him we love him and he might as well get this gift of salvation before his customers get it. If they get what we have they won't be coming to him; because they won't want to lose the high of knowing Jesus. We should to the bars and buy soft drinks and buy people a drink (because it is not what goes into the body that defiles it but what comes out) and talk about Jesus; talk about the awesome service we had; talk about how people got healed and delivered; and anyone can get delivered. They don't have to be straight or in a church. My nephew got saved at a party. His friend. got saved when he was drunk. He drove over to a preacher's house and woke him up and told the preacher he wanted to get saved. He was saved before he woke the preacher up, but the preacher got to participate.

As I lay there thinking of these things, I realized this was part of what happened to me. My drug dealer got saved. I went and paid him for a bag and was going to get another one on credit but he said he was a Christian and wasn't dealing. Later I got drunk and went to his house with my brother in law and asked him about this 'Christian thing' I don't remember this and he had to tell me, but the point is, it made an impression on me and got my attention. Later of course (five or six years) I became a Christian.

Christ knew he had all power and He washed the disciple's feet. This is how we are to act. Knowing we have all power and still serving. Going everywhere and telling everyone the Good News. Telling them boldly and with love. Helping everyone we can who will let us. Telling them the reason we are doing what we do. Because God has put love in our hearts that is overflowing to them.

The problem is, sometimes because of envy, fear, or jealousy we haven't allowed ourselves to get filled up and overflowing. Some of us may should work on that first... but even when we do, we can still share what love we have. We can show people we have peace in the storm. Maybe not as much peace as we could have, but more peace than we would have if we didn't have Jesus.

Repentance

For some reason we think repentance is a hard thing and it means giving up things we want to do. Repentance is to turn from the things you were doing that weren't working for you and start doing things that will. Stop hanging out with people who are getting you in trouble and start hanging out with people who have your best interests in mind.

Stop doing things that are hurting you (drinking, cussing, overeating) and start doing stuff that will be good for you (eating right, sleeping during the night). The Bible gives us instructions to live a happy, healthy life; so repent (change) and follow the instructions. John 10:10; Satan comes to steal and kill, but Jesus came to give life; life more abundantly. Living for the Lord is the better way; so we repent to live better and easier.

My More Exciting Life as a Christian!

June 9, 2016

Yesterday, I mentioned an area where Tony and I and another guy were knocked off the road by a state trooper after a high-speed chase. If it had been filmed, it could have been sold to a movie studio. The next day we made the front page of the weekly paper by having to pay a record breaking fine. I mentioned about being pulled with a chain and a car and running out of chain while trying to pass the lead car and how exciting it was as the two cars were getting jerked sideways on a narrow road.

Later that day I was getting pulled again by Pooch and the car I was in, caught on fire. I don't know why it did because there was no battery in the car, so I couldn't blow the horn to get the attention of the front car. I just had to stick my head out of the car and yell as it filled with smoke. Sooner or later, Pooch noticed the smoke or heard me yell or something and we stopped and got the fire put out. These were just two characters and a couple of days in my life and there are hundreds (if not close to a thousand) such stories with many more characters.

The life sounded exciting; and was; but it doesn't compare to my life now as a Christian. Back then, those things only happened to me every now and again. Not every day; or I wouldn't have been able to survive. Most of the time I was drunk and couldn't remember everything. Most of the time there was also some fear among the emotions I was having at the time. There were a lot of hangovers and fear as the adventures were happening and fear of what was going to happen because of the adventures.

Now I'm excited all the time. I don't have to fear what is going to happen. I don't have to be drunk to have an adventure. I can have one as I'm on Natural Bridge looking at the beauty of the world. I can see a sunrise without a hangover. I don't know how to explain it, but I have a much more exciting life now.

Changing Addictions/ Am I Drunk?

May 2018

I've just come from church and I stopped at McDonald's to get coffee. As I'm walking across the parking lot, a police cruiser drives in. He drives across the lot fairly fast and another one pulls in behind him. I commented a few days ago how I used to think I about avoiding cops, but now I walk right up and say stuff like, "Are you under the Blood?" or "Do you know Christ as your personal Savior?" So now I'm feeling like I want to treat these guys. As I'm going in, I meet a lady who is holding the door for me, even though she has both hands full.

She is smiling and I say, "Thank you" and this seems to encourage me even more to do something for these police officers. Well, they take their time coming in and then they hang back so there is another couple who gets in front of them. All at once I think it would be rude to offer to buy some police officers something and ignore someone else who is there. If I was at home, I wouldn't offer one guest something to eat and ignore the other. I know McDonald's is not my home, but it seems to me I'm at home anywhere.

I tell the server I want to pay for the couple's meal. The guy says, "You don't have to do that." I say, "I know. I don't have to do anything, but the Lord has blessed me; and I want to bless someone." I give the server a 20-dollar bill and tell him I also want to pay for the police officer's food. He says, "Police officers don't have to pay." I say, "Oh." I'm wanting to say more, but I can't think of anything.

I start talking to the crowd and say how thankful I am about having different feelings toward police officers. I say, "I don't know why I had those bad feelings. They were always nice to me and took me for rides in their back seat." This gets a laugh. I tell the officers how I used to get these "feelings of fight or flight every time I saw them and unfortunately the fight feeling won out too often and got me in trouble." I'm glad I don't get those feelings anymore. They say they are glad for that too. I tell them, "I have a Savior now so I have peace." They say they are glad for me. I'm thinking about asking them questions about their relationship with the Lord, but that doesn't seem appropriate. I'm all excited but I don't know what else to say… so I leave.

Now I'm driving down the road and I'm thinking how good that felt. I'm still excited and go in Kroger's in a state of excitement. I see some people from the Winchester church and I'm kind of tempted to start talking to them, but I'm too excited so just say "Hi." I know I'll be off to the races, telling them about the Lord. I know they know Him already and it's late and some people have to work the next day.

I'm thinking how good it felt to interface with the police when I wasn't drunk. And now I'm wondering; am I drunk? and how does one tell if they are drunk or not; and exactly what is being drunk anyway?

I don't know the answers to these questions which seems weird because I have spent so much time of my life being drunk. As I think back, it seems as if being drunk was normal to me; and when I wasn't, I didn't feel normal. I felt as if I should have a cold glass in my hand; so, when it wasn't a mixed drink or a beer, I had a glass of tea. I remember a picture of me at a park in Illinois with my daughter and I was sliding down a slide with a glass of tea in my hand.

So, do we just change addictions? I used to could barely pass a bar without stopping and going in. Now I can barely pass a church without stopping and going in.

Hard to be a Christian

I keep hearing about how hard it is to be a Christian. I don't know what this means. I read the rules and I can't see any that should be so hard to keep for most of us. I think I may see the one that makes it hard. He seems to have a thread of "Trust in ME." That's it. Yet it doesn't make any sense. If I believe He created the universe and everything in it, which would include me, then I would have to believe He would know the best for the universe and for me. Well, maybe He doesn't. I've made things before that I broke. I made a sling shot and the rubber broke and came back and hit me in the face.

Maybe this is the problem. We believe God made us, but we don't believe we are as strong as He may think. He may send us into a place where we will perish. Well He may. He sent Jesus to the cross and He allowed the Hebrew children to be thrown into the fiery furnace, but then He kept them from even being singed. We know all the stories (and most of us believe them), but we still won't do the things He tells us, as we are complaining about how hard they are. Now again, how hard could it be? I don't see anything in those stories that seem to be hard.

In mythology some of the characters are given hard tasks, but in the Bible, God never tells anyone to do anything hard. He may, but I'm not a good enough scholar to find it. He may have given Samson a hard job. He may have told a bunch of them to do things they didn't want to do, but the thing he told them to do wasn't hard. The hardest part of sacrificing Isaac for instance would have been walking up the mountain. The actual act wouldn't have been as hard as sacrificing a bull.

When He sent Jonah to Nineveh, how hard was that? The walk from the boat to Nineveh would have been the hardest part and of course it was harder walking in whale puke because he wouldn't just ride in the boat. There is a moral to this. If you have to do what the Lord wants anyway, why not enjoy a nice ride instead of traveling in the dark hold in a smelly situation.

The point is: He doesn't give us any physically hard job to do. Well is it mentally hard? Well He doesn't make us memorize anything. He gives us the Holy Spirit, to bring to our memory what we need to know. So, what is it? Well I think I saw an example a few weeks ago. A young lady was leading us in some stretch exercises. She kept doing more and more goofy things. More and more of us kept dropping out.

Finally, she laid on the floor and started kicking her feet and hands up in the air. I didn't do this even though I had enough room. Most of the people were too close to each other to do it, so I don't know if they would have or not, but I know I wasn't going to do it by myself. Why not?

I was one of the oldest people there; but I could have done it easily enough. The hardest part would have been to get back up after I did it. Oh, but it would not have looked dignified for an old man to be flopping on the floor. So now we see the only reason I did not do the exercise. Nothing at all about being hard. PRIDE. Or can we even say that? I have done a lot of things a lot more undignified.

Could it just be rebellion? We just don't want to do what others tell us. I think it may be that more than anything else. We don't want to walk into Kroger's and yell, "JESUS IS LORD' we can say what we want, but a UK fan would not have any problem yelling, UK IS NUMBER ONE!!!, anywhere.

We don't live a Christian life because we don't want to. It is that simple. Maybe if we could see that and quit blaming it on all kinds of other things (the devil, our job, our family) we could start doing it. We could repent and ask God to give us the desire to serve Him and to take this spirit of rebellion from us, and then to guide us in our daily walk. We know how He wants us to walk. The Bible has given us all the instructions we need. And even if we didn't have the Bible, if we would just love one another, we wouldn't go wrong.

Dead End Roads

Thoughts I have when I drive up gravel roads.

There is usually a reason they are called Dead End Roads. They end at the cemetery. Or one can be on one that ends in death. The Bible says the way is wide that leads to destruction. In reality, it seems to be pretty narrow. It seems to be too narrow to turn around. One is more like being in a funnel in a downhill spiral.

When I am riding around and I get on one of these roads I am thinking how much trouble it would be to pull over because there isn't enough room. I am also concerned the person I meet won't allow me to pull over. If I don't know where the road goes, why am I on it? Am I looking for his marijuana crop? Well it is too early for that and I don't think too many people make moonshine anymore so that won't be a problem.

I notice that the farther I get up the road, the narrower and rocky it gets. Is this not how it is on the way to destruction? The more drugs we do, the harder the road gets. It seems to be harder and harder to find a place to turn around. One can't just swerve around. One has to pull up and back up several times to turn around. Then one runs into deep ruts making it hard to go on. You have to "gun it" to get past the ruts. This causes damage to the vehicle. Either an automobile or a body. When you get this far along, it gets even harder to get back. But one can. Well most of the time.

Sometimes we need help to get back. It costs money, time and energy to go up these roads and come back. It seems as we are going up these roads, it is forever, but when we turn around and come back, it doesn't seem to be that far. It also seems the road is easier coming back and the main roads are wider and smoother after one has been on one of these off roads.

There are good and bad things about getting off the main road. We may see things we haven't seen before. We may also get stuck and have to stay there longer than we wanted. Life is an adventure. Some good adventures and some bad ones. We learn from them all.

Is Contentment a Blessing?

October 7, 2016

Being content. What a blessing? Or is it? Well it is a blessing to be content, but it is not like someone blessed you with contentment. It is just accepting how things are and being content with that. One cannot be content with how things are, but the reality won't change and then we are unhappy with the circumstances. To be happy one should be content. Is not being contented a sin? Of course. And worse it causes others to sin. If one were contented with what they had, they wouldn't want to steal, to be covetous, to commit adultery; to have other gods before the Lord, or to be jealous. When we are contented other people want to be around us. When we are discouraged about everything, no one wants to be around us.

Just think of a baby. People brag on the baby when he is content. He is easier to take care of. If the baby is fussy, this causes the caretakers to be stressed and aggravated. When we are not content it causes our loved ones to worry about us; to try to do things to make us happy; to buy stuff they can't afford; and the list keeps on going. Us not being content mostly distracts our loved ones from concentrating on doing what they should to make the world a better place. It keeps them from growing.

Does being content mean, we are just to stay where we are? I would say no, because we are supposed to be growing, so that means we are to grow in the rate we were created to grow. Most of us grow at different rates. So be content at the rate you are growing while doing what you can to grow. Don't be upset because someone else is growing faster or slower than you are. We can be content to do what we can to make this world a better place and not worry about the results. We are not in control of the results. We are only in control of what we can do and how we react to situations.

We can't control the situation, but we can decide to be content in it. Paul said he was content in any state he was in. He happened to be in prison when he said that. And then prisons were horrible places.

When Jesus said, do not worry about food and drink, he was telling us to be content with what we have. There is no reason for anyone I know not to be content. We have plenty to eat. We have so much stuff we have to pay for a place to store it. We have so much stuff we worry about it and it's the reason we are not content sometimes. We can worship wherever we want. We have so many choices. This should give us contentment, but it probably stresses us.

When we don't have much to eat, we just eat what we have and are happy. When we have a choice of three desserts, we eat them all if we can hold them and then feel guilty. So maybe contentment is not having more than one needs.

CHAPTER SIX

SERVICE

Wash the Feet; We Have to Humble Ourselves to be a Servant

We know about Jesus washing the disciple's feet just before He was to be betrayed and crucified. He washed all the disciple's feet. Not just the ones who deserved it or earned it or couldn't have done it for themselves. He washed the feet of the people who were going to betray him, doubt him, and run off and hide when danger approached. None of them had gotten the message He was trying to impart. None of them deserved for the Son of God to wash their feet. He did this after He had been given all power and He knew his hour had come. It seems this was a very important thing. A thing he wanted the disciples to do after He left.

The good thing (and the easy thing) is we don't have to make decisions about who is deserving to get their feet washed. We just wash everyone's feet whose are dirty. Whose is that? Everyone who has been in the world. We cannot walk in the world without getting our feet dirty. There is dirt out there we are exposed to. The other good thing is, it isn't hard to wash feet and it doesn't take a long time. The bad thing (at least for some of us) is we have to get down on our knees, and we have to see and smell the dirty feet. That is the only way we can wash them. We can't pay someone; we can't pray them done; we can't do another deed of service.

We have to humble our self to be a servant and to get even lower than the person we are serving. it isn't like serving in the nice restaurants and wearing a neat outfit as we serve someone a filet mignon and ask them if they would like more sparkling water in their nice crystal goblet; and then expect a nice tip. No tips, no recognition, not even learning anything from this, not even an act of penance. No one will understand why you do it; and your fellow workers in the Kingdom may say, "You shouldn't lower yourself that way".

When one has worked on a house, they can drive by and say to their buddies, "I worked on that house. Because of my labors that family can live a safer and drier life." They will say back to you, "That is nice. You are a good man. I would like to do that someday." But if you are driving down Skid Row and you see a bum and say, "Hey guys, I washed that guy's feet once," I doubt anyone of them will say, "Cool, man I would like to wash someone's feet someday".

There is no glory in washing feet and no sign of results. If the house doesn't get burned down I can go by there or take pictures and show someone what I did. I can't show anyone a clean foot of a guy whose feet I have washed because it gets dirty again as soon as he gets out into the world. The good thing is if I get down on my knees, I can look into his eyes, I can show him I don't consider myself above him, I can find out things about him I never could otherwise and I can show I came to serve instead of just sharing something out of my abundance. When I just give someone something it is usually something I didn't want anyway.

Let's go be the servants we were called and designed to be and wash some feet. In Colossians 3:23 "and whatever you, do it heartily, as unto the Lord……" so we wouldn't have any trouble washing Jesus' feet. And if we wash each other's we will see the Jesus in each other.

Let's All Be Servants

July 2018

Christians confuse me. Maybe I'm confused by the name. I thought when someone says, "I am a Christian," it means they are a follower of Christ; and they are trying to be like Him; to imitate Him; to be a servant of Him. I hear them say, "I want to hear the Lord say, enter in good and faithful servant." So, when I hear this, I think they are saying they are servants and Christ is the Master.

Well, I know what servants do. They serve. They don't serve only the master; they serve whoever the master tells them to. The servant serves whoever the master has invited to his table. The servant doesn't get to say, "well if I had known you were going to invite Miss Snooty, I would not have come to serve tonight."

If they did say that to the Master, he would say, "Not only did I invite Miss Snooty who thinks she is better than anyone else and she finds fault with everything, I invited a bum who doesn't smell good. I invited some people with tattoos and have coarse language. They will be riding in on their bikes any minute. They drive those stupid Harleys that leak oil, so in the morning I'll have you clean up the oil spills from the driveway. I have invited people from all cross sections of life. I have invited people who don't speak good English (they may not speak any). I invited people who think they know more than me., I invited all of humanity. If there is anyone you can't serve, then you should leave.

I am going to make it stronger, "if you can't or won't serve them with a cheerful heart, then depart from me." You will serve whoever I put in your path doing whatever they need. This will go from serving them food to cleaning up their messes. I may put you in a nursing home to take care of some invalid and you know what that entails. You don't get to pick the job or the people you serve if you truly want to hear me say, "enter in good and faithful servant."

I want you to be all in on this or all out. I don't want you to serve half heartily. OK, now I have told you, you are to serve everyone and be of good cheer doing it. I'm going to tell you the hard part. You are going to have to serve with whoever I put alongside of you. So, if you have any problems with any other servants you best get rid of them. I am not going to have my servants squabbling among themselves." Uh, oh, does the Lord have any servants? Well I'm sure He does. Just not near as many as profess to be.

Are you a servant? Am I a servant? Hopefully, we are even though we may be struggling to be good and faithful ones. One of the things I like about being a servant is I get to meet a lot of people I would not have met on my own. The Master sent them to me or me to them. another thing I like about being a servant is I get to learn new skills I may not have pursed on my own.

Let's all be servants and meet new people and learn new things. If we get in the right mindset it isn't hard. It is a little messy. Washing feet and backsides is a little messy, but women do it for babies all the time. So, all we have to do is realize that at times we all act like babies. We are dirty, aggravated, sick, hurting and don't know what is hurting us or how to even describe it so we are acting out. At our best we are all babes in Christ, so it shouldn't be hard to help others who have not grown as far as we have.

Maybe they are still infants on the milk and we have advanced up to solid food. We definitely have not grown to where we can tell the Master what to do (even though we do sometimes). We still must lean on Him and not to our own understanding. The Master will never send us to do anything too hard.

We may have to walk some, drive some, study some, serve some food, give someone a drink of water, tell someone the good news about how you came to know the Master, brush someone's hair wash someone, and other duties as assigned, but the Master does the heavy lifting. He is the one who touches the heart and convicts people to follow Him. All we have to do is follow the instructions and allow Him to work through us.

Disclaimer: I didn't reference any scripture because it seemed it would take away from the flow of the narrative. Most Christians know the scriptures this came from anyway. If not, I will be glad to look them up for you.

Responsibility

April 21, 2013

We are responsible for what we can do and we are not responsible for what others do, so don't worry about what they do. I never do all I can do to help the world get better. I never do all I can do to promote the Kingdom of God. I am so thankful for grace. I will take responsibility for my actions today and try to do all I can do to make the world a better place.

Why am I lying? I know I am not going to do all I can do. I won't keep a smile on my face all day. I won't speak to and uplift each person I see. But I will do better than I did yesterday and I will attempt to do better and I will be thankful for grace when I don't do all I can.

Share Some Life Lessons With Each Other

February 27, 2015

I wake up this morning at 4:30 and think about sleeping longer, but after a while I feel like getting up. I go downstairs and two guys are up doing their devotions. One of them tells Mona the cook, the plug won't work. Nosy me has to get into this. She goes in kitchen and asks me to help. She says the devil is giving her rough time. I tell her, 'Don't give him any credit. If we submit to the Lord and resist the devil and he will flee." Of course, we usually forget that part, "Submit to the Lord." If we were submitting, we wouldn't be bothered in the first place. I ask Mona if I can do anything and she asks me if both coffee pots are full. Well, after I get a big cup out of one pot and pour the rest into the other pot, one is empty.

Looks like I had done my part by drinking some coffee. One thing leads to another and now I have to make a pot. Mona has a big pot but the breaker has tripped and this is one of the things bothering her. I look for the breaker and go into gym where they have pallets of food to be given away. There is no light switch at the door, so I go toward the exit sign figuring there will be switch beside the door. I trip over pallet on the way not spilling much of my coffee but realize walking around in a dark room with cup of coffee might not be a smart thing.

No switches there and I walk to front of building where I find some. I turn them on and find the breaker tripped. Reset it and come out front doors where I knock a sign down that says, "Food bank closed." I go in and tell Mona to plug in big coffee maker again. It works…well for a few minutes and it trips again. She says, "I'll unplug it and just leave big warmer on" I reset it and it trips again. I bet the big warmer is too big. Don't guess I am a hero after all, but at least we found the problem and I learn a lesson about walking around with coffee in my hand.

Mona and I share some life lessons with each other. I tell her a lot of things I learned before I was a Christian have come into play. One about priding myself on not spilling much of my drink when I fell while I was drinking liquor. Who knows when what we learned years ago will come in handy? Of course, usually by the time it would come in handy, I will have forgotten it. But, I usually do remember it quickly.

If This Lady Wasn't in Poverty, She Would be Rich

Whitley County, Kentucky

We are working on a house today where CAP is adding a couple of rooms. The lady has six grandkids who she is taking care of, so I guess she could use a couple more rooms. I met her this morning. I didn't know anyone was there and I was beating on some of the walls putting on siding. She came out and said, "I didn't know you were coming and I agreed to work for someone in a convenience store today." I told her, "Well, go to work when you can." She didn't seem so enthused with it; and said she was only working because he had promised someone so they could take the day off.

I could see where she was coming from. She had to take her grandchild to Whitley City to the babysitter and then she had to go to Somerset which is in the next county to work. She is in between these two towns, so she had to go south to Whitley City then go to Somerset and then do this in reverse when she got off work. It is over 60 miles round trip for a few hours of work at minimum wage and paying a babysitter for at least two more hours than she will get. Hard to see how this is a winning proposition.

The lady lives in a beautiful place. She has a pond in the front yard. Behind her house is a holler with a pump house so I figure her water comes from a spring. She lives just past a place where there is a neat Arch and hiking trails. I hiked a little and climbed on the Arch a few weeks ago. The road she lives on dead ends at Cumberland Lake. Cumberland Falls is not too far away.

I guess the irony of this is; if this lady wasn't in poverty, she would be rich. She lives in a natural wonderland. It's like Mitch Barrett says, "we want to make money so we can live like we are poor."

Our Brother's Keeper

I saw a picture of a deer and two skunks sniffing each other and these were the thoughts I had. If these guys can love each other as different as they are and with no reasoning and no Bible; and maybe no conscience, why can't we humans do it? Are not we our brother's keeper? So, we don't do as we are commanded due to fear of the others. It seems; just as fear is learned by the skunk and deer; it is learned by us.

I don't think babies hate each other because of their skin color or religion of their parents. the problem is, after we fear; it is very hard (maybe impossible to unlearn). It's kind of sad because we are commanded to not fear. Does this mean we have to let the Lord in our heart to keep from fearing?

Walk in the Spirit, Not in the Flesh

April 29, 2015
Mississippi Coast

We are told to walk in the Spirit and not in the flesh. Another example of what good advice the Bible gives. I wake up this morning and my body WANTS, it always wants. It is so needy. It wants to rest more; it says it is sore, it wants food. Having a body is a pain. Then you throw a vehicle in and you are almost totally occupied. If wants gas, it wants oil, it wants one to drive it and keep it under control as you are riding. You have to have almost total concentration when you are in a vehicle. Then it breaks wherever it takes a notion and it usually isn't where you were wanting to be.

A few days ago, it broke in Dunlow, West Virginia. But as usual in my life, a semi miracle happened and I was going again. I testified once, "not only do I believe in miracles; I depend on them." They happen so often and they are not completely unnatural. Maybe I should call them semi-miracles.

I'm on the Mississippi coast and the same thing seems to be a problem with the vehicle. The same wheel is smelling because the brakes are sticking. The caliper has been replaced and new brake shoes were installed so how can this be? Is a vehicle like a body? Feed it; fix it; whatever; and it still needs the same things again? Well, they both have to have maintenance. So that means they both need fuel. At least the vehicle doesn't ask for food when it is at rest.

The body does. When it awakes from a rest, it says let's break this fast. Break the fast; you have been asleep. You haven't been fasting. You thought; I was asleep, but I was doing respiratory and cardiovascular functions; I was rebuilding cells. I was doing all kinds of things I didn't realize. My brain was being more active than if you had been awake watching TV; if watching TV can be considered being awake.

Let's eat. We are on the coast, let's eat some *Oysters Rockefeller,* but first let's have some coffee. See what I mean about the lusts of the flesh. It doesn't just want what it needs for maintenance (water and lentils). It wants stimulants (coffee) and unclean foods (oysters). It is trying to make a deal with me and say, "Okay boss, I was just teasing about the oysters, how about going to McElroy's and get some pancakes with blueberries; you know you can eat blueberries to keep you from getting Alzheimer's." My body is reminding me I'm old and having to worry about dementia but it is just doing this to get what it wants.

Later it will have me lusting after some young thing in a bathing suit if I wander onto the beach. Well, even if I don't, it will bring up the subject wherever I see a female. It uses the Bible and says the Lord created everything and called it good. That lady is good; in fact, she is very fine. Doesn't it say males and females are supposed to cleave on to another?

Just one example of how the flesh uses the word of God to get its way. I guess I could blame it on Satan, but I think my natural flesh doesn't need much help from him to have me doing the unhealthy things. Later it will be saying, "Hey man, you can eat those oysters, because we are not under the dietary laws. Hey man, let's eat those biscuits and sausage gravy, there isn't much pork in there."

Besides, aren't you under grace? YES, I AM. I have the grace to resist temptation and grace to be forgiven when I don't resist it.

IT TRULY IS "AMAZING GRACE"

Everyone Can Do Something That I Can't Do Esteem

June 25, 2015

Thinking how all most every verse of scripture can be uplifting and helpful. As I'm thinking this, "esteem others higher than ourselves" popped into my mind. And I'm thinking about how does this help, how does one do this, why would one want to do and what does it mean? Well the whole scripture is Philippians 2:3, "Let nothing be done through strife or vainglory, but in lowliness of mind let each esteem other better than themselves." The whole verse is even better because we definitely don't want something to be done through strife.

So how do we do this? I'm thinking about homeless people and how do I esteem a homeless person higher than myself? I realize everyone can do something I can't do; and this is true in everyone's life. No matter how smart, talented one is, there is always something they can't do. They might be able to sing opera but can they gut a fish? A homeless person can endure stuff I can't. He might be able to scrounge up food when I would be hungry so I esteem him. I admire the trait in him I don't have. I tell him that and affirm he is valuable for the things he does and the Lord loves him and I love him.

I think I have this figured out how to esteem others. Well, I get shown differently. Some guys are discussing what is going on in the country about the controversy over the rebel flag and one of them says, "we ought to kill all the niggers and the Mexicans." I am not totally taken aback because I know the guy who made the statement but I'm trying to think of a statement that I can say to show him he is in error. I say, "why would you want to do that?" and of course this is not the right response because he can automatically give me dozens of reasons. "they are taking our jobs" "they are ornery" "they are just using any excuse to stir up stuff."

I can't add anything to this conversation, so I have to leave. The guy who said this in not holding anything against me because he may not even know it is upsetting me. To him it is just a fact and if I disagree it is only because I'm not a true southerner or I'm ignorant, or whatever. No hard feelings. I'm okay even if I'm dumb about the situation. I'm very grieved for too many reasons to list; but the one freaking me is 'how do I esteem this guy higher than myself"

Now I know I said earlier about seeing something he can do that I can't do and I'm sure he is a better carpenter or chain saw man or whatever, but for some reason this doesn't seem to apply. So, I think, and I pray, and I sleep on it. Then I wake up and it comes to me. I should admire his boldness; his willingness to say what he thinks regardless of what I think, his conviction even when it is based on nothing but his feelings. Hey mine is based on my feeling also (compassion, love.)

So, I knew I blew it. I looked up a verse in II Timothy 4:2. "Preach the word: be instant in season, out of season, reprove, rebuke, exhort with all longsuffering and doctrine" If I would have had his boldness and conviction, I could have said something like, "Well I don't really think killing a bunch of people would work, it hasn't in the past and besides the Lord created all of us for a reason."

He created everything for a reason; even if I have no idea why he created things to irritate us. And he commanded us to love one another so I'm working on that. I know He loves me and He loves you and he loves all of the blacks, Mexicans, Muslims, gays, and it bothers Him we can't get along. I used to hate people who took advantage of people; CEOs who made decisions to pollute or take advantage of workers. I may be still dealing with that, but I know I have a Savior who died on the cross for me....and for you...... and for everyone human on this earth and maybe a few animals too.

Before I would have said all of this I could have said, "I admire your boldness and conviction, now let me tell you a little about how I feel." it is sort of like gossip or any other negative things, I should respond in love. I can't blast someone who is gossiping, I should say something good about the person who is being talked about and tell them how I feel. "Hey, I used to do that but now I get a bigger kick out of uplifting people and seeing the good side of them"

Well anyway I blew it, but I will get another opportunity to interface with this individual (and a lot more who believe like he does) so Lord let me have the words to speak in love to make one think there may be a better way than violence. Help us "reason together" *Isaiah 1:18*. we have a scripture for everything. Help us use them instead of going by the hurt feelings, media, excitable friends, or whatever else that motivates us to be less than loving.

Compassion: Talk Heart to Heart with People

Jan 6, 2018

We had a conversation last night about not being able to help more people or to give more help to people. We talked about Mr. Jones. We pulled out of his house because it was too dangerous. There was a leak in his house and the water had run down and rotted out a header that was holding up part of the roof. I guess sometime there had been a room added onto and the old wall had been removed and a header installed in its place. There was a bunch of his floor in the bathroom rotted out also. I was hoping we would tarp his roof so no more water could come in. I didn't think it was such a big deal to replace the header. I know all kinds of carpenters who could knock that out in a half day or in an hour or so. But they aren't here.

The organization has to worry about liability. I get so discouraged by these kinds of things. The ironic thing is, Mr. Jones was so moved by what we had done, he kept thanking the volunteers as he was crying. A bunch of sheet rock had been removed and it was a lot cleaner and neater looking then when we went there. I didn't see the finished product but I was there the first day we worked and saw how sheet rock was on the floor and pieces still hanging from the ceiling. Mr. Jones was living in one room with the walls gutted out so mold was all around him. It is somewhat less moldy now, but if we were to work anymore we would still have to wear respirators.

We can't do anymore for him. We can't do anything about the little girl who lost her parents. We can't do anything for the homeless guy who lost his trailer he was sleeping in. It wasn't his anyway. It was just a cargo type trailer someone had let him sleep in. We can't help people who don't have anything. How does one do that? So, what can we do?

I guess we start off by having compassion for them. To try not to judge them. We don't judge the little girl because she had no control about the storm, but we may judge the homeless guy and the guy with the hole in his roof. If they had made different decisions they wouldn't be in this situation. So why do we judge? Is it to justify us not doing anything? And if not to justify, at least to not feel so bad for not doing anything? I don't know, but I do know we need to feel more compassion. I think the reason I may judge is because I don't want to feel compassion.

Maybe that is the reason we do it. I guess the next question would be, "why we don't want to feel compassion?" Well it is not very comfortable. Sometimes it may cause us to feel guilt. Guilt because we have so much more, survivors guilt, guilt because we know we could be doing more than we are. The list goes on forever.

I think sometimes why I don't feel compassion is, I think it will interfere with what I'm going to do. Just give me another job, I will possibly make someone else' life a little better. I don't need to feel compassion for people. I just need to do something for them. Of course, I have it backwards. Doing is not near as important as sharing the people's feelings. I could roof Mr. Jones's house and he would not be as moved as seeing young people coming into his house and taking their time to make his house a little better.

It is about relationships and how one talks "heart to heart" with people. We can only do this with compassion. That is why we should have compassion instead of being judgmental. It doesn't really change anything (well except for the person feeling compassion and the recipient) but it makes us better people. It makes us more feeling people. And it may make us think of something that can change people's circumstances.

Do We Really Want to Be More Like Jesus?

I hear people say they want to be more like Jesus. I don't understand why they say this when they are not trying to do it. I am pretty sure I do not want to be like Jesus. If I did, I would start doing what the Bible says Jesus did. Well, it's not hard to have the opportunity to act like Jesus. We don't have any lepers around to touch and heal, but there are dirty homeless people who we could go hug and tell them we love them. There are divorced women who have been in multiple relationships who we could go visit and tell them they are loved and they could be great workers for the Lord.

If we want to be more like Jesus and say, "forgive them," as he said while hanging on the cross, we could start off by forgiving the people who didn't vote the way they should or said something in church that hurt our feelings. If we want to be more like Jesus, we could stop griping about taxes and say, "Hey, the money we have is printed by the government, so it is theirs anyway. I don't care how much taxes I have to pay.

The birds aren't worried about it because they are provided for. The way they are provided for is; they have twigs to build a nest. I'll take the stuff other people don't want and build me a house. If we want to be more like Jesus, we could take a little bit someone has given us and bless it and share with whoever is there. If we want to be more like Jesus we would look at the refugees in the camps and try to feel compassion. Jesus looked at the multitudes and felt compassion. We may not be able to do that, but we can start trying.

If we want to be more like Jesus, we can start by forgiving whoever has done things to us, we can share some of the stuff we have, we can stop worrying about things we can't do anything about anyway, we can be friendly to people who other people shun. We can encourage little children, we can lay hands on the sick and pray for them, we can tell people who don't have hope that they are blessed. We can go into the slums and talk to people and tell them they are blessed because they are in the image of God. We can lay hands on drug addicts and pray the spirit of addiction will leave them and tell them they are loved, and the list goes on.

We know Jesus loved everyone, so we can start out by trying to love everyone. Are we really ready to be like Jesus? I don't love everyone and have compassion for less people, but I would like to want to be more like Jesus. I believe it is a good concept because it takes a lot of pressure off of us. It is a lot easier when we don't hold grudges and we don't worry about our food or jobs or what is going on the world.

While I'm not ready to forgive someone who is driving a nail in my hand, maybe I can forgive someone who is putting a needle in their arm. Then maybe I can work up to people who are putting needles in other's arms. Maybe I can even forgive big pharm for making so much money off of people who are diseased. Maybe I can say, "Forgive them Lord because they don't know what they are doing" I doubt I can because it is hard for me to believe they don't know what they are doing.

It is hard for me to believe the politicians don't know what they are doing when they keep the electorate in fear of everything. I think they study out what will generate fear and use that to stay in power. Maybe I can say, "Lord, forgive me for getting tore up about the things I do. Help me not worry so much. Help me share what I have. Help me see the needs of others and then to do what I can to lessen their needs. Just help me Lord to be a better person. Amen'

While that prayer isn't asking for me to be very much like Jesus, at least it is a start and we know the longest journey in the world starts with a single step. So maybe I can at least do one thing Jesus would do. I can try to meditate on what Jesus would do when I'm upset because I'm in line and someone in front has coupons or looking for loose change. I can realize being like Jesus takes work and time. It takes work and time to forgive people, but it is worth it. The more we forgive, the easier it gets.

A Drop of Water

June 2018

A drop of water is not much. Sometimes when one is trying to do something, someone may say "you are only a drop in a bucket". Well some friends of mine wrote a song about that; and in the song, it mentions, the bucket goes into the stream and the stream flows into the river and the river flows into the ocean and it all started as a drop.

I knew a bunch of drops could make a lot happen, but I wanted to concentrate on one drop. One drop laying on a piece or steel can cause the steel to rust. One drop falling on your head can encourage you if there has been a drought. And likewise, one drop can warn you about a storm coming. One drop in your eye might wash out a dust particle. One drop on your tongue will help if you are thirsty. One drop can carry various things; microbes and dust, so it can scatter bad stuff or wash away bad stuff or carry nutrients to a plant. One drop of water on a plant may be plenty for an insect to drink

Water has a weak gravitational attraction so it can hang on a plant or the bottom of a rock. In a cave a drop of water forms because of condensation. The drop slowly goes to the lowest part of the cave ceiling and then drops. As it drops it leaves a minute part of what it has flowed over and after a while one can see this rock called a stalactite hanging down from the ceiling. The drop is still carrying a minute amount of this material which builds up on the floor to form a stalagmite.

Finally, after enough drops have ran down these two rock formations meet to form a column in the cave. On the other hand, if there are no minerals for the drop to pick up the drop makes a hole in whatever it falls on. A drop at a time makes a groove in concrete or rock.

I think the best thing is when one sees a drop on a leaf. The drop can reflect the light and at the same time make the leaf look greener. It seems to magnify the leaf making it easier to see the veins or pores on the leaf. There was a picture of a drop hanging on the underside to a leaf. There was a reflection of everything around it on the drop of water. Someone said, "one could see the universe in a drop of water." When light shines through a drop, it acts as a prism and one can see a rainbow.

A drop of water on wood causes it to rot and makes it easy for termites to eat the wood. A drop not moving is stagnant and all kinds of bad things may grow in it. A drop seems to have to be moving to be effective in a positive way. And even moving it is not always good. It can erode land and carry off good topsoil. A drop can be all muddy; it is not always clear. It depends on what it has traveled over.

We may be just drops but a drop of water has no control of where it goes and we do. We can build up or tear down, we can encourage, we can make things look brighter, magnify beauty, give nourishment to others. We can just roll along, picking up good things and depositing them where they will encourage others and help them grow. Of course, we can just stay where we are and stagnate.

Again, the choice is ours. We can bond with other drops and because of the weak gravitational attraction we can still be our self and don't have to become so like-minded we become brittle and break. We can flow into places most people can't get to. A long time ago I was with an organization that said instead of being flexible we should become fluid. Being fluid is a lot more effective. We can reflect the love of the Lord while we are carrying nutrients to others.

Let's keep flowing along at a regular pace. Otherwise we are like a double minded person; sometimes doing good; and sometimes not. There is a Chinese water torture where a drop of water is dropped on a person's head at various times. It is irregular so it is torture not knowing when the next drop is going to fall.

"I sure ain't skeered"

4/14/ 2017

Wake up this morning and I feel depressed. Sounds like a pretty harsh word. Am I really depressed or just tired? Or is this the same. Physically tired or tired of nothing changing. Tired or not accomplishing something. Tired of seeing people going from one problem to another. Tired of not seeing I make a difference in people's lives.

It works together. We get physically tired and then it goes into mentally tired. And that leads into depression. It is kind of weird. I almost never get enough sleep when I'm on a mission trip. Too many people to talk to at night and in the am before breakfast. Too many things to share. Beyond that I am so excited. Something is getting done. Lives are being changed. Then it ends and everyone goes home. Back to their 'real' lives. Back to watching the news and being depressed because of all the things going bad in the world. Back from the mountain top experience to being in the valley. Well I know the answer, "Yea though I walk in the valley of the shadow of death, I shall fear no evil" Does this mean I will not get depressed? Well maybe not, because I am somewhat depressed and I sure ain't skeered.

I'm not even depressed. I can make a difference; and I am. It just isn't as obvious to me as I would like it to be. This is Good Friday (what a misnamed day) and this is the day Jesus was crucified by the people He helped. This shows us the effects of doing something a person thinks is good, may not show up immediately. Maybe it isn't so bad I'm a little depressed because all the things I wanted to get done this week didn't get done.

At least I'm not on a cross. I know the resurrection is coming. It already has. Winter is over, but there still will be stormy days in the spring. There will be hot days and there will be cold days; and then it will be summer and one can stay out in the night without a jacket. Things change. We are happy; we are depressed but because of the seasons we grow. Hopefully, we are always in a growing season; but even for growing season, the seed has to be dormant for a while.

I don't know if any of this makes any sense to anyone, but I'm feeling better than I was an hour ago.

CHAPTER SEVEN

WORK

Don't Let Circumstance Stop Us from Helping if We are Able

Houston after Hurricane Harvey

I'm not even sure where we are working. I know it is the north-east area of the Houston metro area. I know out of the 87 people who died because of Hurricane Harvey, 17 of them lived in this area so 20 per cent of the people who died; lived in this area. What I didn't learn until today was, they didn't die from the hurricane. The hurricane had gone by dropping 50 inches of rain on the area, but water filled up the reservoirs and the water from the reservoirs had to be released so they wouldn't break or overflow. For some reason, the people in the area where we are working were not notified of this.

Maybe it was an oversight. Maybe there was some miscommunication. Maybe anything. Who knows? What I do know is, this is a poor area. As far as I could tell there were only mobile homes in the neighborhood. And it was one hundred percent Hispanic. The lady we are interfacing with seems to have a pulse on the people who need help but she is deaf and doesn't speak English. (you can see how this might cause some miscommunication). Most of the trailers don't look like they were in good shape before the flood. The one we are working in had to have the floors removed and I see rotten wood in various parts of the house. All the sheet rock and insulation has been removed. Some of the windows are broken and there is no front door. It doesn't seem like it would be worth repairing, but we have to work with what they have and there may not be any other option. I am kind of amazed they will be allowed to rebuild.

There is no electricity or water at the house so we walk to the Valero station a few blocks away to use the bathroom. Everyone we see seems friendly but reserved. Fences and big dogs are common. I see a couple of new trailers, but they are not fancy. I see people working on their trailers, but I don't see any construction company trucks in the area. I smell wood burning as some of them are demolishing their sheds and burning the wood that can't be salvaged. Tonight, we had to pull our generator to where we have our tools stored. It is a few blocks away and at first, I thought they were teasing. I kind of enjoyed it. Well, that's because I wasn't one of the people pulling the generator.

I didn't enjoy it at all because I was wet and cold, I was glad to get the experience of walking through that part of the neighborhood because it was in the opposite direction of the station. What was wild was, I'm looking up at the trailers which meant the water to flood them had to be 15 feet deep at least. I saw one where they had removed all the siding, so the studs were exposed. They have studs and a roof; well I guess it's better than nothing.

It appeared they had jacked it up also. Guess it would be a lot easier to jack up when siding and sheet rock has been removed. Not near as heavy. I saw some trailers that will not be able to be rebuilt. There are sheds moved around all over the place and some of the sheds had plastic on the sides to cover them. I don't know whether this is to protect possessions or someone is living in the sheds.

There all kinds of things I don't know. There is not much I can do, but I am thankful I am here doing what I can. I'm thankful I can share with others what little I know and encourage them to help others. One almost always never knows the circumstances, but you can almost always see the needs. Does it matter what the circumstance is? Maybe. But the main thing is to not let circumstance stop us from helping if we are able.

We Don't Want Your Prayers: Do Something

In the Bible study class on Sunday, I heard the leader comment on this. He said there was not going to be any gun control because there were four guns for every person in the US. It seemed the group was sad or shocked that somebody didn't want prayers. Well, I didn't comment because I would have said the same thing. If I am in trouble I don't want your prayers. I want you to do something to help me. If I am hungry, give me something to eat. Don't tell the Lord I am hungry. He already knows it.

Now I do believe in prayer. I believe it is our most powerful tool. The problem is it seems most of us don't really pray. Or at least not what I think is prayer. I know we know what prayer is. Everyone I have ever heard comment on prayer said, it was a conversation with the Lord. Well, unless I don't know what conversation is, I don't see very much of this. I don't think conversation is someone running up to me and yelling (or whispering) what problems they have to me and then taking off before I have a chance to tell them anything.

I think the conversation would be when I told them it seemed they could handle the problem or I might actually tell them how to fix it, or I might tell them what tools they needed and maybe even offer to loan or give them the tools, or I might even say "OK, I'll take care of it." But one thing for sure, if I didn't get to say anything, I would not consider it a conversation. I think prayer is the same way. If I tell my problem to someone and he says he would pray for me, I would like to think he would get an answer.

KJV James 5:16; "The effectual fervent prayer of a righteous man availeth much." NIV says, "The power of a righteous man is powerful and effective," so we know prayer is powerful if a righteous person does it. What makes one righteous? Doing the right thing, thinking the right thing, basically obeying the Lord. It isn't necessarily perfect, because it the same verse it says, "Confess your faults to one another and pray for one another"

NIV says, "sins' instead of faults. We are to bear each other's burdens, pray for one another and do what the Lord tells us to do. Later James 5:17 references "Elijah who was a man subject to his passions as we are" Elijah prayed fire down, but he obeyed the Lord and did what the Lord told him to do. If a person who confesses his faults and obeys the Lord wants to ask the Lord to do something for me and is willing to do what the Lord tells him to do or to tell me what the Lord told him to tell me I am grateful. Now if he is praying for the Lord to bless me financially and isn't willing to help me himself, I am doubtful the Lord will bless me with finances because this person told Him to. He blesses me because He loves me and sometimes I may do what He wants.

I guess I'm like the lady who said, "If you are not going to put any feet on your prayers save your breath." If you are not going to wait on the Lord to tell you what you can be doing in the situation then don't bother yelling at Him when there is a problem. He knows we are the problem. When His disciples told him the crowd was hungry, he told them to feed the crowd. He has left us with His authority. Some people say Jesus lives in us, so that means we should do what He would do. When we pray we should be asking for strength, patience, wisdom and mainly His direction so we can do what we can about whatever problems we encounter.

So, what does that mean to the original comment? What does the Lord want me to do? Well, he probably wants me to be nice to the lady who doesn't want my prayers. He says in Isaiah.1:18 "Let us reason together." We should talk to each other and to God with reason. We should not be making fun of others by forwarding Facebook messages making fun of the other side of the argument.

Let's reason with each other to encourage each other, "esteem others above yourself, "do everything as unto the Lord." I think we know how we should treat each other, but we forget in the heat of the discussion or argument. It is the reason we should be in constant prayer. This is the prayer we should be making, "God keep my tongue bridled. Show me the good in this person. Show me what You would have me to do".

The gun people are right. A gun by itself doesn't hurt anyone. Now as a person, what can I do to keep a person from using the gun in a negative way? What can I do to keep a gun from a person? What can I do to encourage others to think they don't have to own a gun? What can I do to convince people "we are not given a spirit of fear, but of love and power and a sound mind?" II Timothy. 1:7.

How can we use this power and love and sound mind to do what we can to keep others from being so violent? Mainly how can we not be violent or promote violence and fear? Well, we know how we can do that. We can rejoice in the Lord, we can bear each other's burdens, we can uplift instead of putting down. I could go on forever. Mainly we can pray and ask God to guide us in our walk and thoughts.

How to Make Work Easier

The Bible is a book of instructions for us to live a better life. An owner's manual. There is a scripture that covers anything we may run upon. If we don't read it enough, we may not realize, or in my case, not know where to find the scripture. One of the good things is there are hundreds (maybe thousands) of scriptures good enough to live by if they were the only one we ever read. A friend of mine said when she first met me, I told her I tried to live by Colossians 3:23 "And whatsoever ye do, do it heartily, as to the Lord, and not unto men".

Now I can't remember saying that to her, but it has inspired her so it shows how important what we do and say is. My actual go to verse is Romans 8:28 "All things work together for good.........". I sometimes use this to justify when I make a bad decision. It may not be good, but it will work together with something else for a good outcome. When bad things are happening to me (of my own doing) I will learn and get stronger because of them.

The last two days I have had to work harder than I can remember. I have been shoveling mulch and pulling weeds in the sun. I had a choice whether to do this as to the Lord or as to man. Man happens to be my boss; and it happens to be me and my fellow workers. I don't especially enjoy working hard in the sun. When I do, I won't be so happy. If I do it unto my boss, I will work like a maniac while he is there and sluff off when he isn't. If I work as unto my coworkers, I may agree with them, it is a horrible job and then take longer breaks than I'm getting paid for. But if I'm doing it onto the Lord, I will be doing as good a job as I can. Hey, if it was me and Jesus shoveling I would want to be as efficient as I could so we could get finished and talk. There are a lot of questions I could think to ask.

For a while, this scripture kind of scared me because I thought it meant we had to be perfect. God wasn't satisfied with anything except perfection. Well, if we are worried about things being perfect, it is hard to enjoy ourselves. Because the scripture said, 'do it heartily' it sounds as we are to enjoy it, to put our heart into it. Our heart is an organ of love. If we believe the Lord loves us and is telling us what to do because He loves us and wants us to become better people, then we can do what He says heartily, knowing it is for our benefit. It is always better to enjoy your work. When we do it heartily we will look for the best ways to do things so we can become more efficient, so we don't waste time and money. If I love someone and I'm doing something for them, I will do it better and I will enjoy doing it.

He also wants us to take care of our tools because we can't work as 'heartily' with bad tools. There are the tools our body uses, (shovels and hoes) and then our body is the tool of our spirit and mind so we take care of it. The Lord created us with a mind to think and built in warning signs. If we are thirsty, it is time to drink. We have already got dehydrated so our body is telling us it needs water. The more we sweat the cooler we are as the breeze goes over us, so we have to drink to sweat.

Man, did the Lord prepare us to work or what? If our muscles get too sore, we rest them. If we exceed the manufacturer's recommendations on our body and ignore the warning signs (we don't have to look for a low fuel light, our body will tell us it needs fuel) the Lord is not any happier with this than he would be if we didn't do anything to start with.

We were given a body so we can "work heartily as unto the Lord" until we become old. I don't know what that is but I remember reading about Caleb saying, "I'm 80 and 5 and I'm as strong as I was at 40." If we take care of our tools (our body and mind) they will last a long time. They will be sharpened by studying the Bible. They will definitely need more maintenance. They may need better fuel to keep the arteries and veins from getting clogged up.

It is easier to break a tool and harder to repair as it gets older, so we need to be careful but again that is why we have pain; as a warning light when we are overdoing something. When we get hot we should cool off, get out of the sun and cover up with something to avoid getting sunburned. Sun helps provide us vitamin D but we are not supposed to stand in the sun all the time. If the Lord had meant for us to do that, He would not have made a tree taller than us. Trees are made for us to enjoy their beauty, their coolness, the oxygen they produce and so many other things. Well, maybe He would have made it a little taller so we could get an 8-foot 2x4 from it.

If we do everything as unto the Lord, we will be happier, healthier, and more efficient.

I can't let a one and a half leg guy do what we can do with some equipment Rupert West, Virginia

Working in Rupert, West Virginia. It was quite a drive from Camp Hope, but it is still in Greenbrier County. It is the second biggest county in WV and the road was getting repaved so we were delayed. We cleaned out a basement that had two oil tanks. The oil tanks had oil in them. We have no way to dispose to the oil, so we had to leave them and tell the owners they would have to call someone who can recover the oil. Maybe if the people give them the tanks they will do it for free.

We are also taking out the carpet in their daughter's trailer. They shared how their daughter was only given four days to live on Oct 15 of last year and how much she has improved since then. She still has short term memory loss but is getting better. We get lunch brought to us, but this job was so far away we were going to buy it at Rupert. There was a barbecue place on the corner so the guys wanted to eat there. the couple offered to buy us pizza but we declined. Kind of a touchy thing.

We want to help and not hinder people to cause them anymore trouble, but we don't want to offend anyone by not accepting their offer of food. The businesses need help to recover also so one should patronize them when they can. I was so hungry. I am not a barbecue fan, but that was the only option. They had a small and large option of taco barbecue. The lady said she hated to make the small because it was hard to get all the ingredients into the container. I got the taco thing because it had jalapenos. When I saw it getting made, I realized, even as hungry as I was, I wasn't going to be able to eat all of it. Our lead had ordered the same and he couldn't eat all his either so we went back to the house to eat it.

The next-door lady comes over and gives us some dried apples with cinnamon. The homeowner asks if she had any damage. She says, "Yes, but it wasn't much. So many others have it worse, so I figured I wouldn't turn it in." I told her to turn it in so FEMA would have a list of all the damage and they could get more help for the area. This lady's response is common here. "other people have it worse." It is refreshing to work somewhere the people are so thankful and appreciative and self-sufficient. It is a good thing because this flood was so widespread and the volunteer agencies can not cover near everywhere; and they are leaving because they can't get enough volunteers.

After we got back and were having share time, the assessor was telling us about one house miles away and there was a long switch back road to his house. Part of the hill side had slid down against his garage. The guy was in a wheelchair because he had lost part of one of his legs. I guess the assessor may have implied that we couldn't help because the place was so hard to get to, and it wasn't his house that had been damaged. The guy told the assessor, "it doesn't matter if anyone helps or not, I'll dig it out by myself." Well that is a challenge, we will get the backhoe up the switch back road and we will dig out the building. We can't let a one and a half leg guy do what we can do with some equipment.

We had two groups today but they were small. The other group lead said a lady came over and asked if he was the assessor who was supposed to be there. He said no, but he could assess her situation. He looked at it and decided we could do the job. Just as he got finished, the assessor with the organization who was really supposed to do the job came up. He was glad we were going to be able to do the job because Saturday (today) was the last day they were going to be here.

Christ in Action is going to be here until Aug 16 and Samaritan's Purse is here until Aug 6th. Don't know how long Southern Baptists, Rubicon, Christian Aid Ministries are going to be here, but they are here now. I think the Mennonite Disaster Response is also here. West Virginia and the relief agencies need prayer, volunteers and money.

Workfest with Christian Appalachian Project 2015

This is the third week of Workfest. We have a much smaller team because fewer colleges came down. One of the ladies on my team (the green team) came down last year. (this is her third year) and worked on my team. Of course, she recognized me and asked if the house we worked on got finished. I recognized her face but couldn't remember her name; or where we worked. That was embarrassing, but I figured it out fairly soon. This is the third of three awesome teams. Anyone who is willing to give up their spring break to come to Kentucky (or go anywhere) and serve is awesome in my opinion.

Then again, if anyone realized what a blessing one gets out of service, I feel there would be a lot more volunteers. I am amazed because when I was these people's age, I doubt very much I would have gone anywhere to work for free. Not only do these guys work for free, they have to pay money to come here.

Our project is to fix a leaky roof. Leaky may be an understatement. Part of the roof was pretty much rotted out. When we got on it to assess and repair, we put 4'x8' pieces of sheeting so we would not fall through the roof. This worked fairly well but one guy did run his foot through the roof. The lady who lives there said she heard a commotion and looked up and saw a foot coming through the ceiling. The guy didn't hurt himself so it wasn't a big deal as we were there to repair the roof. The reason the roof was in such bad shape was due to various reasons.

The bad roof is over two added two rooms. When the rooms were added the roof didn't have enough slope for the rain to run off as soon as it should and a blowing wind might blow water up under the shingles. Where these rooms were added they were not tied into the house as they should be. There has to be metal flashing between a wall and a roof and that wasn't done so this allowed water to blow under the shingles. Then along with leaking, the water laying on the boards causes the wood to rot. Obviously, the bad wood has to be replaced, so it would be easier to just build a roof over the old one and by adding a knee wall we could have a correct slope so water could run off rather than get under shingles and rot the wood. This water leaking has ruined other things in the house; most notably the sheetrock in the ceiling of the laundry room and the kitchen.

And even though this roof is a big deal, this isn't the major problem the homeowners have. The family is great. The son is going to a community college, the oldest girl is in high school and is taking junior ROTC to prepare to get into the armed service. Then there two little girls, (three and two) who are a pleasure to be around. The three-year-old is full of energy and tries to pull the shy act every time she comes out. The two-year-old watches the older one and kind of impersonates her.

All of that is good news, the bad news is the father has a disease so rare there would be a better chance of winning the lottery. It seems like the disease is 'gastroparesis'. Food won't digest so he has to use a feeding tube and he has to take a lot of medication making him sleep a lot and be kind of out of it otherwise. He has to have some kind of apparatus that causes his body to digest food. I know nothing about the disease, but I know it seems painful and uncomfortable and I was amazed at the attitude he had. He said no once knew what he had and then a doctor came upon the scene who figured what he had and he was thankful for that. He also says he is getting better even though he still spends a major part of his time asleep.

One day we worked in the house due to the weather being so bad and he slept on the couch as we were tearing out ceilings and the three-year-old was getting some of the young ladies on the team to ride her on their backs through the house. While we are working on these houses during Workfest, we have a family appreciation dinner on Thursday of each week. The whole family came to it the first week except for the father who stayed home.

This last week, they couldn't come because their car was getting hot from water leaking. That part was bad enough but they had to go to Louisville, (a 2-hour drive) the next day to get a feeding tube installed. The lady said she hoped she could borrow a car to take him. This morning I was happy to hear they managed to do that. I also heard the crew chief tell her CAP would make sure they got to the appreciation dinner this week if they wanted to go.

We still won't have all the work done at the end of Workfest, but the family will have a dry house. The first week we put up rafters, built a knee wall to hold up the new roof, and installed most of the roof sheeting. The second week we finished the sheeting, installed most of the shingles. This week finished the shingles and installed fascia and soffit.

Does the Lord Want Us to Work?
Adam names the animals

July 5, 2018

I hear Christians say, 'It is not about works to have salvation. It is about having faith in the Lord." Well I guess one can be an heir without working, one is born into it, so I guess after we are born again according to Rom 8:16-17" .... we are children of God. If children, then heirs—heirs of God and joint heirs with Christ...." So as heirs, I guess we can work or not, but I know the Lord wants us to work.

In Gen 1:15, "Then the Lord God took the man (Adam) and put him in the garden of Eden to tend and keep it" in verse 8 ".... the Lord God made every tree grow that is pleasant to the sight and good for food." Now that is a big garden so it would be some work to tend. God knew it would be a tough job for one person and in verse 18 "And the Lord God said, "it is not good that man should be alone. I will make him a helper comparable to him" verse 19 "And out of the ground the Lord God formed every beast of the field and every bird of the air and brought them to Adam to see what he would call them. And whatever Adam called each living creature, that was its name"

That had to be quite a chore, naming every bird and beast. And Adam had to do it by himself. I wondered why God didn't wait until Eve was there so she could help him name them. Then I realized how hard it is to name something when two people get involved. One person wants to name a pet dog, Killer, and another wants to name him Fido; and the argument starts. So now we are talking about thousands of names. It probably took Adam months or years to name them all. If Eve had been there arguing, they may not have them named yet.

I think Adam had a system, so he started with the letters of the alphabet. Of course, there were only 26 letters so he would have to start again. I imagine that is why the first one was aardvark because it starts out with double A's. But I can see Eve saying, "There is an anteater." And Adam saying, "Of course that is what he does, but we have to give them unique names." Then we get to B and Adam names the next animal baboon. Eve probably didn't have a problem because the animal looks like a baboon.

Than Adam came to C so he named the animal cat. Eve would have been saying the animal should be named Fluffy and Adam would have to be saying well the animal is kind of fluffy but cat is quick to say and sharp so that describes it. Then we have D so we have Dog and now the Fido and King and all of the other cute names would come out. Adam says, "No, this animal is slower and laid back more than a cat and we can stretch the name out to be like dawg so that fits him.

The next animal was big and it had to be a long name, Elephant and by the then argument would have got so bad, the animal would never have been named, so God knew what he was doing when He had one person naming animals instead of some committee.

We can see what happened when they started naming their kids. They had been kicked out of the garden and Adam had named the woman Eve, because she is going to be mother of all living. Before that he just called her woman (or wife), but now there will be other women around and he can't just yell "WOMAN" when he wants something.

So, they have children and Eve calls the first born, Cain. Now you know this gave him some kind of complex. He has a name that seems to be a troublemaker (raising cane) or a stick sitting in the corner and one only uses it when they are old and feeble. Sure enough, comes the next baby and they name it Abel. Well to Cain it sounds to him like he wasn't able, so they had to get another kid who was.

If Adam had named them, he would have called Cain "Boy" and then it would have been the same for Abel. Fathers don't remember names. They just yell, "BOY." Mothers on the other hand, want kids to have two names so they can call them Mary Elizabeth to make sure the right one comes because one of the girls may watch a baby while another bakes or sews. Guys don't care which one comes. They just want them to lift or open something. They know if they yell the wrong name no one will come to do anything so 'Boy" works well. And if both boys come, all the better.

Eve, like all mothers, gave Abel her whole attention and Adam didn't play with Cain like he did before Abel was born. Cain can't know they treated him like Abel when he was little because he can't remember when he was little. Then they send Cain out to raise food and Abel tends sheep. Cain has the hard job, tilling, planting, watering, weeding and picking.

Abel can just sit in the shade and play the harp. Maybe had a sheep dog watching the sheep.

When it came time to make a sacrifice to the Lord, Cain brought some fruit and Abel brought the firstborn of the flock. I would guess that was a little lamb. Well, God was pleased with the lamb and not so happy with the fruit. So now Cain had the last straw. He tilled, planted, and plucked some fruit and all Abel did was pick up a little lamb after the ewe had done all the work delivering it. I bet Cain thought God was a vegetarian anyway because he had put Cain's mother and father in the garden to tend it.

Cain grabs a rock and smashes Abel in the head. He probably didn't aim to kill him. I'm sure growing up he had hit him a few times before and he may have never seen anything die before. But whatever, Abel was dead and Cain had to leave. Cain left and built a city. Adam and Eve had another son, Seth, and then about 10 generations later Noah came along.

The Bible doesn't say too much about the guys between Seth and Noah but it does say they were herdsmen and craftsmen and one of them Enoch, walked with God. If one is walking with the Creator of the universe that would be close to work. Noah with his three sons built an ark to hold two of every creature and seven of each clean creature and enough food to feed them and the animals for a year. That was a big boat.

The point is, God had Adam tend a garden and name the animals. He had Cain and Abel farm and raise sheep. He had Cain build a city and Noah and his boys build such a big boat. With all these people building cities, starting crafts, tending flocks, and farming He is pleased when we work. He gave us dominion over the earth. This means we are to take care of it. This is a pretty big responsibility. So far, we haven't done it so well. I don't imagine He is so happy with polluting, mountain top removal, clear cutting and other wasteful practices. He made the earth pretty much like He wanted it to stay.

Maybe That Is One Reason I'm Here
Stuck in Wharton, Texas

Oct 22, 2017

I'm stuck in Wharton, Texas because the transmission is messing up in my van. For a while I'm confused about what to do. Then I realize I'm only three hours away from where I left so I'll just go back there and work some more. The bus doesn't leave until 3:00 and I have to check out of the motel at 11:00 so I can explore the town (well the part I can walk to). First, I'm going to get a bus ticket which is 37 dollars (lot better than the $168 to go the other way). But I don't have enough cash and the ATM at the bus station won't work.

I see a filling station up the road near the street where the van is parked and I have to walk to the van and take some clothes back from the suitcase and get some Christ in Action T-shirts. Yesterday when I was leaving, I just grabbed a suitcase and started throwing stuff in it, and it already had a bunch of tees. I also didn't think about going back to work then so I hadn't gotten but one pair of jeans.

I walk up the street with a bunch of loose clothes and go into the store with them on my arm. The ATM doesn't work there either. Is there something the matter with my card? I get a tall Arizona green tea with honey. It is $1.07 and the owner tells me to just give him a dollar. This is the second time today I have been told that. He also asks if I want a plastic bag and has the cashier get me one.

Okay, now I don't look so homeless and I can use that bag to bring my Christ In Action T-shirts and my pants back. I get to the van and when I open the door, I realize I need my boots. (I don't want those sand spurs on my ankles again), but I can't carry my slippers and boots so I leave the slippers and put the boots on. Just before I got to the shop I saw a St. Stephen Baptist Church with some stuff out in front. Across the street I see a Primer Iglesias Baptiste. Seems like this is Spanish for First English Baptist.

I decide to walk down some other streets to get back. For one thing, I hope to find an ATM. I see the Assembly of God Church which appears to have water. There is a mobile clinic at the WIC place and furniture outside. I see furniture drying out everywhere and small piles of debris everywhere and I can smell the mold as I walk by. There are some really nice-looking houses that don't appear to be affected. Well maybe they got them cleaned up and looking down the street it appears they may be a little higher. The library is across the street and FEMA and the SBA is there in the community center. It looks like they didn't get water.

I know I shouldn't walk into a library because I'm always wanting to read. Sure enough, I see a bunch of books about Texas and Indians, one by my favorite author Larry McMurtry. It is about massacres (whites, Indians, and Mormons). I thought it was new because I hadn't seen it before but the copyright was 2005. Because he is a Texas author, more of his stuff may be in the libraries here. I notice there is a little newspaper (The Good News just keeps coming) which is free. I notice religious papers, songs are everywhere.

These people are really into guns and God. I noticed people all over the place. A lot of new windows. I wonder as they were gutting out did they discover termite damage around windows because I know the water didn't get that high. I'm getting concerned about getting back in time and finding a working ATM. I was kind of concerned about my card. I go in the CVS and it works there but it is telling me to take my receipt and I didn't get one, so it may be malfunctioning. Well I got money..

I come back buy a ticket. The lady was about to send to Killinger for some reason. She was concerned about how much stuff I had. I told her I was putting the bag I had into the suitcase. It was a tight fit, and I was going to eat the kolaches. They had cooled off since I got them earlier but they were good. So, I ate two delicious things today. A breakfast taco and two spicy Bohdan Kolaches.

After I got my ticket, Freddy, the owner came in and asked me if I was going to Corpus Christi instead of South Carolina and said it was a good idea. I saw he was changing the floor mat and I asked if water had got into everything in town. He said the reason he was changing mats was because he couldn't get them clean from the mud.

This morning when I talked to the pastor of the College Baptist Church he told me there were so many houses to repair and be gutted out. He said the Southern Baptists and Rubicon were still around but the needs will be forever. I told him I was trying to inform churches to get with local churches in Texas and commit to taking offerings every so often and sending groups down to churches. He said a group had stayed at his church. I didn't see the church when I was walking around. He was working on his house today taping and mudding as a lot of people are.

So maybe that is one reason I'm here. To see (and tell others) there are hundreds of towns that are damaged. Some of the poorer people will never get theirs repaired. I did see where FEMA was extending the time people could put in claims. Seems pretty wild when I had heard there had already been over a million claims submitted.

The bus station closes at 3:00 pm which is before the bus gets there. I'm not sure when it is supposed to come except it is three something. I'm outside writing and I hear the bus stop out on the street and the driver comes over and says he almost didn't stop because he didn't think anyone was there, so he apologized for me having to walk so far to the bus. He took my luggage and I was just thankful I wasn't stranded there. Of course, that would just have been another adventure. I thought about asking him if he thought I was some Mexican squatting there with a sombrero. I didn't think about it much. I needed the ride and south Texas is not a place to make Mexican jokes.

I Need to Go on a Mission Trip to Get Some Rest

I went to Legacy Adult Bible class. Celebrated a woman's 88th birthday. Was invited to dinner. Served "Sensational Salad" (a local name for a delicious salad). The place setting was so beautiful it should have been in a picture.

After lunch I go to Port Hudson and sit on a levee. Feel a breeze I think is from Hurricane Irma. Have conversation with black guy about the state of the world. As we are getting into this deep conversation, he mentions there is a lady who is in a photo shoot and is on her third set of clothes and he is wondering how she keeps changing. There are no trees or anything to change behind (hey, we are on a levee). I look at her and she does have a black outfit on. The next time I look up she is in a red outfit. Both are tight. (hey, it is a photo shoot). I leave the same time as they do, but I don't have the nerve to ask her about the different dresses she wore.

Go up to St. Francisville to a jam session of the "Fugitive Poets" at the *Bird Man Coffee Shop*. Listened to Blues Music on Hwy 61 which is the Blues Highway. Buy a CD by Steven Judice who I met and listened to the week before.

Monday morning, I leave Denham Springs, Louisiana, but first I have to eat at the *Whistle Stop Café* at Laconte and get some hot pickled quail eggs. Stop in Hattiesburg, Mississippi to meet a Floridian evacuee who is an author from Kentucky and a Facebook friend of mine who I had never met. We swap some stories about people we knew in common. I get lost in Hattiesburg get off the highway. Get back on finally and get to Meridian, Mississippi and run out of gas. Get rescued by a guy who takes me to his house to get a gas can. Get gas and go on to Tuscaloosa, Alabama.

Tuesday get lost in Nashville, Tennessee where I had to drive under a building to get to a parking lot and I saw the tallest steeple I have ever seen on the Woodmont Baptist Church. Go by Vanderbilt University and think about how neat it is to be in the traffic and see all the stuff one would miss otherwise. Of course, this looking at everything results in me missing my turn. Get to Kentucky late.

Go to doctors appt on Wednesday. Annual wellness exam. Didn't do fasting so I had to come back on Thursday for blood work. Had good sermon about remembering on Wednesday night.

Thursday get lab work and go to Grandparent's day at granddaughter's school where we eat lunch. Go to church on Thursday night.

Friday go to Servant Farm in Wilmore, Kentucky to volunteer at the River Rock Festival. Meet songwriter and buy his CD. Park cars and have interesting conversations. Get to listen to the News Boys. Drive back to Stanton.

Saturday, drive back to Wilmore. Find out they have plenty of volunteers so I can just enjoy the festival. Listen to some good music. Meet lady who sang "Fearless," buy her CD and get picture with her. Have some neat conversations with some people who had mutual friends. May have made some contacts with other people who do volunteer work. Come back to Clay City and go to church.

I think I need to go on a mission trip to get some rest.

What I Learned When Making a Mess of Making Coffee

I am not sure what happened when I tried to make coffee this morning, but I know it was a mess. It may have been the worst one I've made while making coffee; and it definitely was the worst one I've had to clean up.

So how did it happen? I have no idea. I was doing everything as normal, putting in filter, coffee, water, pot in the coffee maker. All at once, I see the coffee is not coming out in a straight stream; something is making it spew all over the place so it is not all going in the coffee pot and it seems to have a lot of coffee grounds in it. I think, maybe if I get a pitcher with a bigger opening to replace the pot I can catch more. That doesn't work well either because it is spewing past that opening also.

I have to get the container holding the coffee grounds out and then at least the water will come down straight. Well it is full of hot coffee and grounds and it overflows and burns before I can it put in the sink. The hot coffee doesn't hurt me but it makes me jerk and spill more. Now there is all kinds of junk on the floor. I get some paper towels and start to clean it up, but it is on the cabinet doors, countertop and floor, so where to start. I start on the floor so I won't keep stepping in it and make it worse. Then I wipe the doors of the cabinets and I also have to wipe the insides because the coffee ran into the cabinets and then I drag the waste can over to wipe the grounds on the countertop into the can.

I start to make another pot while trying to figure out what went wrong. I can't really figure it out so I do the same thing I did at first except I take more care making sure the filter doesn't collapse. I remember one of the guys saying those filters were not big enough. As I'm making another pot, I notice more stuff to be cleaned up. The first mess seems to have made another mess.

So now comes the lesson.

When we make a mess, there is a good chance we will cause other messes. We can't undo a mess without a lot of clean up, and still things will not be the way they were. Sometimes we have to wait until things have run their course before attempting to fix the mess. Jumping in too quickly sometimes makes things worse. If we don't have the right equipment for the job there is a good chance we will make a mess. But we have to work with what we have. We have to plunge ahead trying to do everything as well as we can to keep the mess down to a minimum and to get the best results we can.

Now we have coffee. Everyone is happy (maybe). The coffee probably has a minimum amount of grounds and I have learned a lesson. I wouldn't have learned anything if it was not for the mess. Messes teach us things. Sometimes, it is not to get involved again. Sometimes it is to be more cautious next time. Sometimes it is to make us realize there are consequences to our actions. And sometimes it is to realize a mess may be unavoidable, but the job must be done, so the result is worth the cleanup.

God is in Control and He has a Job for All of Us

June 30, 2015

I'm in Hope Arkansas. and I drove on the Highway of Hope getting here. I'm filled with so much love as I drive. I could see God's creation, smell the pines, feel the wind, hear the birds. Man, what a moon up there. I realize He made each one of us unique so I can't be upset with a group of people because they are all individuals created for a unique calling and I should do what I can to see they make that calling.

I can only do this if I open my heart to love. Right now, it is open. It is free of all anger, fear, envy, and I'm happy. God is in control and he has a job for all of us.

Weird Things Happen to Me
Where is that Preaching Coming From?

Sept 27, 2017

So many weird things happen to me, I figure I will never be surprised. Well tonight, I'm going to Walmart and listening to NPR and I hear something else playing in the background. I'm wondering if some way or other my CD is playing also, so I push eject. What is in it ejects and I still hear it. I can also hear it clearly because it is a black preacher. Walmart isn't far away. I pull in and turn the motor off. I still hear the preaching.

Well, the radio keeps going until the door opens, so I open the door. I keep hearing the preaching and wonder if maybe there is some street preaching going on. Now if it is, someone could hear a mile away, but then who knows?

I get out and can't hear anything out there, but I still hear the preaching. I'm concerned now because this is going to cause my battery to run down. As fast as it seems my battery has run down before I'm concerned it may run down while I'm in Walmart. I'm only there to get a couple of things, so I go in and then can't find a short line. Of course not, I'm in Walmart. I get in the shortest and the lady in front of me lets me in front of her. People here seem so nice. She says, "God Bless You."

I go outside and walk back to the van. The preaching is not going on now, but something is playing but I can't comprehend. I have the CD ejected, the radio turned off, and I still hear something playing, it is just too low for me to hear coherently. I don't know what to do about this, but at least I will be back at the church and there are plenty of vehicles to give me a jump tomorrow.

As I'm coming back, I'm thinking about how many church groups are here and I was wanting to drive by to see the name of one. I think they may be Catholic because it is the Sisters of Mary, Joseph, and Jesus, or something like that. I want to get it right before I write it down. Well, forget that, I am close enough and I'm not going to take a chance on the battery going down.

Before I get to the church we are staying at, Church of Hope, I pass the one next door, St. Andrew's Episcopalian. When we went to work yesterday, I saw some plastic animals next door. There were giraffes, elephants, flamingos, and I don't know what else but they were in a line two by two and then I see a sign "The Ark", so then the animals made sense.

I pull in the church parking lot and the sound from the radio stops. I pull up and turn the motor off and I don't hear anything. Now I'm clueless about what all of this was about. Could it have been a demon and was scared to come back on the church property? I can't hardly remember if it started the preaching when I was on church property or not. Oh well, I'm happy it quit. Now I know to watch and won't be surprised if it starts again. Just one more mystery I guess.

Emotional Fatigue: Emotions making me sleepy

Oct 4, 2017

Monday night I went to sleep as soon as we finished supper. I don't know if it was because there was no coffee when we came in from work, or whether I was tired from the excitement on Sunday, or if it was because of emotional fatigue. We had worked on two houses on Monday. There was a little boy at the first one who was autistic. He, his mother and father were living in the upstairs bedroom that had been converted from an attic. It was weird because, they built the staircase over the carpet, and my job was to get the carpet from under the staircase.

That wasn't my only job. I removed sheetrock from the room behind the staircase where I discovered the bottom of the wall was rotted out. It wasn't from the storm but from an air conditioner in the wall. The bad news was the wall was rotted out. The good news was, it had been discovered so it could be fixed. The lady seemed to be doing pretty well. I didn't get to meet the father because he was working.

The grandmother was there singing with the young boy who would be six in December. He threw a fit while we were there. His grandmother told him it was okay to be angry but it wasn't okay to hit people. The mother has to deal with living upstairs in one room over a moldy house and worrying about the repairs and what the insurance company in going to do. She said she didn't know exactly how to explain to her son what happened, but it seemed he understood better than she thought he would. When he sees a big pile of debris or a house that is torn up, he says, "the hurricane tore that up" and she agrees the hurricane tore up a lot of stuff.

We prayed with the lady and her son before we left. The next house was only a few blocks away. Two gentlemen lived there. They had left during the storm and when they came back the front door had blown open and the wall at the end of the house had been blown loose. The bottom part was off the foundation where one could see daylight at the bottom of the wall. There was an interior wall between the two rooms and the outside wall was torn loose from the interior wall. One reason for this was the sill plate was broken. It was actually broken in both rooms because there were windows with air conditioners in each room and the condensation from the air conditions had caused the sill plate to rot out.

This saved the wall because it may have broken sooner and let the air out before the whole wall blew out. So of course, the gentlemen wanted the wall to be repaired. I didn't think it would be hard to do. There was a tree close to the wall so I figured one could take a jack and put a 4x4 against the wall and jack the wall back into place. The tricky part was getting the interior wall to fit back into the exterior wall and the bottom plate unto the foundation. Carpentry is *Christ in Action's* forte, so they decided not to try it.

There are so many houses to be gutted and demolished but the time and effort it would have taken would have taken away from their main focus. I was kind of depressed about this; especially since I know groups that could do this so easily. They are not here so it is irrelevant. When we came back to camp and shared the situation with the director, he said they would get in touch with the Mennonites and see if they could repair the wall for the gentlemen. This cheered me up some. But there are just so many people who need help. Most of them have other problems besides the storm; autistic children, sickness, financial problems or martial problems and the results of the storm puts more stress on them.

Today I heard about a guy who went to the hospital for some kind of abdominal problem. While they were operating, they punctured his intestine. The day they operated on him, the hurricane struck and destroyed his house. When your house is destroyed you have to pay approximately 10 grand to get it completely demolished and piled up to be picked up. The guy was barely walking around and still has to have another operation when he gets in good enough shape.

When he heard *Christ in Action* would demolish his house for free, it took a huge load off of his mind. Even though it is depressing seeing so many people needing help, it makes me feel good they are doing something to help someone. I know it sounds weird to be depressed and encouraged at the same time, but it seems this is what happens when one is involved in a disaster. Well actually I guess one swings back and forth from being depressed to being encouraged, but it happens so fast sometimes it seems like both are happening at the same time. It almost sounds like being bipolar. It sure gives one plenty of things to pray about. We can pray while thanking the Lord for the protection He has provided.

The Cogs in My Head are Turning

November 26, 2017

I woke up this morning and I could see the predawn light the sun was about to come up in Georgia (and a lot of other places). Seems weird to say, "The sun is coming up." It has been there all the time. We are the ones waking up and turning to it. Sounds like there is a sermon in that. Then I see the wheels turning on a semi next to us. I feel the wheels turning on our bus (if that is possible). Everything is turning. The earth is turning, the sun is turning, the wheels on vehicles are turning and the cogs in my head are turning. Everything is in perpetual motion, so we are to be in motion too.

When we stop, we are not moving with the flow. Of course, we are to stop to sleep, rest, regroup, think things over, but even when we do, other parts of us that are turning take over. Our healing, visions, revelations, are doing their thing and we wouldn't notice if our other parts were running full speed.

Our body is truthfully a wondrous creation. It has three distinct parts, physical, mental, and spiritual. They all work separately and together at the same time. That doesn't seem possible but it is. One can be in prayer or meditation and one's digestive and respiratory system (and a bunch of others) are still working. That is the reason for fasting and being still so these systems are not interfering with the spiritual or emotional parts.

We need to forgive and be calm so the emotional part isn't interfering with the spiritual part. Yet we can be running from a bear, with fear and anger so our physical and emotional parts are on overload and we can still have a spiritual connection. It kind of overcomes the others by giving us 'peace beyond understanding' and supernatural strength where we can lift vehicles off people or outrun a chariot.

Can Man Affect Nature?

Sept 9, 2017

The world is big and man is small. Well, one man is small, but when we talk about millions and billions, what then? We move mountains, build mountains, build dams to stop the water and straighten out rivers to make the rivers run faster. We build on marshes and wastelands, we cover grass with asphalt, we cut trees down. Who knows what one Walmart may do? How much water runs off the roof into the parking lot. How much heat is reflected off the roof or is absorbed into the blacktop. How much carbon dioxide is released into the atmosphere just from the vehicles that drive there, and the list goes on. So multiply that by millions and it would seem not only do we affect the atmosphere, it is amazing we don't affect it more.

If it wasn't for the Lord creating nature to repair itself, we probably would have destroyed everything by now. Trees put oxygen into the air after taking in carbon dioxide. Seeds grow up in all kinds of places when they have been displaced by man.

After floods, plants rebound and produce more seeds than they did before. It seems they know they need to repopulate the area. They bloom wherever they are planted and we could learn from that. Bloom wherever you are. Do the best you can with what you have. Another phenomenon of nature. As the seeds grow, it makes more soil so more seeds can grow. Nature makes things to replenish their selves. We could do the same thing.

If we use what we have, to the best of our abilities, more stuff will be given to us to do more stuff with. Hey, it is never ending. There is a plan if we don't mess it up; and even if we mess it up there is a plan to rebuild. If we destroy the earth it will replenish itself. If we break a bone it heals itself. There is a plan for restoring to the original design. But we can overdo it. The trees will only absorb so much carbon dioxide (especially if we are cutting them down). Seeds will replenish but not so well on asphalt and even worse on concrete. The list goes on.

I think this is enough for now. I could go on forever. The challenge is, how can we build today? Can we pick up one piece of trash or say one kind word? I'm here in Corpus Christi to try to help clean up after a storm. Maybe we can clean up after some storm in someone's life. In nature it seems are not so many storms; and they can be pinpointed. In humans there are all kinds of storms about all kinds of different things. They are harder to see; and sometimes harder to fix. We are all in this together so let's try to calm someone's storm today.

We Are All in This Together

We hear a lot about culture when we are here. What does it mean to be an Appalachian? It doesn't really mean anything. We are all in this together. Everyone here is from various cultures. Family is a big thing in all cultures. If it wasn't there could be no culture. There could not be anything if we didn't help each other and realize there is a common goal. People move from the places they were born and raised. There is nothing wrong with that. One can keep their culture. It seems the Jewish people have done that quite well. The main thing is to keep the value of your culture; which is family, friendship, learning from your elders; and telling their stories.

Hopefully, you have learned something from the elders here (from Jay, or Larry, Don or Jimbo.) You might have learned to not act like us sometimes. You can learn from anyone. Hopefully, you learned something from the families. Anytime we interface with anyone we should be able to learn from them. If we don't it is because we are not listening. The point is to learn and to build on that. One of the things I hope you learned is things can be fixed. You don't always have to out and buy a new thing. Your old thing may be functional. Hopefully, you have learned that happiness is not judged by how much money you make. It is judged by following your heart.

Every one of you was created to do a certain thing. You were given talents and skills and a personality to do what you were designed to do. I don't know what that is; and you probably don't either, but I know it was to help the world be a better place. you may have to move to do what you were called to do. You may be called to stay and help your neighborhood. There is nothing wrong in moving. Most of us or our ancestors moved somewhere; or we would not be here. CAP tries to get you to come here. Amy moved here. She didn't stay in Texas. But you should pray about any move. I think she prayed for about five minutes before making her decision.

Grief is Part of Healing

We worked in Rainelle, West Virginia today. It seems as if the whole town was flooded. It was isolated by the water. No one could get in or out. We met an amazing lady. When we got to her house she wasn't home, but there was a sign that said something like "thank all the volunteers for helping. I have lived in Rainelle for 72 years, but now I think I'm ready to leave the 'Rain' part".

Just as I finish reading the sign, a lady drives up in a pickup truck with license tag "GAILGIRL." A lady gets out with a limp (I find out later she has a wooden leg) and thanks us for being there and hopes we haven't been there long. She tells us she and a couple of young guys have taken out a bunch of stuff. She said, "I couldn't do anything for a few days because I was feeling sorry for myself," but she knew "Jesus wasn't happy about that."

We assured her that grief was part of healing when a disaster happens. She let us in the house and sure enough a lot of sheetrock and paneling had been removed. There was a picture of Jesus on the wall. She said, "I couldn't take that wall down because Jesus is my man." As she walked by, she blew Him a kiss.

She was telling us that she and her husband had been married for 25 years, but he acted bad and she put them in a time out for 25 years. (pretty long time out). They got back together and he bought her this house. She owned the one next door and had been doing some young lady a favor by renting it to her. Well because it is a rental, FEMA won't give her anything to repair or demolish it. She said, "They were supposed to demolish it, so I'm wondering if they are going to do it this afternoon. I told her, "I'm sure they aren't going to do it today." She said, "Maybe Monday." I didn't say anything. She was wanting to get everything to the street because FEMA was going to quit paying a contractor to pick up debris on the 27th.

This has people in a tizzy because a lot of them don't have their houses gutted out yet. I didn't have the heart to tell her that so far, FEMA hasn't agreed to pay to dispose of demolished houses. Christ in Action has 40 houses to demolish and 20 days to do them (that is if they got approval Monday, which I don't think is likely).

The lady was a hoarder and didn't want to throw anything away. Well, a person is going to accumulate some stuff in 72 years. We didn't finish taking out sheetrock, paneling, and flooring so we have to go tomorrow. I was aiming to leave in the morning, but I'm staying one more day because there are so few volunteers.

She didn't want us to come before noon, because she ministers to the people in the nursing home at 11:00. She says they allow her because she has a big mouth and the old people can hear her. We said we could come over before she went and work while she was gone. We shouldn't have that much to do, so we probably will get through before she gets back.

Created to Be Hurt; Created to Be Healed and Created to Help Others Heal

May 2018

I was grieving Sunday am about not being able to do the high ropes course while I was on the Elder Retreat because I had stitches in my hand. Then I had a revelation that I was created to be hurt. I was born in pain; created with feelings. If I was not to ever be hurt, why would I have these feelings? I was sewed up and, in a week, the stitches will be removed. My body is created to heal itself or the stitches would have to stay in to hold the skin together. I will have a scar to remind me I was hurt. It can remind me to not to something like that again.

Hurt can help us gain knowledge and wisdom. Hurt can give us compassion and empathy. If we were never hurt we would not know how others feel when they are hurt. After we are hurt and then healed we can help others go through the type of situations that hurt us. We can share with them what things make healings go faster; and what hinders healing,

What is kind of weird is, physical hurt can be healed quickly and one doesn't have to do much to allow it to heal (rest, protect the wound for a few days). There are scars to see that one has been hurt so others can realize a person has been hurt. An emotional hurt on the other hand doesn't heal itself so easily or quickly. It usually involves more work. The hurt person has to do something. They have to forgive. They should get focused on something besides their pain. Most of the time they can't avoid the thing that caused them emotional pain because that was people (usually relatives and friends) and they are everywhere and can say hurtful things that open wounds that were healing. It may be emotional healing is a continuous process because of this.

We go through things so we can learn and help others. Sometimes this is very frustrating because it seems not everyone wants to be healed. They seem to want to stay where they are; and they won't appreciate the things we do to help them heal. Sometimes they try to hurt us because they don't understand what to do to get out of the situations. People in pain are not always rational, so we should not hold that against them. Hurting people hurt others.

We were created to help these hurting people so they won't hurt others so much. Most of them won't appreciate it. We know Jesus came to heal people and to tell them we could have "life more abundantly," yet the people he had healed said "crucify Him". I can't imagine how much physical and emotional pain He was in then. No wonder we have troubles getting motivated to helping people heal. Some we help heal will leave us; others will hate us. Oh well it is what we were created to do. The joy we have when we help one person is worth the pain we have for all the times things didn't work out.

Fences

So many stories. Lady telling about her son saving her. Water was up to her neck because she is so short. Her son is tall. She says he grabs her and says, "You ain't going anywhere yet." He tells her they have to go next door but there was a fence they would have to climb over. All at once he looks and the fence is gone. He says this was the miracle to him.

He also comments, "A lot of fences had come down in his neighborhood. He meant; the neighbors were being more neighborly.

The End of My First book

"I guess I need to write a book (or two or three). I would have to get more concise and say they are fiction, because no one would believe I do all the goofy things I do."

Printed in the United States
By Bookmasters